To Kathleen

LOVING AND LEAVING WASHINGTON

a wonderful
friend and a
great asset at
SOLES
with warm
regards

JM
Nov 2016

LOVING AND LEAVING
WASHINGTON

Reflections on Public Service

John Yochelson

Potomac Books
An imprint of the University of Nebraska Press

All rights reserved. Potomac Books is an
imprint of the University of Nebraska Press.
Manufactured in the United States of America.

Library of Congress Cataloging-in-Publication Data
Names: Yochelson, John N., author.
Title: Loving and leaving Washington: reflections on
public service / John Yochelson.
Description: Lincoln: Potomac Books, an imprint of the
University of Nebraska Press, [2016] | Includes biblio-
graphical references and index.
Identifiers: LCCN 2016001678 (print)
LCCN 2016015071 (ebook)
ISBN 9781612348247 (cloth: alk. paper)
ISBN 9781612348353 (epub)
ISBN 9781612348360 (mobi)
ISBN 9781612348377 (pdf)
Subjects: LCSH: Yochelson, John N. | Civil service—
United States—Biography. | Civil service—United
States—History—20th century.
Classification: LCC JK693.Y63 A3 2016 (print) |
LCC JK693.Y63 (ebook) | DDC 327.730092—dc23
LC record available at http://lccn.loc.gov/2016001678

Set in Sabon Next Pro by Rachel Gould.

CONTENTS

PREFACE

This reflection on public service in Washington began as I walked the beach in San Diego. Two goals moved me.

First, I wanted to see if I could tell a story. Writing had always played a big part in my life. The skills that I developed, however, had nothing to do with building a narrative. My strength lay in compression, not elaboration. I knew how to distill for a demanding audience. Perhaps digging into my own past would finally allow words to flow.

Second, I was eager to provide a resource for men and women who are thinking about a future in public service. I stumbled into my career without much guidance. The lack of a doctorate cost me the standing of an expert. But as it turned out, being a generalist had its advantages. I changed fields and worked with some amazing people, instead of sticking to a single area. My experience was worth sharing with others.

I feel a sense of urgency because so many Americans are disillusioned with Washington. Count me among them. The rise of partisan warfare in the 1990s didn't just turn me off; it pushed me to look for an exit strategy. The one that turned up led me to leave a rewarding nonprofit job in DC for the West Coast. With federal support I traded the world of policy for a grassroots cause. The new opportunity tested me personally and professionally. To stay the course, I found that I had to work the Washington bureaucracy all over again.

My concern is that the beleaguered public sector won't attract its fair share of talent. The generation that is coming of age has more options than I could have fathomed a half century ago. Their choices will be fateful. With luck my journey will nudge some to step up to today's most pressing challenge of public service—restoring faith in government.

ACKNOWLEDGMENTS

A bicoastal writing project produces two sets of friends and colleagues to thank. I did much of the thinking and drafting in San Diego. Paula Cordeiro, a University of San Diego dean, and Jim Rohr, a navy engineer, inspired me with their commitment to expanding educational opportunities. Building Engineering & Science Talent board members Irwin Jacobs and Anne Petersen both made helpful comments. Brenda Sullivan generously volunteered communications help. Others to whom I am deeply grateful for advice, feedback, and support include Jessica Brown, Mark Cafferty, Howard Hian, Larry Krause, Heather Lattimer, Sallie Marshall, Alan Nathan, Diane Peluso, Sedra Shapiro, Larry Veit, and Bob Wolfson.

I drew much of my content from Washington. There Bob Black helped shape the manuscript with timely editorial guidance. Max Stier and Tim McManus made me welcome at the remarkable Partnership for Public Service. Andy Rich opened the door of the Truman Scholarship Foundation. John Kamensky gave generously of his time and expert knowledge. Hedrick Smith shared his deep understanding of the changes that have taken place in the Washington political arena. Ted Alden, Eric Iversen, Scott Moore, Debbie van Opstal, and Bruce Stokes provided invaluable insights. Others to whom I owe special thanks include Kianoosh Akhlaghi, Theresa Bourgeois, Lucy Charles, Alex Coccia, Pablo Eisenberg, Erica Greeley, Miles Kahler, Andy Keefe, Don Kettl, Sara Jacobs, Lori Lawson, Peter Lees, Laurel McFarland, Lena Nour, Carlos Rodriguez, Peter Rooney, Greg Treverton, and Tyson Tuchscherer. In addition, Max Angerholzer of the Center for the Study of the Presidency and Congress enabled me to discuss an early version of the manuscript with Dave Abshire, the mentor who changed the course of my life.

Ann Corwin made possible my illuminating dialogue at the Woodrow

Wilson School with Sean Chen, Emily King, Harry Krejsa, Ethan Lynch, Kevin McGinnis, Jamie Morgan, and Meagan Reed. During that visit senior lecturer Stan Katz, in addition to providing valuable perspective, put me in contact with Victor Brombert, a professor of French from my Yale days who made the life-changing suggestion that I spend my junior year abroad.

George Reed, now dean of the School of Public Affairs at the University of Colorado, Colorado Springs, introduced me to Potomac Books at the University of Nebraska Press through acquisitions editor Alicia Christensen. The team there has helped a first-time author learn the ropes. Although copyeditor Elizabeth Gratch worked wonders with the manuscript, I bear sole responsibility for omissions and errors of fact.

My sister, Bonnie, the author of many books in her field, made a decisive contribution to this one by suggesting that I balance my personal story with analysis of the bigger picture.

Most of all, I wish to thank my wife, Diane, and daughters, Lisa and Laura, for standing by me. I would not have seen this through without their love.

1 CALL TO ACTION

Every family has a defining narrative. I grew up on the story of my parents' hard-earned success. The children of immigrants, they lived the American dream in a single generation. Their only son got all the advantages they never had. The edge they provided made me grateful. I wanted to give back.

The youngest U.S. president put my feelings into words. I had just turned seventeen when John F. Kennedy took the oath of office in January 1961. I watched him on the grainy black-and-white screen in the den of our home in upstate New York. Near the end of his inaugural address, standing without a coat outside the snow-covered Capitol, he moved millions with an elegant turn of phrase: "And so, my fellow Americans, ask not what your country can do for you—ask what you can do for your country."

The messenger gripped me as much as the message. The handsome war hero brought a glamorous First Lady, wit, and intellect into public life. JFK had written two best sellers, one in college and the other as a U.S. senator. He looked and lived like a Boston Brahman. He also spoke with a Beantown twang and never forgot that his family had crossed the Atlantic to the New World just a few decades before mine.

Kennedy's short, stirring speech wrapped his call to action in the flag. He addressed a global audience, not just the American people. With a finger now on the nuclear trigger, he wanted friend and foe alike to know where he stood in a divided world. The next generation of Americans, he declared, would pay any price to ensure the survival of liberty. We would check Communist aggression, shore up old European allies, and fight Third World poverty. The leadership of the Free World demanded personal sacrifice and engagement.

The president didn't need to elaborate. My generation knew that Soviet power threatened our way of life. The Russians occupied Eastern Europe.

They backed their massive army with a growing atomic arsenal. They led the space race. In the spring of 1960 they shot down a U-2, the most advanced U.S. spy plane at that time. A few months later their crude premier, Nikita Khrushchev, banged his shoe on the table at the United Nations and vowed to bury us. His peasant bravado evoked bad memories. Pogroms had driven my grandparents out of the Russian empire before communism.

Kennedy's appeal to serve won me over instantly. My family owed everything to the land of opportunity. Of course, the national interest counted more than self-interest. I would head off to college in the fall. Nothing I could do with my future could match serving the public good. That meant winning the Cold War. I'd probably end up working for the U.S. government, which led the struggle against the Russians.

More than a half century later I heard a former cabinet officer discuss the impact of global warming on worldwide food production. Crisply, she outlined the problems and possible solutions. Her concise analysis reflected years of accomplished public service.

I asked her afterward about channeling the energy of young people to crack the challenges she had laid out. I half-expected her blunt response but still found it jarring. "It's really difficult to advise young Americans to go into government," she said matter-of-factly. "Times have changed. Washington doesn't work the way it used to. Congress is impossible. Don't get me started."

The encounter turned my clock back to the world of 1961. A shift in my father's career led our family to relocate to the nation's capital when I finished high school. Dad became a federal employee. The new neighbor who beat me regularly in Ping-Pong had a big job in the space program. A close family friend told stories about bringing electricity to rural America. The daughter of the secretary of agriculture came over to babysit my sister. Washington seemed full of capable people doing important work. Seven out of ten Americans trusted the government to do the right thing most of the time. I saw the human face behind the statistics. Public service was an easy sell.

The calling I felt didn't have a set career path. I studied U.S. and European history at Yale. Junior year in France kindled my interest in transatlantic relations, the field in which I decided to specialize. A master's degree in public affairs from Princeton honed my skills but left me with little grasp of what public service really meant.

Good fortune smiled. The army sent me to Europe at the height of the Vietnam War. Following my release from active duty, I caught another break. Jean Monnet, one of the architects of the European Common Market, asked me to draft a monograph for him. The celebrated visionary, frustrated that Europe was moving too slowly, wanted to jump-start the process of political integration. His friend the British prime minister might help. Perhaps a paper on the American experience of balancing a strong central government with states' rights would point the way forward.

To my astonishment Monnet treated me like a colleague when we met periodically in his office near the Arc de Triomphe. He never let me hold a door for him. Deference, he said, was for old people. He liked what I wrote and published it to make one final push in his twilight years.

A decade later I began to assist Henry Kissinger at his Washington base, a think tank called the Center for Strategic and International Studies (CSIS). The Harvard professor who restored the heights of American diplomacy kept an office there. Twice a year he met privately under the CSIS banner with a small group of international business leaders. They hung on every word of the former national security advisor and secretary of state. He invited newcomers to call him Henry, disarming them with humor at his own expense. His ever-present security detail and packed schedule radiated power. I suggested topics and speakers, scripted introductions, and intervened as needed to keep the discussion flowing. My bit part conferred status. All it took was being at the table with a name tent.

Opportunity knocked again. Paul Volcker, the most respected career government official of his time, agreed to chair the CSIS Advisory Board. He made his name as chairman of the Federal Reserve by breaking the back of inflation during the Carter and Reagan administrations. He had moved into investment banking in New York when I served as his go-to person for keeping current on policy issues. Rainmaking on Wall Street didn't interest him much. He loved teaching about the global economy at his alma mater, Princeton, though he worried that the university was allowing costs to get out of hand. Public service was his passion—with fishing not too far behind.

The greats handled fame differently. Monnet wanted nothing more than to continue his life's work. His cause, unifying Europe, gave him all the recognition he needed. Kissinger yearned for the spotlight. He used his achievements as a platform to build his reputation as a living legend. Volcker resisted the high life. His no-frills style sent a message of uncompromising integrity. Reaching the pinnacle of success didn't change these men. It simply brought out who they were.

My chance to interact with all three icons stemmed from where I was, not who I was. I had a desk over the garage of the Atlantic Institute in Paris when Monnet asked the director for help. I had a real office at CSIS when I drew the assignment of working with Kissinger and Volcker. Like me, they were drawn to a public policy nonprofit that excelled in high-level networking. I was part of their support package.

I came to CSIS from the State Department in the late 1970s to escape being pigeonholed as a European security analyst. The Iron Curtain looked like it would divide East from West indefinitely. I'd be hemmed in if that happened. I was doing well at State but chafed in a bureaucracy that limited my options. The go-getter culture of the think tank at the center of action appealed to me more than the government route. I'd try to serve the public interest by stationing myself at a place that brokered dialogue between high-level policy makers, scholars, and business leaders.

The cofounder of CSIS, David Abshire, took a chance on me. A graduate of West Point, he liked my army experience and ease with French. I won his confidence on a mission to Japan that clinched an endowment from Toyota. He was looking for a point man to engage the corporate community on its concerns in the fast-changing global economy. He let me leave politico-military affairs behind to reinvent myself as CSIS director of international business and economics. I didn't have to be a PhD economist as long as I framed the issues well and expanded the funding base.

I learned how connections build careers. The paper for Monnet put me on the track to State. That job opened the door to CSIS, where my portfolio made it possible to work with the U.S. trade representative and congressional leaders. Supporting Kissinger paved the way for outside consulting with European bigwigs. The clout of CSIS led to a spot on the President's Export Council. I climbed the ladder in the think tank world as the consummate organization man—traveling a lot, managing meetings, cultivating donors, and getting by on op-eds rather than scholarship.

Volcker brought my seventeen years at CSIS to an end in 1995 with a promotion. He recommended me for the presidency of the Council on Competitiveness, a small DC-based forum of high-powered CEOs and research university presidents, plus a few labor leaders. Their Team America approach to strengthening the U.S. economy fit me like a glove. The council offered me my first leadership opportunity, heading a staff of fifteen. In my excitement I accepted the offer before asking about the salary.

The council pushed a bipartisan policy agenda to strengthen the U.S. economy as a whole. My marching orders were to develop recommendations that would enable U.S. products to win in world markets while keeping wages high at home. Council members gave me an open field to look at federal spending, taxes, trade, regulations, and workforce development.

We hit upon building the U.S. capacity to innovate as a signature issue. The council had made its name in the 1980s calling for a let's-pull-together response to the rise of Japan. We needed a fresher theme that reflected the new realities of globalization. The rest of the world was catching up fast at the high end of the value chain. The United States had to dominate that space in order to maintain the world's highest standard of living.

The council ran with innovation. My top hire drafted a groundbreaking report on the global forces at work in key industry sectors. The world's best-known authority on economic competitiveness, Professor Michael Porter of Harvard Business School, designed an innovation index to compare national capabilities. A summit hosted by the president of MIT engaged the White House and high-ranking elected officials from both parties. Behind the scenes I chased down the private email of Vice President Al Gore to persuade him to keynote. The event made the front page of the *Wall Street Journal*.

I rode the crest of the council's success to retool again—this time as a way to leave Washington. I decided to check my advanced degree in big ego management. The DC power game was getting rougher and more partisan. My wife wanted a change of scene. I had signed up at the council for a cause, not tenure. After giving everything I had, I couldn't imagine what came after the race to innovate. Like scholar Francis Fukuyama, I felt as if I had reached the end of history.

The opportunity to disengage grew out of an impromptu conversation with Rita Colwell, the director of the National Science Foundation. Her agency invested billions each year in basic research. Second-class treatment in graduate school gave her a passion for broadening the participation of women and underrepresented minorities in science and engineering. She wondered if the influential Council on Competitiveness might consider getting involved. I jumped at the chance to submit an unsolicited proposal, alerting her that I planned to relocate to the West Coast if the endeavor were funded. My board gave me backing to launch my own 501(c)(3), Building Engineering & Science Talent, or BEST.

BEST received $2 million in federal seed money in 2001 to spearhead a national diversity campaign. I got the okay to set up shop in San Diego, where my four-person operation had solid local support. Armed with a congressional mandate, BEST convened over one hundred experts to scour the country for effective programs to deepen the pool of domestic talent in the fields of science, technology, engineering, and mathematics (STEM). The two-year search turned up incredible personal stories and scattered pockets of excellence. The STEM education system as a whole, however, failed to develop the potential of two-thirds of the population. The diversity challenge exposed the soft underbelly of American education. This fight would take a generation or more to win.

My strategy to sustain BEST misfired. As federal seed funding ran out, I approached private foundations to help us move the needle. One after another they patted me on the back and said their priorities lay elsewhere. BEST teetered on the brink.

The Department of Defense saved the day. DoD employed more scientists and engineers than any other federal agency. A deputy undersecretary at DoD, John Hopps Jr., wanted to expand the supply of homegrown talent rather than simply drawing it down. BEST's body of work and friends in high places impressed him, so I recast BEST as a government contractor. We competed successfully for a grant to help ramp up DoD-sponsored educational activities across the country.

Thus my old stomping ground drew me back, not to weigh in on policy but to produce videos, fund robotics competitions, pay teacher stipends, and provide management advice. Stable funding and direct contact with volunteers in the field offset the constraints of working within a large, layered bureaucracy. I couldn't, however, meet the needs of the Pentagon by staying full-time in San Diego. The bicoastal commute that started in 2007 continues to this day.

I never expected to answer President Kennedy's call to public service outside the government. Unwittingly, I moved into the fast-growing non-profit sector just as the federal workforce came under relentless fire. That shift gave me a front row seat at the dividing line between public interest and self-interest. I kept my eyes open and learned how to make my way in a DC arena brimming with ambition.

Despite serving on a presidential advisory panel, I never punched the tickets that bestow the highest status in Washington. A reputation for competence wasn't enough to win me a White House job or a Senate-confirmed political appointment. By holding partisan politics at arm's length, I marked myself as a niche player.

But the niches I found were more varied and absorbing than I had ever thought possible. Changing fields from European security to economic policy to education on my own timetable ranked as a proud achievement. Each change allowed me to immerse myself in a different content area. My experience ran counter to conventional wisdom. I moved up by downsizing. Moving to smaller organizations with reduced management burdens freed me to work on substance. Along the way I crossed paths with many remarkable people while doing what I believed in. Who could ask for more than that?

Still, jumping forced me to prove myself every time. My wife and daughters lived with the strain. I took pride in clear thinking at work yet found it difficult to explain my career at home. I struggled to describe how and why I spent my day networking, writing, and raising money. It pained me to see that my girls weren't sure when teachers asked what their father did. I saw colleagues dig deep and grow. Some wrote books of enduring importance as they moved in and out of government. Others stayed in federal service and rose to the top. I missed out on this kind of success.

Like many others, I tried to balance ambition, family commitments, and public service. The trade-offs I made were typical, not exceptional. They raise three questions that aren't mine alone.

Where do you focus to make an impact? I felt the difference between trying to change a policy and trying to change a life.

At the Council on Competitiveness, for example, my chairman, Ray Gilmartin, and I called on the majority leader of the Senate to make the case for increasing the $80 billion federal investment in basic research. The door knock gave us a half hour with Senator Trent Lott of Mississippi. Gilmartin, the CEO of Merck, explained that companies like his were in the business of creating new products, not new knowledge. The private sector built off government-funded pure research by throwing its resources into applications. Federally funded R&D was indispensable. Lott understood perfectly. He told us about his friendship with a professor of materials science at Mississippi State University who received federal grants. We could count on the majority leader's support. The council scored a policy win.

In contrast, at BEST I paid for a seventeen-hour bus ride for a robotics team made up of low-income, minority kids to compete in a national championship in St. Louis. A rookie team from East Orange, New Jersey, the students were the first participants to come from their school. Coached by DoD volunteers, they won an invitation by placing well in a regional tournament. No big policy issues were at stake. BEST's mission to expand the talent pool justified cutting a check for a few thousand dollars. There was no other way to give ten high-needs high school students the opportunity. A colleague and I cheered them on. Their touching thank-you video summed up the trip in a word. Unforgettable.

The Senate meeting and the bus ride would be easy to compare if all that mattered were personal satisfaction. But BEST couldn't have intervened in East Orange without a congressionally funded DoD program. Success on the front lines required policy-level support. The choice between walking the corridors of power and taking direct action in the field was deceptively difficult.

How far do you go to raise funds in the nonprofit world? The quandaries of donor influence proved inescapable. Once I saw a revered mentor court a key ultraconservative backer of CSIS. He walked a verbal tightrope to connect with the longtime supporter without locking himself into extreme positions. Sometimes I found myself on the tightrope too. We made every effort to protect the independence of CSIS by diversifying its financial base, roster of experts, and research projects. It was a constant juggling act.

Foreign and U.S. government funding raised sensitive issues. The $1 million endowment from Toyota that I helped raise at CSIS caused a stir. The Japanese were buying up choice American real estate. Were think tanks on the shopping list too? Would the CSIS Japan chair holder pull his or her punches? I kept my distance from Japan, Inc., in spite of my close ties to Toyota's top management. However, I had no qualms assisting a Rothschild with his foundation or writing think pieces for an Italian industrialist. Europe hardly looked like an economic juggernaut, and my assignments weren't business related.

The founder of the Council on Competitiveness, John Young, took a position in principle against any support from the U.S. government. A hero in my eyes, he felt that federal contracts might sway the positions that the council took. But the business model I had to work with left a shortfall in revenue that had to be filled. The ideal collided with the real.

Naively, I held onto the belief that think tanks competed in the marketplace of ideas and resources. The cream was supposed to rise to the top. That may have been true once but not anymore. Today donors call many of the shots, creating public policy nonprofits with distinctive brands for which diverse in-house views create problems.

The contrast between then and now raises the most troubling question of all. Are careers like mine still possible? The arena in which I got my start in the mid-1970s had plenty of drawbacks. Congressional power barons operated top down. Pork barrel politics lubricated the system. Insiders controlled the flow of information. Nevertheless, deals across party lines were the norm. Divided government worked because partisanship gave way to the national interest more often than not.

That world has disappeared since the mid-1990s. Winner-take-all politics, big money, and round-the-clock media have changed the game. Moderates have lost their stabilizing hold on the political balance. Trust in government has tumbled into the teens. Opportunities to cash in on federal experience have increased nonstop. An astute observer, *New York Times* writer Mark Leibovich depicts "this town" as a gilded capital where the trappings of power count far more than serving the public good. Many believe that's the new normal in Washington.

Today's landscape casts a long shadow on public service. A tour in government has become a well-traveled path to financial gain, not the act of self-sacrifice that JFK evoked. Growing numbers of political appointees and contractors have reduced the role of career officials. Advocacy has displaced consensus building as the most sought-after skill. A universe of appealing options to make a difference has opened up outside government. These changes are sapping the strength of the federal enterprise that I grew up believing in.

I can't accept the inevitability of federal decline. Conversations with Millennials pick me up. They face different choices than my generation, but they have both the capacity and the will to serve the nation well. They aren't, however, going to make commitments with their eyes closed. That's what prompts me to share my experience—to start a frank conversation about the rewards, costs, and urgency of drawing talent into the federal sector.

2 SURROUNDED BY STRIVERS

Stately elms lined the streets of Buffalo, New York, in the 1950s. They almost blotted out the summer sun, making houses seem grander than they really were. Ours was a midsized Cape Cod bungalow. The picture window in the back looked out to a well-kept lawn, elevated garden, and detached garage. A dramatic wall-length reproduction of Titian's *Sacred and Profane Love* hung above the maroon velvet sofa in the living room. A handmade breakfront fit snugly into the dining room next to the paneled kitchen. There were four compact bedrooms upstairs, including one with carved twin beds for guests.

Kathryn and Sam Yochelson took great pride in 394 Woodbridge Avenue. They bought it in Dad's hometown on the eve of World War II in 1939, not long before he was called to five years of military service in the Army Medical Corps. When they came back with a two-year-old son in 1946, Mom turned it into a jewel. She and Dad had come a long way. He topped the list of local psychiatrists. She found her own niche in the arts while raising two kids. Our home was the emblem of their success.

My parents' courtship had a storybook quality. The setting was New Haven, Connecticut, in 1929. Sam, a Yale graduate student on full scholarship, calls on Kathryn, a striking young art teacher who lives with her family a few blocks from campus. She already has a wealthy suitor, who will one day inherit a chain of movie theaters. Kathryn falls in love with the scholar, picking him against the wishes of her father but with her mother's approval. They marry at twenty-three, living on scrambled eggs and hard rolls. Sam completes a PhD degree in psychology, earns a medical degree, and trains in psychiatry. Kathryn teaches elementary school to make ends meet and audits classes at Yale Art School. By all accounts that's the way it happened—a familiar plotline for thousands of American-born children of Yiddish-speaking immigrants.

Dad tried to enlist the day after Pearl Harbor. He was turned away for poor eyesight at first but was inducted soon enough to draw on his psychiatric training. He spent most of World War II as Major Yochelson in Camp Kilmer, New Jersey, where he screened soldiers for combat in the European theater. Mom, who had wanted to start a family for years, got pregnant with me in 1943. I was due on Christmas Day but arrived late. Dad ran red lights rushing to get her to the hospital on January 2, 1944.

The decision to return to Buffalo after Dad's discharge made sense. The 1950 U.S. Census ranked the city as the nation's fifteenth largest. Millions of European immigrants passed through on their way across the Great Lakes. No one knew that our hometown was peaking at midcentury—its port to be bypassed by the St. Lawrence Seaway, its steel plants shuttered by foreign competition, and its trees felled by Dutch elm disease. We lived in a vibrant, down-to-earth place where ten-year-olds rode the bus alone. Only the lack of a major league baseball club left Buffalo a notch below Cleveland and Pittsburgh.

My parents' life experience shaped their ambitions for me. Both came from large families of modest means. Dad's scholarly father, Sholom, never realized his dream of becoming a rabbi. Fleeing Vilna, Lithuania, as a teenager, he needed a way to support himself that required less preparation. He settled for *schochet*, or kosher ritual slaughterer. A pillar of the synagogue, he observed the Sabbath so strictly that my grandparents paid a non-Jew to turn the lights on and off on Saturdays. His ambitious wife, Fannie, with her trademark mink coat, always seemed to want more than she had. Their three sons and daughter worked their way through college—two doctors, a lawyer, and a teacher.

The American-born Yochelson boys eagerly shed the baggage of the Old Country. Their rejection of Orthodox Judaism stirred conflict. Dad rebelled against Sabbath restrictions that kept him away from sports, splitting his head open on the edge of a table trying to avoid his father's belt. Middle brother, Morris, changed his name to Young, left for the West Coast, and was disowned after marrying a devout Catholic. Youngest brother, Leon, won grudging acceptance when his fiancée converted. A disappointed father saw all of his sons leave their faith behind.

Mom grew up in a more loving home. Her father, Nathan, a dapper scrap metal dealer, managed to support four boys and two girls without learning to read or write English. When times were good, he bought made-to-measure suits, smoked Cuban cigars, and shipped smoked fish home from New York. Affectionately, he called his daughter Kathryn his "little duck." Mom adored her mother, Esther, a fragile beauty whose taste for learning and culture had a defining impact on the family. Esther's failing health forced Mom to anchor the household in her teens. My grandmother's early death from rheumatic heart disease left Mom—then a newlywed—devastated.

Mom's brothers changed their ethnic-sounding family name from Mersky to Mersey as World War II approached. Two boys went into business, and two went to graduate school on the GI Bill. Mom's younger sister studied nursing in Philadelphia, where she met her physician husband. Mom spent two years at normal school to earn an elementary school teaching degree. Her side wanted to make it in America, just like Dad's.

My parents saw education as the key to my future. More than anything, they wanted to groom me for an establishment that had been beyond their reach growing up. Their time in New Haven laid the foundation for all the good things that followed. Dad, however, had been denied an entry-level undergraduate teaching post on religious grounds. The university sent him to medical school instead. My admission to Yale College would make up for the slight. Then we'd be a real Yale family. Mom and Dad would give me every edge they could. My part was making the most of the opportunities.

This unspoken bargain led me to the progressive Park School at the age of three. When I had a rocky start, my parents rejected the principal's recommendation to hold me back a year. Dad had begun first grade young and graduated high school when he was sixteen. Mom had crammed eighth grade into a few weeks of intensive study after staying out of school most of the year caring for her mother. Yochelsons didn't lag behind.

I hit my stride in the elementary grades. Mom used to wait for the school bus with me, counting the number of times we tossed a red rubber ball back and forth without a miss. The ritual was fun, its message indelible. Mom proudly kept my fourth grade report card, which read that I was "very happy, contributing to the class, and doing above grade-level work."

Mom and Dad pulled me out then. Nichols, the elite boys' day school a few blocks from our house, looked like a better bet for Yale. Nichols served prominent families in the community from fifth grade through high school. Ivy-covered buildings, a circular drive, and a hockey rink set the school apart as a bastion of privilege. Its all-white student body and faculty reflected the norm for private schools in the 1950s. In that era a nod to diversity meant that Catholics and Jews made up about one-third of the entering class of fifty.

Nichols knew what it took to get its graduates accepted by the most selective colleges. The dress code called for white shirts, coats, and ties. Teachers pushed us hard, knew us well, and followed the protocol of calling us by our last names. Every student had to write out and sign a pledge on the cover of every exam booklet declaring on his honor as a gentleman that he had neither given nor received information. Good manners, a strong work ethic, and personal integrity were nonnegotiable.

No one got lost in a school our size. Everyone had the chance to build a record in studies, sports, or an after-school activity. That's what $800 per year in tuition paid for. Decades later the Bill and Melinda Gates Foundation invested tens of millions making public schools smaller. "The well-to-do figured out what succeeds in education two centuries ago," Tom Vander Ark, the founding director of the Gates program, told me. Typically, the top quarter of every Nichols class made it into the Ivy League. I was getting an inside track with the admissions offices of all of them.

The student body of four hundred gathered in chapel every morning at 9:00 a.m. Early arrivals propped up pencils at the end of each pew and rolled marbles to knock them down. Mr. Boocock, the bow-tied headmaster, conducted a twenty-minute service with warmth and dignity. After opening announcements he read from the Old or New Testament and had us recite the Twenty-Third Psalm. It felt uncomfortable singing his favorite hymn, "Onward Christian Soldiers," but we all joined in. He dismissed us for class with a crisp "Have a good day, gentlemen."

Mr. Kleiser, a fixture known to everyone as "Doc," introduced fifth and

　　　　　　　　　　　　　　SURROUNDED BY STRIVERS

sixth graders to Nichols's traditional methods. His white hair parted high, he peered over our shoulders in a required penmanship class to check the columns of small and capital letters we wrote out. His notorious weekly exams in civics class tested our capacity to spit back facts. I learned by heart all the stops between Albany and Buffalo on the New York Central Railroad. The facts themselves didn't matter, but putting in the hours and paying attention to detail did.

The curriculum included two years of foundational Latin in grades 7 and 8, which Nichols called Forms I and II. The assistant headmaster who taught us had been named after the Roman philosopher Pliny. He brought the military campaigns of Julius Caesar to life with toy soldiers. He also explained how the hundreds of vocabulary words we had to memorize had found their way into English. The connection he drew between the present and the past stuck with me.

The school didn't do as good a job linking its math and science courses to the here and now. The 1950s was a decade rich in discovery, engineering feats, and technological challenges. The development of the polio vaccine, the construction of the interstate highway system, and the space race could have shown why algebra, biology, and physics mattered. None of my teachers connected the dots. I didn't do as well in these subjects as liberal arts, where I easily grasped the value of structured thinking and writing.

Nichols practiced the survival of the fittest in the classroom. Teachers piled on homework, term papers, and tests. Learning started with discipline, not curiosity or inspiration. Weak students had nowhere to hide because monthly grades were posted in the halls for all to see. Mr. Boocock recognized honor and high honor students at school assemblies after every marking period. Eager for approval, I ranked near the top of my class in this hypercompetitive environment.

Sports softened the focus on individual performance. Teamwork won games. Coaches drove this lesson home to all students—everyone had to participate in the sports program. I never made the cut as a real jock because I didn't play football or hockey. Soccer, basketball, and tennis hardly counted, even though I made varsity in all three. The scoop on the Yoke, as I was called, was "Good athlete, lacks toughness."

Sports provided my only contact with less advantaged kids. Once we scrimmaged a vocational high school in our brand new gym. The all-black team arrived in worn clothes with its white coach. The players' eyes widened when they saw glass backboards. They were better athletes, but we played them about even. We shook hands afterward. The scrimmage gave us two hours of common ground.

My other extracurricular activity, the *Nichols News*, triggered a lifelong interest in national politics. The start of my tour as coeditor coincided with the Kennedy-Nixon race for the presidency in 1960. With the country glued to their first-ever televised debate, which put me in the Kennedy column, I got permission to invite the candidates to a follow-up at Nichols. Their pro forma regrets didn't have any news value. Getting responses on White House and Senate stationery, however, was a first for any high school in the area. A front-page story reprinting the correspondence won a local award.

On the eve of my fiftieth reunion I strained to recall any personal relationships that had made an impact. The values that Nichols instilled made a much greater impression on me than classmates or teachers. Others were in the same boat. Few of them had kept up either. Half the class of 1961 came from around the country to give the school credit for later accomplishments. Nichols had changed with the times by going coed, easing rules, and adding technology. The basics, however, hadn't changed much at all. Today's educational reformers have rediscovered them: high expectations, skilled teachers, personal attention, and school accountability.

My parents supported me every step of the way. Mom prepped me for tests and hired a tutor when I had trouble with math. She asked the family handyman to build the model car I used to crash test a new safety device called the seatbelt. She attended every home game in every sport I played. I could do no wrong in her eyes. Whenever I had a success, she used the expressive Yiddish word *kvell* to describe how her heart filled with joy. She shrugged off my sarcastic reaction, determined to make her belief in me a fixed point.

It took years for me get an insight into Mom's unconditional praise. She waited until I was about to be inducted into the army to tell me about the infant she had lost two years before I was born. Following a smooth pregnancy, she woke up from anesthesia to learn that her baby daughter had strangled on her umbilical cord during delivery. After that awful blow,

Mom felt doubly blessed giving birth to me at the age of thirty-six and to my sister almost nine years later. Bonnie and I were her own personal miracle, proof that God made up for her loss.

Mom made room for my sister easily, hiring a live-in housekeeper to make sure that she could meet all of her commitments. In effect she raised two only children under one roof. Her separate but equal parenting, together with the gap in age, removed sibling rivalry. As Bonnie grew older, she developed her own close relationship with Mom. That shared closeness drew brother and sister together.

Dad, my most important role model, took a different tack. Eager to prepare me for life's challenges, he never let me slack off. The rule around the house was "Take an aspirin and go to school unless your temperature hits 101." Expecting that I would be an only child, he made sure that I went to two months of overnight camp starting at age seven. No son of his was going to be tied to his mother's apron strings.

Dinner was our most important time together. Over Mom's delicious comfort food, Dad used his powerful mind to sharpen mine. We started with a review of my day at school. I held the floor, recounting the high points of every class. Then we turned to current events and sports. No matter what the topic, Dad found something to analyze. I picked up his most precious gift, the capacity to break down problems.

Work came first in Dad's world. He left the house early six days a week to see patients, chain-smoking his way through the fifty-minute sessions without a break for lunch. He never broke away from the office to watch me play basketball, even though we had bonded shooting hoops in the backyard after dinner. Helping people straighten out their lives paid him back in ways that leisure and material things could never match. "Your patients worship the ground you walk on, Sam Yochelson," Mom used to say with admiration and a touch of regret.

Sometimes Dad couldn't keep his own competitiveness in check. His fierce will to win brought me to tears as a little boy when he gloated over winning a backyard game of croquet. Yet he drove through the night to be at the head of the line to visit me at camp when Mom was pregnant. For years he left a standing instruction with his secretary to interrupt whenever I telephoned. His office number was su-3636.

I found myself between two strong parents, one expressive and the other cerebral. I had a special relationship with both. Years later my sister observed that I took naturally to the middle position—accepting the Yochelson ethic of hard work and high achievement without a second thought. My success at school kept the cycle of high expectations and high praise going. I was the son who never pushed back.

Mom and Dad downgraded religious training as much as they stressed my Nichols education. The lite option was Temple Beth Zion, the large, hundred-year-old Reform congregation where most of their friends belonged. Six years of going through the motions provided little grounding in Jewish ethics, history, or practice. I soon forgot the Torah portion in Exodus that I had memorized for my Bar Mitzvah. The shallowness of my religious education was par for the course for Jews at Nichols, where the headmaster knew the Old Testament better than any of us.

A month in Israel during the summer of 1960 offset my indifferent experience at Temple Beth Zion. Mom, who had established herself as a local champion of Israeli painting, promoted the trip. I traveled with a group of thirty streetwise public school kids from New York, marveling when one of them sat down at the piano and reeled off Gershwin's "Rhapsody in Blue" from memory. This was also the first extended time I ever spent with girls my own age. Some were sexually aware and showed it. I had a lot of catching up to do.

Israel touched and challenged me deeply. Jews were making the desert bloom to build a nation. Their achievements made me very proud. Native-born Israelis, however, threw me on the defensive. They asked why I wouldn't move to the Jewish homeland if I felt a sense of belonging. Israel was living within its UN-mandated borders in 1960, a small and vulnerable democracy. Why didn't I want to devote my life to the cause? Maybe I didn't have the heart. Americans were so soft. Why else did they wear sunglasses all the time?

The criticism stung. I could identify with the Holocaust survivors and refugees from Arab lands. But my family's immigrant experience was over. I had so much to be grateful for. Americans weren't soft. I weeded orange groves until I dropped when we spent a few days at a kibbutz at the end of the summer. The rich English cousins whom I stopped to see in London gasped when they saw my blistered hands. They told me I should have worn gloves.

A paradox hit me on the way home. I felt a stronger attachment to the history of the Jewish people than my own extended family. The Yochelsons and the Merseys were too busy getting ahead to create ties that bind. My aunts and uncles spread out from Boston to Pasadena. A few warm memories lingered, but family occasions had a competitive edge. The grown-ups compared careers and kids. The cousins never got to know each other. Dad picked family members apart afterward, while Mom never got along consistently with her sister or any of the women who married into the family. One time Dad and two of Mom's brothers ripped a dinner check apart fighting for the right to cover the whole tab. Nobody laughed.

Surrounded by strivers, I was a striver too. I had no burning desire to lead. I wanted to serve, not to be in charge. Most of all, I didn't want to disappoint. A rejection from Yale would be my worst nightmare.

Nichols delivered. The acceptance letter thick with forms to fill out confirmed the Yochelson bargain. My parents gave me every chance to succeed, and I held up my end. I'd earned the opportunity but not on a level playing field. I owed something in return. That's why President Kennedy's call rang so true.

As graduation neared, Dad made a made bold career move that brought public service much closer to home. He decided at age fifty-five to make a clean break from private practice. Having provided for the family, he was ready to take on a larger challenge. The National Institutes of Health came up with one. The federal government needed better research on what made criminals tick. Dad had the clinical skills to find out. Taking a steep cut in pay, he accepted a civil service position as director of a criminal behavior project at St. Elizabeths Hospital in Washington DC. We were going to the nation's capital.

Mom took the move in stride. She and Dad delayed picking up stakes until after my commencement. Then, with my eight-year-old sister in tow, they relocated to the DC suburb of Chevy Chase, Maryland. As I left for New Haven, the Buffalo chapter in our lives ended and the whole family turned a page.

3 PEGGED AS AVERAGE

I arrived in New Haven full of self-doubt. Underneath the brave front I put up when my parents drove off from my freshman dorm, Wright Hall, I wondered whether I'd be able to measure up.

The sharp contrast between Yale and its surroundings struck me immediately. The historic Old Campus, where I'd spend my first year, took up a city block. Its gates marked the boundaries of Yale College in the 1700s. The university had grown to three hundred acres since then. Handsome Gothic structures built in the 1920s and 1930s unified its core. Boldly designed new buildings, such as Eero Saarinen's whalelike hockey rink, added a creative touch. The narrow streets that crisscrossed Yale provided ready access to shops and restaurants. I could walk from one end of my undergraduate world to the other in fifteen minutes.

Yale flourished within its inner-city perimeter. Outside I saw familiar signposts of failed urban renewal—dilapidated buildings, empty lots, and overcrowded public housing. Walking west where Mom grew up could be dangerous day or night. She wouldn't have recognized the city she had known as a child. My sheltered life in Buffalo spared me from seeing how the urban underclass lived. New Haven forced me to face it.

The all-male entering class in the fall of 1961 highlighted the thin pool from which Yale drew. One thousand freshmen averaged six feet tall. All but a handful were white. Three-quarters were Protestant. The Catholic and Jewish chaplains joked about which group had the larger quota. The turmoil that would turn Yale upside down in the late 1960s seemed nowhere in evidence.

The old order protected Yale's social hierarchy. Nominally, all of the members of the class of '61 were treated alike. We roomed together in dorms on the Old Campus, ate together in the Commons, and took many of the same introductory courses. After this gigantic freshman mixer, we'd spend our remaining years in one of twelve residential colleges. Each was supposed to reflect a cross-section of our class.

The egalitarian side of Yale had an opposite twin that celebrated status. Membership in exclusive secret societies marked the pinnacle of peer recognition. Ten percent of every class received coveted invitations. Those left out of this senior year rite of passage never got the full undergraduate experience. The secret societies admitted star athletes and extracurricular standouts. Meritocracy, however, had its limits. Graduates of elite boarding schools filled most slots. The entitlement often passed from one generation to the next. Lacking a pedigree, I wouldn't be part of the in-crowd unless I made a name for myself beyond academics.

A routine meeting with a dorm advisor during orientation week set my priorities. The brash law student who lived on the floor below in my dorm looked up from a folder when I walked in for a ten-minute counseling session. After a perfunctory welcome, he informed me that I had been pegged as an average student based on my transcript and College Board scores. He hit the raw nerve of my deepest insecurity. I flushed with embarrassment at the put-down.

I retreated from my counseling session without a word of objection. It never occurred to me that the advisor might have used the same crude motivator with everyone. I took him at his word and vowed to prove him wrong. Not just wrong but dead wrong. I'd been passive in our face-to-face meeting but got very angry afterward. No one had ever called my academic ability into question.

A pickup basketball several days later clinched my decision to put studies above everything else. The freshman class had taken buses to the state park at the end of orientation week for sports and a barbecue. Four of us held the court against all comers for much of the afternoon. I made some pretty good plays but didn't come close to keeping up with a couple of my teammates. One, Bob Trupin, was going to play three years of varsity ball and develop into a late-round NBA draft pick. Forget basketball at the college level.

I took the bus back to campus with Bob Levine, an all-state six-foot-five-inch forward from Maine. He had great hands and a perfect touch around the basket. Although he was varsity material, he wasn't going to try out for the freshman team. When I asked why, he said that as a premed he couldn't afford two or three hours a day of practice.

His choice sealed mine. If a truly exceptional athlete was passing up basketball to concentrate on studies, I had no business doing anything but hitting the books. Forget trying out for the *Yale Daily News*. My credentials were as good as any other high school newspaper editor. I just couldn't bring myself to attend an organizational meeting. For better and worse, I pinned my whole college experience on being a top student.

As Yale intended, education started with classmates. Peter Szilagy, the foreign student I requested as a roommate, had an astonishing life story. He had crossed the border into Austria as Russian tanks crushed the Hungarian Uprising of 1956. From there he found his way to England, finishing grammar school and playing a muscle man in a Rock Hudson film. This exceptionally talented future doctor, who worked two jobs on the side, couldn't shake the Hungarian old wives' tale about evil spirits traveling through the night air. He insisted on keeping all the windows closed after dark.

Lee Moore, the southerner who lived on my floor, convinced me one Saturday night that the grits served with our scrambled eggs grew on grit bushes. Charley Benoit, the all-American lacrosse player down the hall, wanted to show me that tough guy jocks had a reflective side. Nick Fessenden, an old-line Philadelphian who didn't want to get by on family ties, confided that a street in Washington had been named after a family member who served in Lincoln's cabinet. My pickup basketball partner Levine asked me to hold his wallet when we walked up Chapel Street to Saturday games at Yale Bowl. Observant Jews weren't supposed to carry money on the Sabbath. The friendly midwesterner with whom I sat down at meals in the Commons turned out to be Bob Woodward of *Washington Post* fame.

Yale delivered a lot more than rubbing shoulders with interesting people for $3,000 room and board. With advanced placement a rarity, no one graduated without taking basic or advanced English, a foreign language at the intermediate level, a yearlong survey of Western civilization or American history, and two semesters of science. Large introductory courses had well-led discussion sections. Tenured faculty taught small sophomore seminars and held regular office hours. An honors program gave upperclassmen leeway for independent study under the supervision of a senior advisor. Access to great minds was there for the asking.

The slide rule, typewriter, and card catalog made up my academic tool kit. Science and math instruction factored in time for computation in the pre-calculator era. Research in the humanities meant combing through library stacks and poring over microfilm to find nuggets of information. Typing with carbon paper took forever. Most interaction with other students and professors was one-on-one. A Yale liberal arts education valued individual achievement over collaboration, depth over breadth, and focus over multitasking.

Freshman instructors asked a lot. Mr. Welsh, a New Englander said to be writing pulp novels on the side, assigned three papers per semester in advanced English. Every one came back loaded with marginal comments on style and logic. He never sugarcoated his criticism, the first of many teachers who pointed up weaknesses in order to show that they took the work of their students seriously.

An imaginative instructor in intermediate French prepared fill-in-the-blank scripts with the lyrics of popular folk songs and the monologues of comedians. I spent countless hours listening to tapes in the language lab to come up with the right words. The Jacques Brel classic about a young couple embracing on a public bench comes back all the time.

My discussion leader in Western European history, Mr. Emerson, camouflaged his keen intellect with an Arkansas drawl. A fighter pilot who had returned to Yale on the GI Bill, he dazzled us with sports talk, profanity, and deep insights. His command of primary documents and his explanations of why they mattered astounded me. I approached him after class one morning to make an appointment. Instead, he invited me to join him for a fifteen-cent White Tower hamburger. That lunch counter conversation made up my mind to major in history.

Learning about the past intrigued me in part because I couldn't trace my own family roots any further back than two generations. If I couldn't put the pieces together on the personal level, then at least I could try to understand the larger forces at work. The big questions appealed most to me. What gave rise to the modern nation-state? Why did Europe nearly self-destruct in the twentieth century? What shaped America's distinctive national character? Putting the here and now into context stirred my passion.

History also looked like the best all-purpose preparation for a career in international affairs. I wasn't cut out for medicine, law, or business. Someday I wanted to help my country lead the world. Europe stood out as the most important piece on the global chessboard. The more deeply I understood the Old World, the stronger my position would be down the line.

I surpassed my academic goal at the end of the first semester. I had hoped to make the dean's list, the top quarter of the class, but wound up in the top 10 percent. Once I opened the small vanilla envelope with my grades, nothing less would ever do.

While trying to prove myself, I discovered that Yale was an incredible intellectual resource. At its heart was Sterling Library, the vast, cathedral-like structure in the center of the campus. The heavy iron doors of Sterling opened a storehouse of archives, books, manuscripts, periodicals, and newspapers. Fifteen separate levels housing millions of volumes defined Yale as a world-class institution. Every scholar at the university knew and used the library. It was always possible to find a quiet nook on the upper floors. The black and brown leather chairs in the reading room were perfect for stretching out with a novel. Sterling made me part of a community that seemed larger and more important than my class.

Freshman year primed me to grow intellectually. As I sophomore, I decided to skip superstar lecturers and look for courses that gave me personal contact with leading scholars. I was still eighteen, but those choices marked me for life.

Allan Bloom, a tightly wound classicist who later gained fame for his critique of American higher education, made me think for myself. Eager to do well, I asked him to read the draft of a paper for his course on modern political thought. He tore apart my analysis of a chapter in *Leviathan*, the seventeenth-century masterpiece of British political philosopher Thomas Hobbes. Puffing nervously on a cigarette, he let me have it. "Have you been listening to me this semester?" he fumed. "I've said time and again that you have to pull the meaning out of the text word by word. So you hand in a draft that cites secondary sources."

Bloom took out his copy of *Leviathan*. Pausing for emphasis, he read

Hobbes's one-sentence definition of *power* aloud: "The power of a Man is his present means to obtain some future apparent Good." Then he challenged me to write at least two pages on that sentence alone. I retreated to the library. Bloom was asking me to do something I had never done before.

Painfully, I marshaled my thoughts. A surge of accomplishment hit me when I got them down on paper. I found it in me to do what Bloom had asked. He jotted a note of qualified encouragement after reading the final paper I turned in. "A vast improvement over your draft," he wrote. "You still have to think through a lot of things but you begin to get inside the text."

Edmund Morgan, the slight, soft-spoken authority on Colonial America, gave his students a taste of the work historians do. He supplemented his polished lectures with a compendium of every known document related to the founding of the Massachusetts Bay Colony from 1620 to 1635. We had to write our own account based on primary sources or compare two of the historical accounts that he included in the volume of documents. Doubting my ability to weave facts into an engaging narrative, I chose the comparison.

Morgan quietly suggested that I should keep an open mind in deciding whether a modern historian had a better insight than someone writing a century or two earlier. That possibility had never dawned on me. I assumed that writing history was a forward march just like the advance of technology. I concluded, however, that the nineteenth-century narrative got closer to what really happened than the twentieth-century account. When it came to scholarship, newer wasn't always better. Morgan liked my analysis but docked me for using the passive voice too much. A good historian, he wrote, figures out who did what to whom and uses active verbs. I should do the same.

Robert Lopez, a renowned medievalist who published in four languages, inspired me with his love of learning. Unlike Morgan, he spoke from notes rather than a prepared text. I found his meanderings incredible. Once he spent half a class period describing the link between the growth of the Roman Empire's goat population, increased soil erosion, reduced agricultural production, economic decline, and political upheaval. His accounts of twelfth-century trade between the backwater of Western Europe and the more advanced Arab world drove home a fundamental point. The preeminence of the West was a five-hundred-year chapter in a much longer story.

A meticulously dressed professor of Romance languages, Victor Brombert, had the greatest influence on my future. Brombert, like the historian Lopez, left Europe during the Hitler era to become one of Yale's leading lights. He taught a sophomore seminar on French literature around a conference table that seated twelve. Conducting the class only in French, he introduced us to Balzac, Flaubert, and Proust with European sensibility and American enthusiasm. Once he broke into an Italian aria to show that Molière's *Don Juan*, the play we were reading, shared the same roots as Mozart's *Don Giovanni*.

I felt drawn to the cosmopolitan Brombert and called on him during office hours. A natural-born mentor, he treated me cordially and asked if I had considered majoring in French literature. When I told him that I planned to study history, he suggested spending junior year in France anyway. "You could learn a lot," he said, "if you see how and why the French look at the world as they do. There will be time for books later."

I was ready for a change of scene from Yale. I hadn't found life in a residential college anything like what it was cracked up to be. Yale's small communities of 250 students were supposed to be the centerpiece of undergraduate life. Each college had its own dining room, library, intramural teams, extracurricular activities, and a senior faculty member in residence.

I was assigned to Timothy Dwight College on Temple Street, named after an early Yale president. For convenience sake I shared a suite with two other serious students with whom I wasn't close. Aside from occasional blind dates that led nowhere, I kept on pouring everything I had into studies.

Nobody warned me what it would be like living with a clique of boarding school bluebloods. A hard core—the kind Dad hadn't been permitted to teach back in the thirties—gravitated to Timothy Dwight. They owned the college. Their assured futures and nonchalance about academics put them in a different world from mine. It was their booze versus my books, their women versus my work, and their good times versus my goals.

One high achiever navigated easily between both worlds. Richard Wheeler Baker III had Groton credentials, played varsity hockey, and was to graduate summa cum laude. He could party on Saturday night and get to the library before me on Sunday morning. Our academic interests overlapped. I admired him greatly, even if he were the exception that made the rule.

The boarding school crowd ignored types like me. Two with whom I shared a bathroom gave me the silent treatment for an entire year. I had never been snubbed before. It didn't take a rocket scientist to figure out why. I disdained the preppies, failing at the time to see what they gained and I missed. They made lasting friendships, while I floated alone. Later they shaped the alumni network, in which I never participated.

Eventually, I found a rewarding way to support Yale that had nothing to do with the class of 1965. The endowment of a lecture honoring Dad's research brought me back to campus regularly. I saw day-and-night changes. The breaking of the gender barrier, the naming of a Jewish president, and the growth of undergraduate diversity made Yale a better place. But the positives that came later couldn't undo the exclusion I had felt sophomore year.

My discomfort at Timothy Dwight prompted me to take Brombert's advice and apply for junior year in France. The program, sponsored by Sweetbriar College, accepted me along with a few other classmates. Instead of being invited into a secret society, Yale's highest social privilege, I'd be able to master a foreign language that still rivaled English and experience a way of life that defined high class. The year away would be the most fulfilling of my undergraduate education.

Before heading off, I returned home for a summer of intensive conversational French at Georgetown University. Our family's eight-room brick colonial just over the District line made a statement. A screened porch off the dining room looked out on a large yard centered by a huge, shady oak tree. Mom's brother Paul flew down from Boston to design the landscaping. Just beyond the back fence was Rock Creek Drive, a two-lane road that wound its way through northwest Washington to the Lincoln Memorial.

Despite the house, Dad remained a small fish in a big pond. While his younger brother, Leon, treated VIPs, he was the other Yochelson bringing home a government salary. Finances pinched. My parents paid a whopping $50,000 in cash for a Chevy Chase address. They dipped into savings for my college tuition. A $20,000 loan to a former patient had to be written off. Dad disregarded Mom's plea to take out a license to supplement his income. He also crossed the line with his new research subjects, inviting one with a long prison record to come over on weekends to do odd jobs.

Mom did her best to handle the stress. Her love of Israeli art opened the door to a friendship with a prominent philanthropist. She toyed with the idea of taking courses at American University. Dad objected, and she gave way. The family always came first. She looked after his needs, entertained friends from New Haven days, and provided the same support for my sister, Bonnie, that she had for me.

I pressed my parents on Bonnie's education. The age gap had always limited our time together. I had been a protective older brother in Buffalo, tugging her around on a snow sled and shooting baskets with her in preschool. She had a lot of spunk, once prompting me to slam a door and break her finger while babysitting. Before bedtime I used to give her confidence-building quizzes on vocabulary, math, and geography. She never failed to get a perfect score. When we moved to Chevy Chase, I taught her how to toss a Frisbee in an open field in Rock Creek Park across from our house. She was a natural athlete and a gifted student.

It irked me that Bonnie might be shortchanged on educational opportunities. Although public schools were stronger in suburban Maryland than they had been in Buffalo, my parents had shown no interest in any of the private schools that would open more college doors for her. It was a question of equity, not privilege, from my standpoint. My pressure eventually made a difference. Bonnie transferred to Sidwell Friends, a Quaker school with high academic standards that later became known for attracting the daughters of Presidents Clinton and Obama.

A more fundamental issue of equity, civil rights, commanded national attention before I left for France. In August 1963 I joined hundreds of thousands who marched from the Capitol to the Lincoln Memorial under the leadership of the Reverend Martin Luther King Jr. My commitment wasn't grounded in direct personal experience. The only African American whom I knew was Elvy Robinson, the mild, hardworking live-in housekeeper who looked after Bonnie and me for several years in Buffalo. Mom and Dad weren't progressive on matters of race. What moved me was whether America, which had been so good to my family, could live up to its own ideals.

The civil rights marchers streamed to the Mall early in the morning of August 28. There were 250,000 of us; most of the marchers were black. I went along with the Connecticut delegation. The loudspeakers weren't up to the job, so we didn't hear much of Dr. King's historic "I Have a Dream" speech. Locking arms with so many others, I sang "We Shall Overcome" dozens of times on that hot summer day. The simple act of solidarity always stayed with me. I played it over in my mind thousands of times, feeling the power of the moment and the cause.

I prepared to leave for a year on a high note. Just as Kennedy wished, I had taken my first political stand for the good of my country.

4 FRENCH CONNECTIONS

Mom and Dad dropped me off in September 1963 at Pier 41 in New York to take the *Queen Mary* for Le Havre. Looking around, I saw a hundred new faces from forty universities. As the Sweetbriar contingent boarded with our footlockers, I felt excited but unsure.

A lot would depend on language skills. English wasn't widely spoken in France. If you couldn't make your way on French terms, you hung out with other Americans. To get us ready, Sweetbriar put us through six weeks of language training before the academic year started in Paris. This warm-up took place in Tours, a city of about 125,000 in the heart of château country. We were assigned in twos and threes to live with host families.

French textbooks celebrated Tours, the site of a great battle that halted the advance of Islam into Western Europe in 732 CE. From its medieval origins the town grew into a flourishing commercial center surrounded by the lush properties of the aristocracy. Although the French Revolution undercut the power of the landed gentry, tourism kept Tours viable. The charm and authenticity of the city lay in its stewardship of French tradition. No purer French was spoken anywhere else.

French provincial life won me over quickly. Tours was small enough to get around on bicycles. I rode into town for class Monday through Friday, pedaling down the banks of the Loire to cross the Woodrow Wilson Bridge. There I discovered the difference between pastries made with shortening and butter, the taste of café au lait, and the wondrous smell of baguettes fresh from the oven. Bread meant so much to the French. The typical baker got up at three in the morning to prepare the day's dough from scratch. Then there were the cheeses. France turned me into a foodie overnight.

Sweetbriar programmed six hours of language class a day. I rated about average on incoming placement tests, well below those who attended bilingual schools or grew up with French at home. Trying to get the language down, I used to walk through the bustling outdoor market in Tours with Janie Pepper, an outgoing blonde French major from Ohio. We wandered from stall to stall, trying out new words and expressions with vendors, who were always looking for a sale.

One day a horsemeat butcher gave us a five-minute lecture on the advantages of eating his product instead of beef. It wasn't just a question of price. Horsemeat was cleaner, fresher, and tastier. My classmate, who rode horses, said that slaughtering them was inhumane. The butcher begged to differ. You couldn't compare riding horses and eating horses. They were totally different kinds of animals. We decided to move on, never quite sure whether the butcher was kidding, rationalizing, or speaking truth.

I teamed up with other Sweetbriar students on weekends to visit the spectacular residences built near Tours before the French Revolution. We reached Azay-le-Rideau, Chenonceau, and Chambord by train and bicycle. Surrounded by moats, the castles reflected the power of an aristocratic ruling class that marked France profoundly. The nobility all had the privilege of using the pronoun *de* in their names to refer to the places they came from. Many of the most famous, such as Amboise and Orléans, were located near Tours. The fields and vineyards of the region accounted for their wealth. As we biked by them on single-lane roads, ripe fruit within reach was fair game.

Weekend road trips couldn't begin to match the value of living in a French home. Host families provided *demi-pension*—our own bedrooms, a separate bathroom, and two meals a day. Families that could afford such amenities were more likely to be interested in houseguests than extra income. Sweetbriar paired me with Peter Smith, a quiet, easygoing French literature major from Columbia.

The family with whom we stayed fit the profile of the French upper middle class. He was a reserved, silver-haired oil company executive in his fifties. She was about ten years younger, stylish, and socially ambitious. Their son was at boarding school, leaving a spare bedroom and bath for my roommate and me to share. Our host family had taken in Sweetbriar students for several years in their comfortable home, mainly for the cachet. Neither spoke English.

Our host took her responsibilities seriously. She was going to make her American boarders presentable no matter what. The dinner hour provided an endless string of teaching moments. Among other things, I learned why it was important to keep my hands on the table at all times, how to hold a knife and fork, which way to tip a soup bowl that is almost finished, and how to peel fruit without touching it. She polished my roommate and me like pieces of silver.

Several couples came over one evening for dinner and bridge. A wise-cracking invitee wondered whether I was a milk or a wine drinker. I replied that Americans weren't the only ones who liked milk. Hadn't Prime Minister Pierre Mendès-France campaigned for greater milk consumption during the mid-1950s? The guest replied that Mendès-France wasn't a Frenchman, using a slang word that I didn't understand. When I looked at him quizzically, he explained that the former prime minister was what you Americans call a "Yid." I let him know that I was one, too, and went upstairs.

Our host received a prized invitation to the annual hunt near Tours toward the end of our stay. She invited my roommate and me to follow along with her. An energetic wild goat kept the hunters and their dogs running in circles for hours. When I ducked behind a tree for a minute, she honked in frustration. Twenty riders charged toward her mini-wagon, mistaking the horn for a signal that "the animal" had been sighted. Withering looks cut down the woman who put so much stock in appearances.

Nostalgia sweeps over me when I think back on home schooling in Tours. The mealtime tutorials pushed me across the threshold from hesitancy to fluency. Etiquette lessons registered. Provincial views alerted me to the stereotypes I'd run up against later on. I took to the role of student ambassador of the United States with my host family. I was ready for the next level by the time I left.

Sweetbriar arranged for another live-in experience in Paris. Almost all of us were placed in the fashionable residential districts that flanked opposite sides of the Arc de Triomphe. We tailored our own courses of study. I took a placement exam that qualified me for a one-year program for foreign students at Sciences Po (short for Sciences Politiques), the well-known institute that led to careers in government, law, and journalism.

The certificate program all but eliminated daily contact with everyone in the Sweetbriar program except my roommates. I liked it that way.

Sciences Po occupied two squared-off buildings on the Rue St. Guillaume near St. Germain des Prés on the left bank of the Seine. Cafés in the neighborhood had been favorite haunts of generations of artists and intellectuals as well as American expatriates. Rebuilt and reorganized by the government after World War II, Sciences Po served as a stepping-stone of choice for nineteen- and twenty-year-olds on their way into the French establishment.

Twenty-five hundred students enrolled in the three-year degree program. They got a generalist credential in politics, economics, and international relations. Many supplemented Sciences Po with a more specialized degree program in law. The most ambitious viewed it as preparation for l'École Nationale d'Administration, or ENA, France's elite school of public service. The infamous ENA admissions exam was designed to rattle every candidate to see who withstood the pressure. Those who made it through traveled a well-marked path to the top of the powerful French bureaucracy. Their counterparts at France's other elite schools, known as "grandes écoles," followed the same trajectory in engineering, academe, and business.

I quickly saw that the top of the pyramid in French education was more selective, merit based, and narrowly focused on the public sector than the Ivy League. The French state was an abstraction but not the students my age who aspired to manage it. They had more poise and a facility with ideas than I had ever seen. I put them—and by extension public service itself—on a pedestal as the year progressed.

The one-year certificate program had an enrollment of two hundred foreign students. More than half of them came from Europe, with the remainder divided about equally among Africa, the Americas, the Middle East, and Southeast Asia. We took elective lecture courses (modern French history and diplomatic history in my case) plus a required American-style seminar on France since 1945. I'd get credit for junior year on a pass-fail basis if I made it through.

Sciences Po had an altogether different feel from Yale. As I approached the Rue St. Guillaume from the Métro, passing the student hangout Chez Basil, I didn't sense that I was crossing any boundaries, as I did in New

Haven. The school fit seamlessly into its high-end neighborhood, an urban campus that offered classes to students who were otherwise on their own. My well-dressed French classmates shared similar interests and were for the most part products of a system famous for weeding out all but a few.

Bringing this group together created a lot of intellectual energy. Students didn't just come and go. Their animated conversations spilled into surrounding cafés and restaurants, a blend of big ideas and small talk that was open to all. Although my French didn't always hold up, I felt part of a student community for the first time.

In contrast, a wide gulf separated students and faculty. Sciences Po had its share of stars. They wrote prolifically in French newspapers but stood aloof in the amphitheaters where they lectured. Professors arrived, read from prepared texts, and left. The give-and-take that took place naturally at Yale rarely occurred at Sciences Po.

The impersonal system could be brutal, as I discovered during an excruciating half-hour oral exam in diplomatic history. The question I picked at random from a pile on the table was obscure. The professor hadn't covered it in his lectures. My weak answer counted for the whole grade.

Happily, the centerpiece of the certificate program was its small group breakout on postwar France. The overview of domestic and foreign policy doubled as an introduction to the French way of writing essays, making eight-minute presentations, and taking exams. It was the brainchild of the much-liked head of administration, Monsieur Henry-Gréard, who led weekly discussions, organized field trips, and made himself available for one-on-one meetings. His warmth and informality were atypical.

The French approach captivated me. All of my professors at Yale had individual teaching styles. Here every paper or talk began with an introduction that framed the issue and stated a thesis. Supporting evidence had to be presented in two parts that fit together, such as causes and consequences, benefits and costs, or successes and failures. The conclusion summarized the argument. The French method stressed capturing the essence of an issue from more than one side. The final exam in the "France since 1945" seminar didn't even pose a question. We had three hours to discuss the significance of the end of French colonial rule in Africa, Asia, and the Middle East. The rest was up to us.

I grasped the French art of synthesis quickly. My role models were the greats I heard and read at Sciences Po. Historians René Rémond and Pierre Renouvin didn't rely heavily on data, but they knew how to put ideas together with originality and flair. That skill, learned as a junior in college, would be the mainstay of my future career. Looking back, I sometimes wonder if I leaned too much on a single strength instead of expanding my repertoire.

Adopting the French intellectual style didn't mean accepting its content. For all its imposing traditions, France didn't have much to offer as a political model. The parliamentary system put in place after World War II had lasted little more than a decade. France changed institutions in 1958, when its brilliant, dogmatic war hero, General Charles de Gaulle, stepped in to fill the vacuum. He soon consolidated power as a strong, directly elected president.

De Gaulle's obsession with the grandeur of France grated on me. He carried himself like a world leader with far more standing than the mid-sized country for which he spoke. His challenges to American leadership enthralled the French and increased his stature abroad. In grave tones he questioned the reliability of the U.S. security guarantee to the North Atlantic Treaty Organization (NATO). No American president, he said, would ever risk the destruction of Chicago to safeguard Paris. American motives weren't to be trusted. France would pursue its own interests by expanding its nuclear capability and keeping its distance from the United States.

The drumbeat of anti-Americanism sharpened my ambivalence about France. There was much to admire in the richness of its culture, the quality of its education, and the universal meaning of its political ideals. Yet much about France wasn't appealing at all. The split between haves and have-nots ran deep. The French mistreated the North African immigrants who did the dirty work. There were troubling skeletons in the closet, including the treatment of Jews during World War II. French insecurity often translated into disdain for all things foreign.

The assassination of JFK in November 1963 left me feeling painfully cut off. The first sketchy reports were broadcast in Paris at about 8:00 p.m. France was not the place to be at a time like this. Kennedy personified so many of the hopes I had for my country and my own future. Dazed, I wandered up to Le Drugstore at the top of the Champs Élysées near the Arc de Triomphe. Hundreds of other shaken Americans gathered there to wait for the international edition of the *Herald Tribune* to hit the newsstand at midnight.

By sheer accident I struck up a conversation with a reporter for the *New York Times*, whose European edition went to press at two in the morning. He invited me down to his offices, where his bureau chief offered me a drink. I volunteered to distribute the paper before it went on sale at 6:00 a.m. to any Americans who had not gotten the word. Stationing myself outside the elegant strip club Le Lido, I gave away about twenty copies. A half dozen hookers expressed genuine sympathy.

My homesickness didn't last long, in part because of the good living situation in which I had landed in Paris. Two classmates from Yale joined my roommate from Tours and me. Bill Benson, a likable science major from Connecticut, wanted to have an outside-the-box experience before going to med school. David Hoy, an introspective philosophy major, was going to find out whether the French were the masters of logic whom they claimed to be.

The four of us stayed with an old-line aristocrat, Madame de St. Maurice, who was looking for company, not income. She lived comfortably in a building designed by her late husband, a well-known architect, on the Avenue de Wagram in the posh 17th arrondissement. Her classically furnished apartment took up half a floor. She and her twenty-five-year-old son, Gilles, had bedrooms in one wing, while her four paying guests shared two bedrooms and a bath in the other. She invited us to use the large entrée, which doubled as a sitting room, with a phonograph and a small collection of classical long-playing records. The Portuguese cook and housekeeper left us a breakfast of toast, juice, and café au lait in the kitchen every morning.

Madame presided over a four-course dinner every evening at 7:45 sharp, signaling the cook with a bell under the carpet. Despite the formality of the dining room, these evening meals were nothing like those at Tours. Madame treated us more like nephews than pupils. She never corrected our French or played explainer-in-chief. Instead, she brought us out with gentle questions about our interest in France and our impressions of Paris.

She brought the meal to a close by asking if we had eaten well. It was a ritual that all of us enjoyed.

Madame was less reserved about her own background than I expected. The crests on the living room wall traced her ancestry to William the Conqueror's invasion of England in the eleventh century. Her Catholic family returned to France to seek refuge during the English Reformation. Her husband had carried on the work of a relative, Baron Haussmann, the civic planner who had remade much of Paris during the nineteenth century. Her great sorrow was the recent death of her eldest son, a diplomat, in an accident in Switzerland. American students raised her spirits, reminding her of the English nanny she had had as a child.

The aristocratic code of conduct that she observed didn't apply to her American boarders. We were free agents who provided a window into a side of French life that she could not allow herself to experience. The relationship I struck up with the baker's family across the street intrigued her. She had been a customer of that bakery for decades and would have never dreamed of making small talk. My roommate from Tours and I, on the other hand, got invited for a glass of wine and leftover pastries on Sunday afternoons.

Madame's fondness for us led her to suggest that we tag along with her son and a visiting niece at a French debutante party. We would not have qualified for an invitation if we were French, but we were a welcome novelty as the Americans who shook the hand of the hostess in the receiving line instead of kissing it. A nice couple invited me to attend a reception a few weeks later. Showing up on time at 7:00 p.m., I waited a full hour before the other guests started to trickle in. My charcoal gray suit stuck out in a sea of navy blue.

Madame used to join me for tea in the entrée as I listened to Mendelssohn's violin concerto on her phonograph. The difference in our ages and backgrounds ruled out deep personal conversation, so we kept it light. Clearly, she was reaching out to me because my interests paralleled those of the son she had lost. In his memory she crossed social boundaries that she had been raised not to cross. This small, conservatively dressed matriarch—about Mom's size—wasn't the last of a dying breed. She was a survivor for whom I developed great affection.

I searched out a different side of French life when I started going to Friday night services at the conservative synagogue in the 16th arrondissement. Curiosity drew me to the quietly ornate sanctuary on the Rue Copernic, which was a short Métro ride away from where I lived. The experience of World War II was still fresh. Paris had been liberated from German occupation less than two decades earlier. I wanted to learn what had happened to the Jewish community during and after the war.

The Jews whom I met at the Rue Copernic did not talk easily about their past. France had not yet begun to come to terms with its wartime history. The country was still reeling from its forced retreat from Vietnam and the loss of its colonial empire in North Africa. The surge of Muslim immigration was only just beginning, leaving the Jewish community of five hundred thousand the most visible religious minority. Young Jews were eager to fit in. One had the unlikely first name of Christian.

I was able to peel back the layers of Jewish identity when I met Marion Rothman, a student of French literature at the Sorbonne. She looked like a pretty young girl in a woman's body with twinkly blue eyes, dark hair, and a bounce in her step. She agreed to go out to the movies and picked me up in her family's Peugeot.

We hit it off. Marion was the first girl I wanted to put my arms around. The attraction was mutual. We went out two or three more times before she asked me over to meet her parents. I remembered the cardinal rule learned in Tours that a dinner guest should never arrive with empty hands. A small box of chocolates did the trick.

The Rothman narrative read like a novel. Marion's grandparents, first-generation immigrants from Poland, had crossed the Pyrénées on foot in 1942 to escape the Nazis. The family separated in Portugal, where their daughter boarded a boat to Palestine. There, at the age of seventeen, she fell in love with a Jewish conscript in the British army who had lived most of his life in Istanbul. Bernard and Geneviève Rothman returned to Paris after the war, where Marion was born. Her mother found work in a dress shop. Starting from scratch, her father became a successful entrepreneur.

Marion's parents rarely spoke of the hard times before they were able to move to the fashionable suburb of Neuilly. After she graduated from a top-ranked lycée, they bought a home farther west of Paris in exclusive Le

Vésinet. The upward mobility and the high priority attached to education struck a very familiar chord.

What set the Rothmans apart was their total attachment to the French way of life. Marion's academic specialty in French theater, her father's avid interest in wine, her mother's eye for fashion, and their getaway apartment on the Côte d'Azur were all part of the package. It was amazing to see the impact of the French values, culture, and lifestyle on a family whose origins weren't very different from mine.

The mix of the familiar and unfamiliar made Marion an ideal match for me. We were both intellectuals but in different fields. She spoke good English, but we got to know each other in French. She was worldly and widely traveled in some ways but as inexperienced with boys as I was with girls. I liked her close family despite their barbs about American cooking ("ketchup is your national dish") and culture ("the soap opera is your contribution to the arts"). And I found her French femininity very alluring.

I headed home to collect my jumbled thoughts. A year of upper-crust French education changed not only my view of the world but also its view of me. I came back more confident and polished than before, an equalizer to being left out at Yale. Yet the country that enriched me challenged the United States at every turn. Should I aspire to be an interpreter of the French, a mediator, or an American advocate? I wasn't sure.

I tried to sort out my French connections in an essay over the summer of 1964. Borrowing a construct from Sciences Po, I highlighted the interplay of continuity and change. The French, I concluded, found strength in their past. And that put strict limits on the pace of modernization they'd accept. My detached style presented France as a puzzle to solve rather than a flesh-and-blood place. Tellingly, I didn't write a single line about my relationship with Marion, even though I couldn't get her out of my mind. It was easier to analyze than to explore my emotions.

5 PATH OF CHOICE

I returned to New Haven struggling to bridge the French-American divide. Cooped up in a single room, I wound down from ten life-changing months abroad while my classmates revved up for their capstone year.

The French-born dean of Yale College, Georges May, taught an advanced literature course that allowed me to keep up my language skills. He knew how to navigate between France and the United States. Yet he only showed his French side when interpreting the poetry of Baudelaire, the novels of Stendhal, or the discourses of Rousseau. I never got close enough to him to share my reflection on my junior year abroad.

I could have gotten by with a concentration in European history but decided to learn more about America's past. I also renewed my apple-pie American interests, sharing many a coal-fired pizza with Howie Dale, the sophomore starting guard on the basketball team. He told me about the calls that had flooded in after he scored thirty points in a Florida high school tournament. The wave stopped as soon as recruiters learned that the wire story listing him as six feet ten was off by a foot. Talking basketball reaffirmed my cultural identity, just as reading the *International Herald Tribune* every day had in Paris.

I guarded one precious link to France—my correspondence with Marion. I hungered for her handwritten letters, which arrived every few days at my postbox in Yale Station. They weren't deep, mostly a running account of how she was spending her days and her reaction to my most recent letter. She always closed with a reminder of how she missed me and that she loved me with all her heart. The certainty that I'd be hearing from her kept a very strong hold on me. I wanted to factor Marion into my plans for the future.

As I mulled over what to do, senior year proved a telling reminder that my choices were trivial in the larger scheme of things. While I was still in France, President Lyndon B. Johnson arm-twisted the Civil Rights Act of 1964 through Congress. The act mandated federal action to level the playing field for minorities, especially African Americans, who had endured a century of second-class citizenship.

Staughton Lynd, a fortyish assistant professor, provided insight into the weight of the past in his course on the history of the South. The son of two widely known sociologists, Lynd combined a scholarly demeanor with a fiery belief in equity. He demolished the view that slavery had been a paternalistic institution. The slave experience didn't produce Negroes with sunny smiles and carefree dispositions. Some of the most telling evidence of the dehumanizing effects of slavery came from studies of Holocaust survivors.

Lynd himself made an extraordinary gesture when he learned of the suicide of a student taking his class. Realizing that he had never spoken to the student, he felt that the death might have been avoided in a smaller setting. He broke the lecture for 120 students into four discussion groups. He led each on his own, more than quadrupling his teaching burden. Some thought he had a Jesus complex, but I didn't. Like other sixties activists, he had his eye on changing a system that he found far too impersonal.

Lynd's course also showed how far removed Yale was from the realities of U.S. race relations. A university that prided itself in developing leaders had virtually no African American undergraduates and token representation in its graduate schools. Marion Wright, a recent Law School graduate and later a celebrated children's advocate, hammered my classmates and me for being out of touch when she addressed our senior dinner. "This may be the first and last time many of you ever have to listen to a black person," she said with controlled anger.

Wright's hard-hitting attack on white elitism hurt, but it was on target. The Yale education that meant so much to me was painfully inadequate in some respects. Worse still, I had done nothing to make up for Yale's deficiencies. It never occurred to me, however, to stop building my credentials for a career in international affairs. I would try to do the right thing in my personal life, but I was not ready to make a professional commitment to civil rights.

A fateful turn in the Vietnam conflict also took place at the start of my senior year. Following an incident at sea in August 1964, Congress gave President Johnson the authority to take military action to protect U.S. interests. Soon after the 1964 presidential election, the intervention that had begun under JFK spiraled into a ground war that put five hundred thousand American boots on the ground by 1967.

I screened Southeast Asia out as I weighed graduate school and career choices. My goals lay on the other side of the world. I wanted to make my personal interest in Marion and the national interest in Atlantic solidarity mesh. One day I might be part of the American team that drew the French back into the NATO fold.

The glamorous jobs that made public service exciting were out of reach. High-powered political appointees filled them. JFK raided Harvard to make historian Arthur Schlesinger a special assistant. He picked undergraduate dean McGeorge Bundy as national security advisor. LBJ named Walt Rostow, a Yale professor whose family had lived near Mom's growing up, to serve as Bundy's successor. There was no way to prepare for being a political appointee. Anyway, that kind of opportunity was many years off for me.

A start in government, however, looked doable. Living in Washington had already given me a leg up. A family friend who worked on Capitol Hill helped me line up a summer internship at the Senate Committee on Aging after my freshman year. Frank Frantz, the able staff member with whom I rode to work every day, gave me a meaty assignment analyzing private health care plans for the elderly. I combed through them one by one, wondering if there wasn't a better way. My thoughtful boss let me get away to look at Senate debates from the visitors' galley. In a few months I knew my way around.

My experience on the Hill left me feeling positive about government. So did my banter with an assistant administrator of NASA, Bernard Moritz, who lived across the street. I enjoyed the shoptalk about federal agencies when my parents' friends came over. None of the government types came across as gray bureaucrats. They were the reliable insiders who often did the heavy lifting. There were thousands of them in Washington. They weren't rich or socially connected, but they bought homes, raised families, and made a difference on their civil service salaries. I could see myself as one of them.

I decided on public administration as my path of choice without giving law a serious look. Who cared whether lawyers ran Washington? Law school would bog me down in endless detail. The study of government and public policy, I convinced myself, would give me a chance to develop into a geopolitical thinker. I was going to be both an intellectual and a policy maker.

I applied to two well-known graduate programs. Harvard's Littauer School (later to become the Kennedy School of Government) and Princeton's Woodrow Wilson School offered two-year master's programs that would equip me for public service. Mistakenly, I thought of both as American equivalents of ENA, which I had learned about at Sciences Po. These were the platforms from which the best and the brightest worked their way up to leadership positions in the public sector.

In fact, there was no French-style career track in the U.S. government. Public affairs wouldn't establish itself as an accredited field for more than a decade. I was simply betting on the old boys' network of a pair of great universities.

The reputation of Harvard couldn't be beaten, but the Woodrow Wilson School offered all of its incoming students a stipend of $4,000 per year. Financial independence trumped prestige. From the time I had been sent to sleep-away camp, Dad had always said, "Johnny, you've got to learn to stand on your own." Here was my first real chance to do just that. When I was invited to a final interview at Princeton in the spring of 1965, along with Dick Baker, my brilliant classmate, I had already decided to accept if asked.

Opening the letter of acceptance from the Woodrow Wilson School was a bittersweet moment. I had worked so hard for it and had paid a high price. Yale gave me the education of a lifetime, yet I was about to graduate without a single close friend. I saw no point driving back to New Haven for commencement. A magna cum laude diploma and a Phi Beta Kappa key came in the mail.

I spent the summer of 1965 learning Spanish. The Woodrow Wilson School built an international work or research experience into the curriculum between the first and second years. Most of the opportunities were in Central America. I didn't expect that learning an additional Romance language would be too hard. I looked forward to the chance to get a firsthand look at issues of economic and political development that had passed me by in college.

The eight-week course offered by Georgetown University met my needs. I drove to the language arts building just outside the main gates of the campus in my own car. Mom and Dad asked me to pick one out because they were saving the money they had put away for graduate school. Not wanting to overreach, I went for a General Motors compact that looked like the best value on the market. I found out that I had made a bad call a few months later. That's when a little-known consumer advocate named Ralph Nader launched his career with a report tagging my new Corvair as unsafe at any speed.

The six-hour-a-day course at Georgetown brought together a varied group of twenty students. Catholic clergy heading for Latin America made up the largest contingent. Government officials and students rounded out the class. A handsome Harvard undergraduate, who seemed a little standoff-ish, always took a seat by himself in the back of the class. As we got into the language, he introduced himself as "Alberto." The exuberant Puerto Rican teacher called him "Señor Gore." Years later, when I reminded then Senator Gore of our time together as he began a run for the presidency in 1988, he laughed and called out at the end of our conversation, "Hasta luego."

I worked hard on Spanish. My comfort level in French helped a lot. Romance languages shared much the same structure and vocabulary. By the end of the course I was able to express myself, follow fast-speaking news broadcasters pretty well, and get the gist of most newspaper articles.

Marion's surprise visit lit up the summer. She spent a week with her cousins, who lived in Chevy Chase. A year of separation drew us closer together. We had continued to write each other twice a week. Neither of us left ourselves open to meet anyone new. I felt ready to think about marriage, with one proviso. Marion couldn't know me without getting to know the United States. If she spent a year teaching near Princeton, close enough for us to see each other every weekend, we would be able to confirm that a transatlantic tie could work over the long term.

I suggested that Marion apply for a teaching position at Bryn Mawr, a prestigious women's college near Philadelphia with a nationally recognized

French program. She had such impressive credentials. I was sure she would be offered a position. My heart skipped a beat when she agreed to apply.

I drove up to the Woodrow Wilson School in early September with John Forbes, a graduate of Georgetown. I had met him during the final stage of the selection process. The son of a two-star general serving in Vietnam, he had a strong physical presence, jet-black hair, and a deep, resounding voice. I liked his serious, straightforward manner right away. We shared the same interest in public service and Europe. When we grabbed a burger on the way up, he kicked himself for forgetting that it was a Friday. Catholics were supposed to eat fish on Fridays.

Princeton, New Jersey, unlike New Haven, had the look and feel of a privileged enclave. Only the mulch seemed to be decaying in this community of well-appointed homes. The campus of the university was more unified, more beautiful, and more extended than Yale's. The graduate hall where most of the incoming single students lived was a good thirty minutes' walk from the Woodrow Wilson School. I would definitely need the car, but there was ample parking in front of the undergraduate eating clubs that lined the street adjoining the school. The rough-and-tumble of Trenton, ten miles south of Princeton, seemed a world away.

The school itself, a modern four-story rectangle set off by a large concrete plaza and an imposing fountain, had all the amenities of the day. The first floor of the functionally designed building had plenty of open space, a medium-sized auditorium, and seminar rooms. The upper floors housed offices, study cubicles, and a well-stocked library. All classes were taught on the premises, reinforcing the school's singular identity.

My forty classmates were going to make or break my experience. All were accomplished, and many had bright futures. Jim Johnson, a national student leader, would become a Democratic insider and CEO of Fannie Mae. Bob Taft, a former Peace Corpsman, would win the governorship of Ohio. John Dyson, who flew his own plane, would serve as a deputy mayor of New York City under Rudy Giuliani. Heather Low, the only woman and the academic star of our class, would become a key player in the financial services industry. Bing West, a burly ex-marine, would establish himself as a leading expert on unconventional warfare.

For the first time I felt no need to compete. What brought all of us together was a shared commitment to tackle big public policy challenges. Public service had as much cachet as any career in the mid-1960s. There were plenty of challenges to go around in a group entirely made up of high achievers. The school fed our egos and downplayed competitiveness with a grading scale that ranged from good to excellent.

A required domestic policy simulation threw the class together during the first semester. We had to find a politically acceptable site for a fourth commercial airport in the New York City area. The gruff assistant professor who ran the exercise, Mike Danielson, skillfully combined role-playing, research, analysis, and political advocacy. We broke into teams to crack a seemingly intractable problem.

The group dynamic that Danielson set up revealed the hardball side of the policy process. Close-in locations ran afoul of environmentalists, airport authorities, military demands for airspace, and city planners. Splitting the difference didn't work. I learned things about my temperament and style that would not change much for the next forty-plus years. I was more adept at advising than deciding, better at planning than implementing, more conceptual than practical.

The school didn't follow up with a national security simulation. Its resources were much deeper in policy analysis than practice. Research universities like Princeton rewarded publications, not government experience and know-how. The respected dean, Marver Bernstein, had his hands full building a multidisciplinary program that offered a fuzzy degree in public affairs. Most of the school's faculty held joint appointments in established disciplines, balancing their interests in policy with their research. They viewed public administration as a field of study rather than a career path.

Few of our professors had war stories to tell about government service. We had little contact with former officials. I would have given my eyeteeth to chat informally with George Kennan, who had no affiliation with the Woodrow Wilson School but was at Princeton. The most influential career diplomat of the post-1945 era came over once to lecture from the rarefied Institute for Advanced Studies. Immaculately dressed in a suit with a vest, the father of U.S. Cold War strategy read from a prepared text that rang clear as a bell. He made a quick exit afterward. I'd have to read his memoir to get his perspective on the difference between representing the United States overseas and making policy in Washington.

Likewise, the school was sketchy about its public service mission. The curriculum focused on skills, without delving into the larger purposes of government. I found no commitment to developing a group whose careers would intersect later on. The school trained individuals, not a class, for a broad range of endeavors. The application process ensured that most of those who attended were interested in federal careers. The work program aimed at producing generalists, not specialists, who could move anywhere within their areas of interest.

I opted to build on old skills rather than acquire new ones. A concentration in U.S. foreign policy allowed me to do more of what I did best—analyze, synthesize, and communicate. There was much to learn about the policy-making process, global and regional challenges, international law and institutions, and diplomatic strategy. I got along well with three classmates who were taking the foreign policy track to prepare for the U.S. Foreign Service—John Forbes, Dick Baker, and Galen Fox, a Hawaii-born graduate of a liberal arts school in California who planned to concentrate on China. We all shared the same worry: that the unique U.S. position of strength after World War II couldn't last.

The teacher whose perspective influenced me most was Klaus Knorr, a German-born opponent of the Nazi regime. His dueling scar and formal manner made him seem more forbidding than he really was. Like other noted German émigrés in the international field, including Hans Morgenthau and Henry Kissinger, Knorr believed that power explained international relations. He focused on the exercise of military and economic power to achieve a nation's goals.

It was a quintessentially European way of looking at the world, but for me it captured the heart of the challenge facing the United States both in divided Europe as well as in war-torn Vietnam. How much, when, and for what purpose should U.S. power be used? Helping my country make the right decisions was exactly what I wanted to do. Nothing I could think of would be more challenging or rewarding than a career at the interface of power and diplomacy.

Knorr's power politics view of the world contrasted sharply with that of Richard Falk, the school's expert on international law. Falk argued that the United States had a commanding interest in an international community based on respect for legal norms. A card-carrying liberal, he gained prominence for challenging the legal basis of American military intervention in Vietnam. I didn't care much for his politics but shared his belief in the rule of law.

Dick Ullman, the faculty member with whom I had the closest rapport, taught the school's foreign policy seminar. A prize-winning historian of Anglo-Soviet relations, Ullman was reinventing himself as a national security specialist. He was smart, approachable, and only a few years older than I was. His determination to fight through a speech disorder moved me. It was painful hearing him stutter at the lectern, but he wouldn't give up. Instead of resting on his academic laurels, he wanted to make policy and to train policy makers. He encouraged me to set my sights high on the State Department Policy Planning Staff or the National Security Council.

My fascination with geopolitics took my eye off the ball in other areas. I failed to recognize the importance of science and technology as a wellspring of power. Passing up the course of a rising star in that field, Robert Gilpin, I would return to the issues that surround technological innovation thirty years later.

I made a more costly error by overlooking quantitative analysis. Others at the school understood that data-driven decision-making could be a game changer. Jan Lodal, a future principal deputy undersecretary of defense, would make an early mark in the Pentagon's efforts to streamline the weapons acquisition process. Bob Wilburn, then an air force captain and a future college president, would crunch the numbers that helped justify the shift from a draft to an all-volunteer army. I continued to believe that ideas meant more than data. As a result, I didn't seek the quantitative grounding that would have increased my effectiveness later on.

As I pondered America's global interests, I conducted my own international negotiation with Marion. She had submitted her application to Bryn Mawr, but her letters made clear that her interest was in me and not an American teaching experience. If she got an offer, she was looking for a commitment from me. She didn't want to come over simply as a girlfriend.

Meanwhile, Dad suffered his first serious health setback. An ambulance rushed him to the hospital in the middle of the night after an apparent heart attack. Mom shielded me from the news until the following day, when doctors decided that gallstones accounted for Dad's excruciating pain. By the time I drove home that weekend, his gallbladder had been removed and he was resting comfortably at home. We played gin rummy by the hour to pass the time together. Mom always said Dad was as strong as a bull when they married. He was paying the price of thirty years of failing to take care of himself.

Filled with uncertainty about Marion and Dad, I left for a summer of field research in Costa Rica, the small coffee-exporting country known as an island of democratic stability in Central America. My only previous exposure to a developing nation had been in Israel, which was politically and economically isolated from its neighbors. Costa Rica, however, was part of a much larger test bed of U.S. development strategy in Latin America.

The topic I chose to study reflected my big-picture interests and linguistic skills but cost me the chance to get a ground-level view of Costa Rica's economic challenges. I wanted to find out what accounted for the peaceful transfer of power every eight years from a left-of-center party of self-proclaimed modernizers to a right-of-center conservative bloc. A hotly contested presidential election, won by the conservatives in February 1966, provided the hook for my inquiry into the relationship between political stability and economic modernization.

Boarding with a middle-class family in the capital city of San José, I found Costa Rica less different and less poor than I had expected. While culturally Spanish, Costa Rica had a different racial makeup from most of Central America. The population of 1.5 million was much more European than Native Indian in profile, not just in the cities but also in the countryside. A pocket of former slaves, comprising about 5 percent of the population, was concentrated in Limón, a banana-growing region on the Pacific coast controlled by the United Fruit Company. With the highest per capita income in the region, a literacy rate of 80 percent, and quite a bit of infrastructure, Costa Rica seemed far better-off than its Central American neighbors.

No bona fide election analyst would have approved of my research methods. Instead of concentrating on election data, I spent practically all my time conducting open-ended interviews in Spanish with people on both sides of the country's political divide. Using the 1966 presidential election to provide context, I asked about the causes, benefits, and costs of the back-and-forth shifts in power that had taken place since 1948. This journalistic approach paid off. More than thirty deeply engaged players, including the president and three former presidents, agreed to share their perspectives on the competition between the left-of-center and conservative blocs. Notebook in hand, I gathered the material for my first published paper in Princeton's journal *Public and International Affairs*.

Why were so many senior people willing to speak with a twenty-two-year-old American? Perhaps they thought a Princeton grad student might have connections in the U.S. intelligence community. I was in Central America, after all. Whatever their motivations, the Costa Ricans wanted to get their side of the story out.

Before heading home, I took a daylong bus ride to observe a local election. There I ran into one of my sources, who invited me on a white-knuckle flight back to San José. A single engine plane swooped into a cleared field to pick us up. I got my first real taste of developing world reality when the pilot threw his cigarette out of the open-air cockpit as he revved up the propellers.

The letter that was waiting for me in San José rocked my world. Marion had backed out of her commitment to Bryn Mawr. She needed to get engaged before taking what she saw as a great risk. I rushed in a daze to the central post office and called Paris. In tears Marion said she would not be coming. She continued to write, refusing to accept that her decision had ended our relationship. Deeply hurt, I didn't respond and struggled to put the whole thing behind me.

6 CALL OF DUTY

I returned to Princeton in the fall of 1966 torn up inside. My personal concerns, however, quickly took a back seat to the conflict in Vietnam. The war was not going well despite the buildup of U.S. forces. I fit squarely in the demographic of single males aged eighteen to twenty-six who were being drafted. Some of my classmates were applying to law school with the hope that they would not have to serve by the time they graduated. Others were heading for the foreign service or other government agencies that were exempt from military service. The third option was to go army.

My thinking about Vietnam had not changed since the escalation of the war. I gave the benefit of the doubt to the White House. To do otherwise would be to question the very foreign policy establishment that I hoped to join. As U.S. forces failed to turn the tide, I suspended judgment on the right or wrong of American involvement. I wasn't sure whether the cause was worth the human and financial cost. What mattered more for me was not shirking my duty. Going to law school would amount to running away. Taking the foreign service exam would be opportunistic because I truly was not interested in becoming an all-purpose career diplomat.

I would take my chances in the army. Dad and three of my uncles had served during World War II. If I could go to graduate school with Bob Taft, whose great-grandfather had been president of the United States when my grandfather went through Ellis Island, the least I could do was answer my country's call. Military service was a duty; public service was a choice.

My second-year classes faded into the background as I tried to figure out how to limit my risks. To avoid losing complete control to the draft, I signed up for the three-year officer program for college graduates. It would take a year to earn a commission, and then I'd serve two more years. If I washed out along the way, I would probably be sent to Vietnam. The only officer candidate schools that remained open at the height of the war were in the combat arms—armor, artillery, and infantry. I chose armor because tank divisions made up the heart of the U.S. defense in Europe. U.S. troops numbering 250,000 were stationed there, mainly in Germany.

A preinduction physical in Newark in the spring of 1967 exposed the yawning gap between the world I was leaving and the one I was about to enter. Five hundred of us stripped down to our underwear, moving through an assembly line of medical stations in a depot in the crumbling inner city. A dozen doctors and assistants in white coats checked our eyes, teeth, heart, lungs, feet, and reflexes with no personal interest. It was a tough, racially mixed crowd, mostly younger than I was. More than a few of the guys were covered with tattoos and scars. Some swaggered, but underneath I suspect most were uncertain and a little scared, like me. Riding the train back to Princeton Junction, I realized that I would be in for a challenge like no other I had ever faced.

I finished up at the Woodrow Wilson School with mixed feelings. I sharpened my career focus on European security and made a small group of friends. The broad-brush curriculum, however, skirted basic questions about the U.S. foreign policy establishment. What skills really mattered? How did careerists relate to political appointees? Where was the line drawn between public service and private gain? I'd have to figure these things out on my own. The school's master of public affairs degree didn't give me the edge I was expecting. I skipped commencement at Princeton, just as I had at Yale.

Mom drove me to Baltimore for my army induction. She chose the car ride to tell me about the child she had lost before I was born. She shared her moment of grief and faith to let me know how worried she was. She left me with a hug and no tears, knowing that I would check in once a week from Fort Knox, Kentucky, where I was slated to go for four months of training.

Fort Knox spread out over more than one hundred thousand acres of land about thirty-five miles south of Louisville. The installation was widely known as the storage site for America's gold supply. It was also the home of the Armor School as well as one of the army's largest basic training centers. The wooded, rolling hills made for perfect tank country and were equally well suited for marching recruits off their feet. Fort Knox had the look and feel of a world unto itself, with its vast training areas, standard issue barracks, and support facilities. This was not a menacing environment, but it was tightly controlled.

Standing in a long line to be issued green army fatigues, w36, l32, it hit me that I was about to have the same melting pot experience as generations before me had. Recruits in their twenties who had enlisted for the officer program only made up 10 percent of our 150-man training company. Most of the rest were recent high school graduates from a radius of three or four hundred miles around central Kentucky. We were all going to come out army privates regardless of race, religion, or family background.

Eight weeks inside Fort Knox put me into closer contact with more different kinds of people than I had ever met as a civilian. I helped good ol' boys from Tennessee write home to their girlfriends. I traded stories with a college football star from California who almost made the Buffalo Bills. I heard the blare of rock, soul, and country music on portable radios during off-hours. There was room in the mix for one lover of classical. The army's shift to an all-volunteer force would whittle away at this draft-era diversity a few years later.

Basic training did not turn out to be the shock I had thought. The army knew how to mold a diverse group of recruits into a functioning unit. They cut our hair alike, clothed us alike, fed us alike, and treated us alike. They worked us hard and built esprit de corps by pitting units against each other.

The veteran African American first sergeant who charged through the barracks at 5:30 a.m. and called lights out at 10:00 p.m. had the routine down pat. He led by example, whether we were standing inspection, learning parade drill, or marching double time. Sergeant Williams was the first black man I had ever met in a position of authority, and he had exactly what it took to command respect: military bearing, strength, and stamina. Once, when our company caught him nodding off in the back of a classroom, we yelled, "Wake up, sergeant." He reddened and shot back, with a hint of a smile, that he was just testing his eyelids for holes.

The physical side of basic training was my strong suit. I worked my way up to twenty pull-ups and forty push-ups. I ran a six-minute mile in combat boots. My hand-eye coordination was good enough to earn a frequently awarded medal for marksmanship. My soldiering skills, on the other hand, were woeful. A good score on the physical training test did not get a rifle clean or make it easy to read a terrain map. Conceptual ability was no substitute for nimble hands, a feel for the outdoors, and an eye for detail.

Alphabetical order came to the rescue. I was assigned to bunk next to Charley Wilson, a soybean farmer and part-time high school teacher from southwestern Missouri who had signed up for the officers' program. Wilson was just five feet six, but he could rip off twenty one-armed push-ups with ease. He had all of the natural skills I lacked. Although I represented everything he had been taught to suspect—sinful city folk, goofball intellectuals, and crafty Jews—we hit it off very well. He patiently taught me how to look sharp for inspection, pack gear, and disassemble a pistol.

Wilson only lost it with me once. A small group of us were running around the barracks on a Sunday afternoon when a recruit whom I scarcely knew began mocking me. Each time we circled around the place where he was standing, he added a taunt. I don't know why I got under his skin, but the challenge was unmistakable. I tackled him the fourth time around, catching him by surprise. We wrestled and threw some punches for no more than a minute or two before the fight was broken up.

When I went back to the bunk with a bruised cheek, Wilson chewed me out for not kicking the guy's head in when I had him down. In rural Missouri you didn't fight like a gentleman. It didn't matter that I had stood up for myself or that the guy who picked the fight came over to apologize. I lacked the killer instinct you had to have where he came from.

Wilson and I stuck together for two months of advanced individual training but parted ways afterward. The specialty we learned was driving armored personnel carriers, APCs, the small tracked vehicles that ferried squads of eight to ten men around the combat zone. APCs with mounted .50-caliber machine guns were the vehicle of choice in Vietnam. This was the kind of dangerous grunt job that made OCS, officer candidate school, all the more inviting to me.

Wilson had the opposite reaction. He would have made a far better lieutenant than I, but he got fed up with army rules and restrictions.

When we were alerted that the Armor School would be closed, making infantry ocs the only available option, he decided to drop out and take his chances. Years later I was greatly relieved not to see his name among the many Wilsons engraved on the ebony marble of the Vietnam Memorial.

An ominous midday message to an instructor on the apc course disrupted the final weeks of my training at Fort Knox. I drove myself off the course in a jeep to the nearest landline to learn that Dad had suffered a major coronary the night before. He was resting comfortably in a hospital in Washington DC. I would not be granted emergency leave because his life was not at risk. I wasn't able to reach Mom for several hours. When I did, she assured me that Dad was getting the best possible care and that she and Bonnie were okay.

Dad's heart attack marked a turning point. He had started to make long overdue changes by the time I completed advanced individual training and returned home to see him. His beloved deli food was out. His weight dropped to about 150 pounds, and he made sure to walk at least forty-five minutes a day. He had stopped chain-smoking cigarettes a few years earlier but could never wean himself away from the pipe that took their place.

Although Dad regained enough strength to resume his commute to work, he was never the same. He remained as sharp as ever, but he became increasingly self-absorbed, and his already firm views hardened further. Mom rarely let Dad's dogmatic side or his critical eye get the best of her. His diminished physical presence made it easier for her to shrug off his criticism. The balance of her relationship with Dad shifted as she assumed more responsibility for his care.

It was Bonnie, by then fifteen, who bore the brunt of Dad's rigid attitudes about dating, women's lib, race, and popular culture. Bonnie wasn't a little girl anymore. She had grown to a statuesque five feet nine, inheriting Dad's height along with Mom's oval face and striking features. She was coming of age in a different generation from mine, one that questioned authority and was ready to fight for social change.

While Dad admired Bonnie's spirit and intellect, he was basically looking for a compliant daughter—a female version of his son. He had little experience, professional or personal, with independent women. His rejection of the Vietnam-era upheaval that Bonnie felt around her was absolute.

She was no rebel, but they clashed whenever she failed to back down. As always, Mom made up the difference by listening and providing hugs.

I missed the full impact of Dad's coronary. My eye was on making it through officer training. ocs was going to be a lot harder in every way than the four months I had spent at Fort Knox. The Infantry School at Fort Benning, Georgia, was widely known to be the most challenging officer course. I wasn't at all sure that an Ivy League intellectual was tough or practical enough to earn a commission.

I drove to Fort Benning, stopping at a motel off Interstate 95 in South Carolina before continuing on. The location of the post in Columbus, Georgia, a midsized community on the Alabama border, left me uneasy. This part of the country had led resistance to school integration and civil rights. I had only passed through the Deep South once, where I encountered graffiti in the men's room of a diner marking its urinal as a "Jew blood bank." Columbus was less than a thousand miles from Washington DC, but I felt that I was entering territory more unfamiliar and less welcoming than France.

Fort Benning turned out to be a world unto itself, just as Fort Knox had been. I spent eighteen straight weeks in its sprawling training areas before earning a weekend pass to Atlanta, where I tried to make up for four months without a Whopper or a Big Mac. A gigantic Airborne jump tower loomed over rows of barracks on the main post. Miles of low hills and swamps fanned out in every direction. The "Benning School for Boys" hosted basic training, ocs, paratroops, and Ranger School—the army's elite survival training. This was a heart-pumping, testosterone-driven place set in Georgia's red clay.

The January 1968 entering class of 175 officer candidates was drawn from an all-white pool of middle-class college graduates. The lack of battle-hardened noncommissioned officers put us on equal footing. About 125 candidates were going to complete the course. The army had a tried-and-true method of making cuts. Those who broke the rules of personal conduct were dismissed on the spot. Everyone else who dropped out of the program did so voluntarily. The key to making it through was winning the respect of others rather than outperforming them.

The insular world of Fiftieth Company revolved around our commander,

Captain Wall, a wiry combat veteran with a short fuse. His charge was to prepare us to lead a platoon in battle. He gave that mission everything he had. With the support of two junior tactical officers, he logged eighteen-hour days guiding, berating, and occasionally praising us. He made up for a lack of physical presence with boundless energy and a tongue that cut us to pieces regularly. Rumor had it that Captain Wall was so hard on his troops in Vietnam that one of them threw a grenade at him during a firefight. I never took that story seriously. In my book he was an awesome professional who pressed us to the limit but knew when to let up.

Captain Wall and every other company commander used the same three-part playbook. First, we had to stand up to the physical grind. Reveille sounded at five o'clock every morning, and the entire company hustled out for a three-mile run around the airborne track rain or shine. The rest of the day was packed with classroom and field instruction as well as physical training. The pace didn't let up until an hour before lights out. Physical tests were ratcheted up until the eighteenth week as a proven weeding-out strategy. The twenty-mile march in full gear and the five days of Ranger training in the post's wetlands were deal breakers for at least fifteen candidates. Although my weight dropped to 175, these challenges didn't faze me.

Second, we had to master battlefield skills. Instructors typically worked with us six or more hours a day on terrain map reading, small unit maneuvers, small arms, and communications. Their approach never varied. They told us what they were going to cover, covered it, and recapped the material they had covered. Battlefield skills were my weakest spot, so repetition was just what I needed. Without "drill and kill" I wouldn't have gotten enough of the fundamentals to survive.

Third, we had to perform under pressure. The flip side of the extended day that tested endurance was the short clock that tested responsiveness: twenty minutes to shave, dress, and get into formation; thirty minutes to get ready for full-dress inspection; an hour to get through the swamp and take up a position on the ridge. The measure of performance that mattered was not individual achievement but whether the unit got the job done. Captain Wall held the officer candidate serving as company commander accountable. Each of us rotated through this position under his eagle eye, and he never missed a chance to swoop.

The ocs playbook masked a huge challenge. How was the army to prepare its junior officers for both unconventional warfare in the jungles of Southeast Asia and mechanized warfare on the plains of Northern Europe? Neither theater could be overlooked. The resulting compromises created a mishmash. Our combat boots and fatigues felt like they had been designed for cold-weather terrain. Live fire exercises also seemed to have been planned before Vietnam. Survival training, however, mimicked rice patties. Instruction focused on countering the military tactics of the Viet Cong.

Our training showed that U.S. infantry platoons didn't have much capacity to cope with unconventional warfare on their own. We lacked technology to provide early warning of ambushes or booby traps. Our semiautomatic M16 rifles were no match for the enemy's Russian-made AK-47s. The big equalizers were helicopter gunships, artillery, and airstrikes. Officer candidates going through Fort Benning today have far more sophisticated and powerful tools at their direct disposal.

I made it through ocs on sheer determination. Failing to earn a commission would have meant falling short for the first time on an important goal. Worse yet, I would not have measured up to the example Dad had set as a medically commissioned major during World War II. To succeed, I checked my intellectual and policy interests outside the gates of Fort Benning at a time of incredible turmoil in American life.

I felt especially isolated standing in formation before dawn in April 1968 as word spread that Martin Luther King Jr. had been assassinated the night before in Memphis. I had been able to take action in Paris the night President Kennedy was killed, but there was nothing to do midway through training. In fact, I wouldn't have known what to do in the face of the rage that set black neighborhoods ablaze throughout the country. But that seemed beside the point. I had no way to feel the pulse or express my feelings.

My army commitment also left me on the sidelines of the antiwar movement. I didn't follow the protests or identify with the protestors who accused the president of the United States of being a war criminal. Their music was okay but not their message. ocs made it possible, at least for six crucial months, to filter out those who wouldn't understand my reasons for serving. Their extreme language and acts of civil disobedience in the name of peace turned me off as much as the head bashing of the police who broke up their rallies. The assassination of Bobby Kennedy in June 1968, weeks before I pinned on second lieutenant bars, confirmed that something was deeply wrong outside army life. But like everyone else in Fiftieth Company, I was more concerned with my personal future than the body politic.

The orders that came down on the eve of graduation spelled relief. The army would honor its initial commitment to all of us who had signed up for Armor ocs. We would head back to Fort Knox for a summer course. Then, after we were commissioned in that branch, the entire group would report to units in Germany.

A few days later I was pulled out of formation for a phone call from Washington. The last such call had alerted me to Dad's heart attack. This time the news was good. Based on my graduate work, army personnel had decided that I belonged in civil affairs—the staff that deals with community and policy issues wherever U.S. forces are deployed. After Fort Knox I would attend the U.S. civil affairs school at Fort Gordon, Georgia, and then report to U.S. Army headquarters in Europe.

This unexpected turn of events thrilled Mom, relieved Dad, and gnawed at me. From my parents' standpoint their only son was going to be out of harm's way. Europe was still divided by an Iron Curtain, but East-West conflict seemed unthinkable. I, however, couldn't shake the discomfort that I was getting a much better deal than everyone else. Military service was about sacrifice. Had Dad asked a brigadier general he knew to intervene? Was it possible to intervene in wartime?

I took Dad at his word when he said he had kept Brigadier General Bennett posted on my whereabouts but that they had lost touch when Bennett left Washington for a tour overseas. Part of me, however, could not help but feel apologetic. It hurt to compare my experience with Charley Wilson, the fireplug mentor who stood by me in basic training. The army tapped Wilson's skills, too, but in his case that meant using his farming know-how to spread the toxic Agent Orange to defoliate enemy supply lines.

The remainder of my stateside training introduced me to two different sides of warfare. The eight weeks I spent back at Fort Knox in the Armor School were all about overpowering the enemy. Tanks were the most potent battlefield weapon in the mid-1960s, before the advent of missile and air-delivered smart bombs. We learned tactics and maneuvered gas-guzzling M60s without the benefit of simulation. Commanding a tank platoon required skills that didn't come easily to me—coordinating with infantry, calling in precision air and artillery strikes, and maintaining heavy equipment.

Civil affairs school, a much easier fit, focused on restraining the use of force. We were trained to advise field commanders in Vietnam on what not to do in combat: don't allow U.S. troops to fire on unarmed civilians, don't destroy religious and other sensitive targets that could undermine support for U.S. forces, and don't mistreat prisoners of war. These weren't theoretical factors a few months after an American platoon slaughtered hundreds of people in the village of My Lai. The civil affairs mission differed in Germany, where the United States had shifted from occupier to ally. There we were briefed on strengthening ties between the U.S. Command and other NATO forces as well as the host government.

I made time during these brief assignments to reach out to the Jewish communities in Louisville and Augusta. A visit to the Jewish Community Center in Louisville led to several dates with a college student who seemed surprised at my lack of interest in a short fling. I was looking for the right girl, not any girl. In Augusta I worshipped and broke the Yom Kippur fast with a family. I arrived in uniform to meet my host in his pawnshop. It felt more than a little awkward to wait while he completed a gun sale before services. That wasn't the insight into Jews in the South I was looking for.

The extra training kept me detached from the home front turmoil of the Vietnam War during the summer and fall of 1968. I was far removed from the bloody confrontation at the Democratic Convention in Chicago, the presidential campaign, and the election of Richard Nixon. I never saw a draft card burned, never heard a policeman called a "pig," and never knew what it was like for a Vietnam vet to be advised to change into civilian clothes rather than return home in uniform. A two-year hitch in Europe would keep me out of touch.

7   TOUR IN GERMANY

My orders to report to headquarters, U.S. Army Europe, in Heidelberg sank in slowly. I had never set foot in the Federal Republic of Germany. Some of my parents' friends refused to buy anything made there.

Yes, West Germany was a fledgling democracy and a vital Cold War ally. But the French had drummed their fear of German power into me. Three wars in four generations had cost them millions of lives and their rank as a global power. More vexing was the prospect of living in a country that had exterminated most of European Jewry. I was sure to meet middle-aged Germans who had turned a blind eye to Hitler's atrocities or worse. Did I have it in me to move beyond the past?

Nuts and bolts pushed my conflicted feelings aside. The chartered military transport plane I took from McGuire Air Force Base, New Jersey, touched down in Frankfurt in January 1969. A welcome desk directed me to the green shuttle that soon lumbered south on the heavily traveled A5 autobahn. Cars zoomed by at one hundred miles per hour. I got out at Patrick Henry Village, a large, gated military housing complex on the outskirts of town. I had crossed an ocean to go from Middle America to Middle America.

My first day at work brought good news. I took another green shuttle to headquarters, which U.S. forces had taken over from the Wehrmacht in 1945. Personnel told me that I was going to be attached to the Office of Public Affairs, whose mission included being a liaison with the German community. As a result, I was not required to be on call in case of emergency. There would be no problem getting approval to live among German civilians instead of in Patrick Henry Village.

I found a good place in short order. A lanky German-speaking first lieutenant, Jim Lange, had sublet the ground floor of a two-family house in Zeigelhausen, a residential district a few miles away. He had an extra bedroom and bath and was looking for someone to share costs. Because we kept the same hours, he didn't mind giving me a ride until I bought a car. Our fifteen-minute commute bypassed the old city of Heidelberg, which was mostly filled with students, shoppers, and sightseers.

Heidelberg didn't look or feel anything like Tours, the French city of comparable size that I knew from junior year abroad. Both were historic treasures, and both had survived World War II intact. But that's where the similarities ended.

Tours commanded the soft, rolling hills of the Loire Valley. Heidelberg was wedged along the protective, wooded slopes of the Neckar, a tributary of the Rhine that cut through the city with whitewater force. The profusely detailed cathedral of Tours stood as a monument to Catholic tradition. Heidelberg's simpler but still imposing Church of the Holy Spirit had passed into Protestant hands during the Reformation. Tours showcased the culture of prerevolutionary France, while Heidelberg shaped modern German philosophy and science. In Europe I finally saw that a few hundred miles could make a world of difference.

My staff job in the Command Information Division of Public Affairs didn't involve any contact with Germans. Command Information served as the headquarters' channel to keep officers and senior noncommissioned officers informed about command-wide issues. Why was the army keeping a quarter of a million troops in Europe in the midst of a conflict in Southeast Asia? What was the role of NATO? Why did the Defense Department want to limit U.S. purchases of German goods and services? I was the designated answer man, filling a major's slot in an office thinned by the rotation of career officers to Vietnam.

I had scarcely unpacked when I drew a weeklong detail observing Operation Reforger, the largest U.S. military exercise in Europe since the Berlin Wall crisis of 1961. An armor brigade from Texas was demonstrating rapid U.S. reinforcement capacity as part of NATO's response to the 1968 Soviet crackdown in Czechoslovakia. Transports airlifted the brigade straight to the Grafenwöhr training area in eastern Bavaria. There arriving units picked up prepositioned tanks and ammunition to counter a simulated thrust from the East. I was to provide a rundown on Reforger for the monthly Command Information brief.

A week of deep snow and bitter cold in Grafenwöhr confirmed that war might be hell but training for it was all about avoiding property damage. The precautions taken to prevent a farmer's field from being torn up or a bridge from being smashed gave Reforger a make-believe quality. I was getting a glimpse of a war game that had little to do with the real deal.

The U.S. show of force meant to deter a Soviet attack was mostly posturing, a small part of the Cold War chessboard I had studied in grad school. But it seemed unlikely that any of the strategic experts writing about deterrence ever got their hands dirty trying to start a mothballed tank. Slogging through the training area, seeing equipment break down, and watching some ingenious fixes had nothing to do with nuclear scenarios. The wide gap between realities on the ground and spit-and-polish headquarters stunned me.

The Reforger write-up I sent up the chain of command passed muster. More opportunities to serve as a roving correspondent followed. I traveled to air force headquarters at Wiesbaden to report on efforts to provide American television to troops in the field; to Brussels to interview the U.S. ambassador to NATO; to the armored division in Würzburg to get a firsthand look at collaboration between the army and the Bundeswehr; and to Berlin to report on the role of the American military garrison.

I relived history passing through Checkpoint Charlie on my way to the Berlin Brigade. A tense confrontation of U.S. and Soviet tanks had taken place in 1961 at this one and only crossing for allied military personnel in the city. The tanks were gone, but the contrast between the simple wooden shed on the Western side and the bristling watchtower on the walled Soviet side told the story of the Cold War at a glance.

My article in the commander's brief to the troops, *Army in Europe*, summed up our military mission. "The Soviets want the Western allies out of Berlin," I wrote, "because it is a showpiece of success. The swallowing of Berlin would be interpreted as a sign to the world of the West's inability to live up to its obligations. That is why U.S. leaders continually affirm our pledge to guarantee the freedom of Berlin. The Berlin Brigade has real responsibilities."

I had a memorable encounter with the highest-ranking military commander in Europe. The occasion was a reception honoring General Andrew Goodpaster, the Supreme Allied Commander Europe (SACEUR), visiting from his headquarters outside Brussels. Arriving a few minutes late to help fill the room, I was amazed to see SACEUR standing alone—tall, white-haired, erect, and a bit professorial in his glasses. It took about ten seconds to size up the situation. Everyone was hanging back out of respect for Goodpaster's rank, so I decided to break the ice. I was familiar with his background as President Eisenhower's military assistant. He was also one the most respected alums of the Woodrow Wilson School.

Goodpaster looked visibly relieved when someone finally walked up to him at the punch bowl. We chatted for a good fifteen minutes about Princeton, the rigors of Fort Benning, and NATO's response to the Czech crisis. He asked for my contact information and followed up with a short, handwritten note—a gesture that said much about his personal qualities.

Although I had no further contact with Goodpaster, a grizzled sergeant major bent my ear about the division Goodpaster commanded in Germany as a two-star general on the way up. Word filtered down that a future chief of staff of the army was going to take command but that he might be too intellectual to be effective. His supporting cast would therefore include a tough-as-nails deputy commander, two seasoned brigade commanders, and the most experienced senior noncommissioned officers in Europe. The army made sure that its chosen succeeded.

In contrast, the self-made major for whom I worked, Guy Holland, had little going for him except a stellar combat record. His drawl marked a humble background from the heart of the Bible Belt. He had served ten years in special forces airborne operations before earning a commission at Fort Benning. A mail-order bachelor's degree followed.

Major Holland's uniform displayed two silver stars, among the highest awards for bravery. He never talked about Vietnam except to mention that it took a half hour of daily stretching just to hold his body parts together.

Leadership, courage, and sacrifice in battle didn't count much behind a desk in Heidelberg. Holland would be measured by his capacity to string sentences together, handle abstract ideas, and play office politics. He and his wife invited me over to their quarters occasionally. One evening he sheepishly excused himself when the only word he could think of in an after-dinner game of Scrabble was "C-R-A-P."

How would the army's up-or-out promotion system treat an officer who wasn't cut out for staff work? I gave him every ounce of support I could. He had given back more to his country than I ever could.

My direct supervisor, Harry Davis, provided a glimpse of what it might be like to work as a civilian in the government. A gifted writer and fluent German speaker in his midforties, he cranked out the monthly commander's brief like clockwork. He didn't have to press hard to get the job done and didn't want to. A secure, midlevel position gave him time to pick up the pieces of his personal life after a messy divorce from a German opera singer.

Davis and I hiked regularly on Saturday mornings to avoid the crowds that came out in force on Sundays. We took the philosophers' walk above the Neckar, where Hegel was said to have done some of his most creative thinking. We explored the Odenwald forest, picking the best wild blackberries and raspberries I ever tasted. We always ended our walks with a good meal at an out-the-the-way place.

One spring weekend we took a short drive to the castle and gardens at Schwetzingen, known throughout the region as a German response to Versailles. This was the heart of asparagus country, so we would top our excursion off at a restaurant. On the way we stopped to see the mounds of dirt the farmers piled up each day to keep their choicest asparagus white by preventing photosynthesis.

The extraordinary gardens blended formal French design, English landscaping, and imaginative small buildings. Our visit was marred by a flock of ducks aggressively attacking a single duck on a large pond. When we failed to scare them off, we alerted a groundskeeper. He listened politely and then replied with a smile that we were trying to protect a female duck in mating season.

Our outings broke the ice for me on Germany. I stopped catching rides to work, bought a used 1966 vw Bug for $500, and enrolled at a technical high school in a "German for Foreigners" class. The class met two times a week. The struggle with German humbled me. My knowledge of French and Spanish made no difference as I tried to learn a language that placed verbs at the end of the sentence. A whole class of nouns that were neither masculine nor feminine but neuter took me back to my two years of Latin at Nichols. I plugged away, eventually reaching the point that I could manage a basic conversation and get the gist of a simply written newspaper story.

Lack of fluency didn't allow me to get the feel for Germany that I had for France. My surface observations highlighted national traits that were new to me but familiar to anyone who knew Germany. Germans had more social discipline than I had ever seen. They set limits on store hours, for example, that would never fly back home. Stores had to close at 6:00 p.m. Monday through Saturday and weren't open on Sundays. Shoppers had no choice but to manage their time, and they did so without apparent complaint. I never saw the law breached. Such discipline was a source of strength, but sometimes Germans went too far in being orderly. Once a shopper scolded me for standing too far behind the customer in front of me as we waited in the checkout line of a grocery.

I also noticed a remarkable degree of social consensus. The two largest political parties, the center-right Christian Democrats and center-left Social Democrats, formed a Grand Coalition to share power in the German Bundestag. Trade unions had a seat at the table in the management of large German companies and a comparatively harmonious record of labor relations. Cooperation in the name of strengthening the country as a whole looked like a bedrock value, perhaps because Germans were so determined to redeem themselves in the eyes of the world.

The workers I saw seemed really serious about getting the job done right. They put a premium on planning, craftsmanship, and execution. They liked their time off but clearly understood that high productivity was the way to earn it. Still, the very qualities that made them productive made it hard to loosen up. They seemed to understand what they were missing. Maybe that's why they liked Mediterranean vacations so much.

Getting to know Germans personally would be the only way to get beyond these surface generalities. Heidelberg University sounded like the best place to find someone interested in exchanging conversation with an English speaker who was learning German. I went there after work one day, half-hoping I'd meet a beautiful, multilingual woman. It felt un-comfortable going in uniform to a hotbed of opposition to the Vietnam War, but the students made nothing of it as I wandered the halls looking for the cultural affairs office. Only one person expressed interest in the exchange I proposed, a lecturer in the philosophy department who was available to meet that weekend.

Gerhard Knauss, whose rugged looks didn't fit the mold of a student of philosophy, showed up at the appointed time and place with his stunning young girlfriend. None of us were proficient in the others' language, but the stiffness eased when we decided to take a walk. Knauss, who looked to be in his early forties, had been a protégé of the renowned philosopher-theologian Karl Jaspers, an anti-Nazi who had spent World War II in a concentration camp.

Knauss had been denied tenure after Jaspers left the Heidelberg faculty. The philosophy department, he explained, wasn't interested in someone who saw shades of gray instead of Marxist red. He had accepted an adjunct position, however, and he liked the idea of reaching out to an American soldier who was ideologically off-limits at the university. We agreed to call each other by our first names—a nod on their part to American informality—and to meet the following Sunday.

I grew sufficiently confident after a few more conversations to ask Knauss about Jews and the war. He answered straightforwardly and without hesita-tion. As a very young boy, he remembered the night that the synagogue in his town was set ablaze. Hitler's brown shirts confronted the firemen when they arrived, and the jostling lasted until there was nothing left to salvage. Later, as the campaign against the Jews intensified, the family next door was left alone because of the father's military record during World War I. Once the conflict began, the Knauss family was so focused on its own well-being that the disappearance of these Jewish neighbors was scarcely noticed. Knauss himself was drafted into an antiaircraft unit at the end of the war as a fifteen-year-old and surrendered to advancing American forces.

I never gave a moment's thought to questioning this narrative. Language problems aside, what would be accomplished by trying to dig deeper? I had no way of knowing how self-absorbed German civilians had been in the early days of the war. The cheering crowds that I had seen in newsreels as Hitler's armies marched across Europe didn't seem too worried. If I had read *The Oppermanns*, a classic fictional account of the impact of Hitler's rise on a Jewish family in Berlin published in 1934, I would have been more skeptical of Knauss's story.

What struck me most at the time was the look of curiosity on his girlfriend, who was in her twenties. She was hearing things that she had never heard before. Her expression told me that this topic might be heavily covered in books and the media, but it wasn't much discussed on a personal level among Germans. I got an impression, rightly or wrongly, of huge gaps in communications between Germans who had lived through the war and the generation born afterward.

Crossing the threshold of the Jewish question didn't create a breakthrough in my relationship with Knauss and his girlfriend. I never asked her to bring a friend along so that we could make it a foursome. We never got together for dinner or a concert. Something held me back. I couldn't open myself up the way I had in France. It was easier to relate to the victims than the aggressors, even though the Germans could only be admired for trying to come to terms with their own past.

I didn't visit any of Hitler's death camps or reach out to Germany's small Jewish population. I made my own personal connection to the Holocaust in the Jewish cemetery in the town of Worms, near Heidelberg. The gated burial grounds occupied a block near the cathedral where the Catholic Church had issued a historic edict rejecting the reformist views of Martin Luther early in the sixteenth century.

The cemetery had survived the Hitler period but was not well maintained. The headstones, dating from the late Middle Ages to the 1930s, evoked the deep roots and gradual assimilation of the Jewish community. The oldest markers were no longer legible, while later inscriptions traced an arc from being all in Hebrew to almost entirely in German. The headstones remembering those who died on the German side during World War I filled me with sadness. I returned regularly with garden tools to do what I could to help keep the place in shape.

A starkly different cemetery brought me back to France in the spring of 1969. As the only French speaker at headquarters, I got orders to represent the command at a ceremony marking the twenty-fifth anniversary of the liberation of Alsace-Lorraine. Crossing the border at Strasbourg, I drove several hours through the mountains on the French side of the Rhine to Épinal, where five thousand American war dead were buried. The American Seventh Army had freed the region after months of bitter fighting. French veterans and civic leaders wanted to say thank you.

The simple ceremony at Épinal took place in a memorial that overlooked fifty acres of perfectly aligned small white crosses and a sprinkling of Stars of David. The grounds were perfectly landscaped in a setting of serene beauty. I stood at attention with my French hosts as a band played the national anthem of both countries. It was hard to hold back tears as young and old stepped forward solemnly to lay wreaths. After saying a few words, I stayed on as guest of honor at a three-hour lunch, listening to war stories and tasting homemade liquors.

As I drove back to Heidelberg, my thoughts turned to my old girlfriend Marion, in Paris. Her family story linked the cemeteries in Worms and Épinal. The Rothmans were Jewish and French. They were victims and survivors. The security provided by American military forces helped make it possible for them to rebuild their lives after the war.

Marion and I had lost contact since our breakup several years earlier. She stopped writing when I didn't respond, but we never had closure. I made up my mind to find out once and for all how things had turned out for her by jotting her a note in French.

My shot in the dark drew a quick response. Marion was living at home completing her doctoral dissertation on the playwright Montherlant. She was pleased that I had not been sent to Vietnam, glad to hear from me, and looked forward to meeting. I was surprised that she wasn't married or didn't seem to have a significant other. She had insisted so strongly on getting engaged if she came to the States that I presumed that's where her priorities lay.

When Marion and I got together, the old chemistry was still there. She hadn't changed a bit. Her mischievous blue eyes sparkled. Her baby face and girlish style belied the serious student underneath. In French we talked through what had happened between us. Subtleties of language had caused a serious hang-up. To Marion engagement meant commitment. To me it meant she wanted me to buy a ring.

Our reactions were identical as we saw each other on successive weekends. If almost five years had passed and neither of us had had a serious relationship, then we were meant to be together. Coming from different places and cultures, we shared the same romantic view of having one true love in life. As far as I was concerned, Marion was mine just as Mom always said that Dad had been hers. I was living in the moment, confident that the long-term issues that we'd have to face would work themselves out.

Impulsively, we decided to get married in a few months. I let my folks know with a brief phone call and a follow-up letter. Neither one threw up a red flag. This was new terrain for them, except that they, too, like Marion and me, hadn't had much romantic experience with other people when they got married. Even though they had never met Marion, they knew how much she meant to me. They also trusted my judgment. The Rothmans seemed equally enthusiastic. They knew me and adored their daughter. I had the education to go places. Marion would be able to continue her studies in Germany. Above all, we wouldn't be far away.

The June wedding was small and elegant. Because the Rothmans didn't have extended family, they invited friends and business acquaintances. The Yochelson party had nothing to do except get to the synagogue on time. Mom and Dad flew over with Bonnie, whom the Rothmans invited to stay for the summer to bring our families closer together. Mom's wealthy friend from DC brought her granddaughter and stayed at the Ritz. Cousins from London came too. I wore my dress blue uniform for the first time.

After a short ceremony, conducted by a rabbi whom neither Marion nor I knew, her parents hosted lunch at a well-known restaurant in the Bois de Boulogne. They judged correctly that a great meal in a beautiful outdoor setting would break the ice between Europeans and Americans who didn't know each other. Marion and I let the guests figure things out for themselves, leaving that night by train for a brief honeymoon at the Rothmans' apartment in the Pyrénées. We stayed a few miles from the escape route that Marion's mother and grandparents had taken to flee the Nazis. Life had turned full circle.

We set up house in a suburb of Heidelberg for the rest of my tour, subletting a furnished two-bedroom apartment. I was determined not to ask the Rothmans, who had given us a wedding present of $10,000 cash, for any financial support. An exchange rate of four German marks to the dollar, together with my housing allowance, enabled us to make ends meet on my pay.

Although our makeshift rental didn't feel like home, my regular hours made it easy to set a routine. I switched to French after work. Marion took care of shopping and appeased the difficult landlady upstairs in her fluent German. We often walked through the garden farms across the way from our place, amazed by the open access to individual plots planted with lettuce, cucumbers, beans, potatoes, and strawberries. Taking advantage of twenty-five-cent-per-gallon gas, we played tourist on the weekend, mostly staying in Germany but occasionally driving down to Strasbourg. Every few months we returned to spend a few days with Marion's parents.

More than ever, this sheltered life kept me out of touch with the sacrifices that others were making in Southeast Asia. A weekend in Paris with my grad school classmate, John Forbes, jolted me back to reality. Forbes was taking two weeks of rest and recreation from his diplomatic post in Vietnam. He had spent a harrowing year in a rural combat zone as an advisor in the U.S.-led effort to create civilian resistance to the Communist insurgency. He asked us to celebrate his engagement to a beautiful State Department staffer whom he had met when he changed jobs to become the special assistant to the U.S. ambassador in Saigon.

As the four of us had dinner in a Vietnamese restaurant in the Latin Quarter, he said that he had seen too much brutality to remain a practicing Catholic. Crossing the street afterward, he got into an ugly confrontation with a French driver that ended in the police station. In comparison to Forbes's hardening, I felt like a hothouse plant.

The easy street that Marion and I enjoyed in Heidelberg had to end. I was due to be discharged in the late spring of 1970. That approaching deadline posed the first significant crossroad in our marriage.

8 THE CLUB

What next? Marion had made her career choice in French literature. Now I had to find a path that protected her options and played to my strengths.

The piece of the European security puzzle that I knew firsthand, U.S. troop stationing, was making news. Some of the most respected voices in Congress were claiming that the number of American forces could be cut significantly without undermining the U.S. security commitment to NATO. The Nixon administration opposed even a token withdrawal, which the White House claimed would send the wrong signal at the wrong time in the great chess game of East-West geopolitics. By weighing in on this debate, I might be able to establish credentials that opened doors.

My supervisor, Harry Davis, offered help. Telling me with a smile that I already knew too much about European security for my own good, he handed me orders to NATO headquarters in Brussels. He had sent me there at the beginning of my tour for an in-and-out interview with the U.S. ambassador. This time I'd stay longer and get a glimpse of the daily routine of the American delegation.

Day-to-day operations reflected none of the drama of East-West military confrontation. The tone in the corridors of the gray, squared-off NATO complex near the Brussels airport felt businesslike. What I observed in Brussels was bureaucracy grinding away—dozens of working groups and committees debating issues of defense spending, weapons procurement, force readiness, military doctrine, arms control, crisis management, and responses to "out of area" conflicts.

U.S. experts conducted a running negotiation with their counterparts on all of these issues. The NATO delegations didn't make final decisions on any of the big questions. They narrowed differences and teed up compromises, leaving the last word to heads of government and cabinet officials at annual ministerial meetings. The NATO agenda commanded top-level attention, even though Europe hadn't been a global hot spot since the Soviets threatened to close off Western access to Berlin during the Kennedy administration. At the end of the day the East-West balance of power mattered more across the Iron Curtain than anywhere else.

My credentials and background were standard for the NATO crowd in the early 1970s. Geopolitics in Europe was definitely a white male's game. Graduates of top military academies and universities ran NATO headquarters. Minorities were underrepresented and women almost entirely absent. I only met one female academic, Catherine Kelleher, who specialized in strategic studies.

Returning to Heidelberg, I looked at the wider circle of organizations that surrounded NATO and found there were too many to count: government-funded institutions, consulting firms, nonprofits, think tanks, and university-based programs, as well as transatlantic networking groups. A well-established circuit of meetings and publication outlets tied this European security club together.

The club attracted great minds and big egos. Prominent members included national security advisor Henry Kissinger, German defense minister Helmut Schmidt, and retired French air chief Pierre Gallois. Each made his mark through the power of ideas. Intellectual capacity and high-level policy making went hand and hand in the field of European security.

Still, there was clearly room for younger people because the Cold War wasn't going away anytime soon. My education, language skills, and military experience gave me a shot at joining the club. This wasn't a secret society. Merit counted as much as pedigree. If I published a timely article that caught the eye of the right people, there was no telling where I might land. The National Security Council, the State Department, the intelligence agencies, congressional committees, and NATO headquarters drew from the same pool. I'd launch my career in public service by playing to my strength as an analyst.

Gathering material wasn't as hard as I feared. The Deutsche Gesellschaft für Auswärtige Politik, or German Council on Foreign Relations, agreed to have me as a visiting scholar for six weeks after my discharge from the army. After that, speaking French with the director of studies of the Atlantic

Institute helped land a paid six-month internship in Paris. At some point I'd get to London. This timetable suited Marion perfectly. She'd stay with her parents while I was in Bonn, meeting me on weekends and finding a sublet for us in Paris.

Before moving on, I extended my tour in Heidelberg until midsummer 1970 at the request of headquarters. U.S. Army Europe marked my release from active duty with a distinguished service medal, the army's way of saying job well done. My tour in Germany produced a win-win. The army got what it needed while giving me experience on which to build.

My brief look at the German foreign policy establishment in Bonn could not have come at a more exciting time. Ostpolitik, Chancellor Willy Brandt's diplomatic opening to the East, was in full swing. As the first Social Democratic chancellor of West Germany, he aimed at easing tensions with the Soviet bloc instead of fueling them. His controversial overtures kept West Germany's provisional capital buzzing and left Western allies waiting anxiously on the sidelines.

Bonn hardly looked like the seat of power of Europe's strongest economy. The choice of a small university town on the Rhine, known for being the birthplace of Ludwig von Beethoven, had been deliberate. Bonn was supposed to be a makeshift solution until Berlin could be restored as the capital of a unified German state. The plain-looking government buildings scattered around Bonn, including the Parliament, were functional but uninspiring. The imposing American diplomatic compound in the choicest suburb served as a constant reminder of the dominant U.S. role in shaping postwar Germany.

The German Council on Foreign Relations, which gave me a desk and typewriter, proved an excellent base. The council, like its model in New York, didn't take sides on foreign policy questions. Its role was to support the German foreign policy community as a whole through meetings and publications. The director set an informal tone by asking to be addressed as "Herr Karstens" instead of "Professor Karstens"—a bold step by German standards. The cosmopolitan staff cheerfully helped guide my search and politely suppressed its opinion of my German.

The real benefit of a desk at the council was entrée to informed opinion. It only took a few good interviews to open the door to others. Government officials, foreign diplomats, scholars, and journalists carved out time to discuss U.S. troops in Europe. These conversations added insights and authenticity to my research. To my great relief, every German switched to English as soon as I opened my mouth.

Without exception the German defense and foreign policy establishment struck the same note regarding the absolute necessity of a large U.S. military presence in Europe. Germans were well aware of the inherent contradictions of their position. Militarily, they had to reassure Europe that they would never rise again while looking robust enough to help NATO deter the Russians. Economically, they had to provide an engine of growth while remaining a political follower within the Common Market. Diplomatically, they needed the leeway to negotiate with the East while remaining firmly anchored to the West. U.S. military forces made it possible to manage these contradictions. West Germany desperately wished to preserve the military status quo in order to create opportunities for movement in other areas.

A foreign officer stationed in Bonn helped me process these German complexities. Jon Kornblum hailed from rural Michigan and still had family in Germany. He had the same gut knowledge of the Germans that I had of the French. We took long walks along the Rhine. He spoke boldly about the options, but the course of action he recommended was always very measured. He went on to become ambassador to Germany and assistant secretary of state for European affairs.

A blond, blue-eyed son of East European Holocaust survivors also caught my eye in Bonn. The perfectly bilingual Josef Joffe had lived in the States as a teenager and was writing a PhD dissertation at Harvard. He was going to explain American foreign policy to Germans and German foreign policy to Americans in their own languages. He had the tools to succeed. Eventually, he became editor-in-chief of *Die Zeit*, Germany's most influential weekly newspaper.

James Sattler, a bombastic oddball who spoke excellent German, stood out in Bonn for the hard line he took against the Ostpolitik. He liked good food, however, and we got together occasionally in one of Bonn's good Italian restaurants. A few years after losing touch, I was stunned to be called in by the FBI for a debriefing on my association with him.

My right-wing dinner partner was being held as a highly decorated East German spy.

I left Bonn for Paris eager to rejoin Marion and start writing. Our first foray into the sky-high Parisian housing market didn't last long. Marion found an affordable, newly renovated studio apartment in the Marais, a historic but rundown neighborhood in the heart of the city that was getting back into fashion. The location was perfect, and our unit had all the right amenities. Nobody told us, however, about the rats that controlled the stairwell of the four-story walk-up. It only took one confrontation with the rodents on garbage pickup day to decide that we weren't going to be pioneers of gentrification.

A second try landed us in a ground-floor sublet on a busy thoroughfare with a rich mix of street dirt and noise. We never opened a window for as long as we stayed there. Marion reintroduced me to the city and way of life that she loved. The everyday pleasures of going to the market, stopping at a café, or walking through a neighborhood were what we enjoyed most. We spent time every weekend with my new in-laws. I respectfully addressed them in the *vous* as we bantered over the dinner table, while they used the familiar *tu* with me.

Marion didn't have a close circle of friends for me to meet. Moving through the French educational system from home didn't push her to network socially the way the American residential college experience does. Her passion for literature gave her great fulfillment. Work-life balance in Marion's eyes meant spending time with me and her family and in the cavernous French national library. Her priorities freed me to focus on trying to get into the European security club.

The Atlantic Institute, where I was going to hang my hat, would not provide much of a window into French thinking. The institute was a throwback to the period before President de Gaulle withdrew from the military side of the Atlantic Alliance. When he forced NATO military headquarters to relocate from outside Paris to Brussels in 1966, the institute remained in place in a stylish residence on the Rue de Longchamp. A handful of Europeans and Americans staffed the outpost, whose mission was to reinforce the alliance with strong political and economic ties.

Nevertheless, my short stay led to an incredible career break. I had barely arrived, sitting in the extra office over the garage, when the institute's president, former U.S. ambassador to the Common Market Jack Tuthill, called the small team into his office. "Jean Monnet needs a monograph," he said. "The subject is American federalism and its implications for Europe. Robert Bowie at Harvard agreed to help, but he's busy. We need to find someone to pull a draft together in the next couple of months. Does anybody have any ideas?"

I spoke up, assuring Tuthill that I had the background to meet an end-of-the-year deadline. What a privilege to assist one of the great architects of post-1945 European integration. Monnet's renown dated back to World War I, when he left the family cognac business and established himself as France's top war production expert. He advised Allied leaders on economic cooperation during World War II. Returning to France as head of planning, he wrote the blueprint for integrating European coal and steel production that laid the foundation for the Common Market.

I met Monnet in his well-appointed offices on the Avenue Foch about a mile from the Arc de Triomphe. His longtime Belgian collaborator, Jacques Van Helmont, ushered me into a parlor, where a small man with lively eyes was waiting. As we shook hands, I wondered how this vigorous eighty-four-year-old without a university degree had won the confidence of presidents and prime ministers for a half century.

It didn't take long to find out. Monnet put me completely at ease from the start. This was not a job interview, he assured me. Ambassador Tuthill would only have recommended a high-quality person. He looked forward to learning more about me, but the purpose of our initial meeting was to explain why Europe was about to reach a turning point.

The larger goal of European economic integration, Monnet continued, had always been to unify the democracies of Europe politically. That was the only way Europe would become a true global partner of the United States. The process had bogged down over petty economic squabbles.

Britain's forthcoming entry into the Common Market had the potential to jump-start European federalism. Britain had an unmatched record of creating strong political institutions. Monnet's close friend Prime Minister Edward Heath was a convinced European. A paper highlighting the relevance of America's historical experience would help motivate him to play a forceful role. Monnet was commissioning other papers on the Swiss and German federations, but it was the American example that mattered the most.

Monnet then floored me by asking what I thought of this project. He had charmed me with his manner, dazzled me with his intellect, and now he was treating me like a colleague. More than any other quality, the lack of self-importance of a truly important man touched me. Monnet never allowed himself to be treated deferentially, even when it came to something as simple as who went through the door first. The more I saw the power game played in Washington later on, the more I appreciated why Monnet was so special and so effective.

The first draft of the essay flowed easily. My customer, Monnet, wasn't looking for footnotes, and those great teachers at Yale had given me a solid grasp of American federalism. The first part of the essay highlighted the failures of the confederation set up during the American Revolution and the adjustments made in the U.S. Constitution of 1789. The second part covered conflicts over states' rights, the impact of constitutional amendments, and the growth of the federal role during the twentieth century. Its message was that a strong but limited central government contributed to America's emergence as a global power.

Whenever Monnet compared European and American historical experience, he came back to the same European stumbling block: the power of the nation-state. National rivalries had brought Europe to ruin. That's why he had committed himself to building a European identity after 1945. He had done so in his personal life by marrying an Italian, embracing the Anglo-Saxon political model, and designing the Common Market. Now, as he made clear in our periodic meetings, he intended to use my essay on American federalism to give his vision of a United States of Europe a final push.

With Monnet's blessing the draft went for comment to Robert Bowie, the director of Harvard's Center for International Affairs. An authority on international law, he had been a top advisor during the postwar occupation of Germany and director of policy for Secretary of State John Foster Dulles. His signature would give the draft the credibility Monnet was looking for.

Bowie wrote back that the paper was fine and generously suggested that I be recognized as coauthor. Monnet's Action Committee for the United States of Europe published it in French and in English in a collection that included a reflection on federalism by Walter Hallstein, the first president of the Commission of the European Community.

At the end of the day Monnet proved far too optimistic about the relevance of the American model and the influence of his friend the British prime minister. European leaders could not be moved to change course by force of personality. It would take two decades to move from a European Community to a European Union with a single currency. Instead of leading the way, Britain opted out of the currency arrangement.

Monnet thanked me for my work and asked in passing if I might consider working with him on his memoirs. He had been looking for a ghostwriter for years. I declined respectfully on the grounds that I lacked the qualifications to take on a project of that magnitude. Still, I would not have traded my few months of association with him for anything. He showed that greatness and idealism could go hand in hand.

The Monnet monograph gave me an invaluable calling card, but I couldn't afford to get sidetracked. I went to Paris to write about U.S. troops in Europe but didn't feel ready to do so. I still had to figure out how France and Britain fit into the European security puzzle.

I covered the French base by making contact with the Centre d'Études de Politique Étrangère (Center for the Study of Foreign Relations), a small think tank with close ties to the French government. The modest offices of the center clearly didn't reflect the ambitions of French diplomacy. The French knew all about the trappings of power. As I rode up the elevator of a nondescript building near Sciences Po, I felt as if I were approaching a research annex rather than a foreign policy hub.

Jacques Vernant, the intense lawyer who directed the center, had a more limited reach than I expected. Although he was a respected authority on the status of postwar refugees in Europe, he lacked policy-making experience and spoke only French. He and his colleagues thirsted for French speakers who could provide insight into American policy toward Europe. How ironic that I was able to engage the insular French more easily than the cosmopolitan Germans. I was pleased to accommodate.

The views I heard in Paris differed sharply from those in Bonn. The French questioned the credibility of the American security commitment to Europe, while Germans believed fervently in it. The French saw their own nuclear capability as a source of political leverage over Germany, while the Germans saw their partnership with the United States as a way to reduce French influence. Yet France and the United States shared the same concern about Germany trying to go it alone in negotiations with the Soviet bloc countries. They also saw eye to eye on the stabilizing role of American forces in Germany. European security had wheels within wheels.

Getting a handle on Britain came next. I had encountered the British at every turn in my undergraduate studies—their institutions, ideas, and power. Yet I never felt that knowing Britain well would set me apart as a Europeanist. The paths into Oxford, Cambridge, and the London School of Economics were well-worn by other Americans. The barriers to understanding British culture, politics, and statecraft didn't compare to the Continent. A few well-chosen meetings would give me the material I needed.

Once in London, I quickly saw that I was missing the forest for the trees. The British stance on European security grew out of a richer and more complex set of international interests than I had realized. Unlike the French and Germans, who conceded that they were no longer world powers, Britain had the tools and skill to play a global game. The British had a permanent seat on the UN Security Council, a special relationship with the United States, a place in the European Community, and a commonwealth of fifty-four nations. They wanted to keep their options open in all of these spheres.

The stately Royal Institute for International Affairs, known as Chatham House, showed how Britain positioned itself center stage. A forum with a royal charter in the heart of London told the world that Britain was globally engaged at the highest level. I saw the same savvy at the International Institute for Strategic Studies (IISS), a think tank set up in the late 1950s to work on nuclear deterrence and European security. Its well-connected founding director, Alistair Buchan, created a niche for the IISS as the most trusted unclassified resource on the East-West military balance.

I left London with the sense that the British were not nearly as committed to Europe as Jean Monnet hoped. They wanted the benefits of economic integration without the constraints of political integration. A U.S.-led Atlantic Alliance suited the British perfectly, bolstering their status as America's junior partner and qualifying their ties to Europe.

Armed with these insights, I sat down to write. Despite the time I had invested in Alliance politics, the angle that looked most promising was the U.S. domestic debate over troops in Europe. On the one hand, senate majority leader Mike Mansfield was calling for a 50 percent reduction in U.S. troops. The Nixon administration, on the other hand, was digging in its heels against any unilateral troop cuts. Both sides marshaled arguments based on U.S. economic, political, and military interests, but no one had systematically compared them.

Instead of taking a position for or against, I examined the limited scope of the policy debate (experts only) and the factors that structured the troop level discussion within and between the branches of government. Then I looked ahead to the middle of the 1970s and suggested why there would be more continuity than change in the American military presence. The framework of analysis was pure Sciences Po, while its content owed a lot to the Woodrow Wilson School.

Curt Gasteyger, the Swiss director of strategic studies at the Atlantic Institute, liked the draft and offered help. He wrote a letter of introduction to Robert Pfaltzgraff, the associate editor of *Orbis*, a respected right-of-center quarterly that specialized in security issues. Pfaltzgraff welcomed an analysis of the troop level debate that had no ax to grind. The publication of "The American Military Presence in Europe" in the fall of 1971 marked my admission to the European security club.

The power of the network came into play again. Ambassador Tuthill wrote on my behalf to his old friend Henry Owen in Washington. Owen had stepped down as director of policy planning at the State Department to head up foreign policy studies at the Brookings Institution, a well-known Washington think tank. Yes, Owen responded, there was a one-year opening as a visiting fellow for Yochelson if he submitted a sound proposal. That was no problem. I suggested an analysis of negotiated East-West force reductions in Europe—the alternative to unilateral cuts that the Nixon administration had advocated all along.

The offer for a yearlong fellowship at Brookings, beginning in the fall of 1971, set Marion's and my future course. I would start in a field that could easily lead to a transatlantic career. Marion had good job opportunities in Washington's French-speaking community. We left her hometown for mine.

9 BREAKUP

Marion and I traveled separately to Washington. There was no point passing up the army's free ride. I needed a couple of weeks to lay the groundwork on housing anyway. After making arrangements for shipping a light-blue VW Bug, purchased at the military discount for $1,300, I took the train to the same side of the Frankfurt airport at which I had landed two and a half years earlier.

The long flight back to New Jersey gave me a chance to think about the social upheaval that had taken place since I left Princeton. The drug culture, the sexual revolution, feminism, Black Power, and antiwar violence left me feeling out of step. Where did a guy belong who didn't smoke pot, wasn't a sexual swinger, and trusted the American political process? Was I inside or outside the mainstream? How would my socially conservative wife react to the American scene? I wasn't ready to deal with these uncomfortable thoughts, so I tried to sweep them out of my mind.

Mom picked me up. The three-hour drive back to Chevy Chase allowed us to catch up for the first time in almost a year. Dad's health remained her biggest concern. Two recent fender benders made her wonder whether he was up to the long commute to St. Elizabeths Hospital. But he was making progress at work. A recent PhD psychologist, Stanton Samenow, had begun to compress Dad's clinical notes into the makings of a book. Samenow, the son of friends from Yale days, was doing just what was needed.

Bonnie, Mom continued, was flourishing at Swarthmore, the small, highly regarded liberal arts college near Philadelphia where she had just finished her freshman year. Her summer with the Rothmans had been a good learning experience, but she had not fallen in love with France the way I had. She was going to major in history with a particular focus on art, a passion she shared with Mom. Bonnie had met a senior she liked a lot, Paul Shechtman, the captain of the Swarthmore basketball team and a top student who was going to study at Oxford on a Rhodes Scholarship.

It took only a few days for the profound differences between Paris and Washington to sink in. The distinctions had never mattered before, but they did now.

Paris, the largest urban area in Europe, showcased the best France had to offer the world. The City of Light combined the attributes of a national capital and a national treasure. The grandeur of the past fit harmoniously with the power of the present. The affluent lived in the heart of Paris, nurturing its most attractive features and streaming out on weekends and holidays. Good mass transit made it easy to get around. The burden of long commutes fell mainly on low-income workers who couldn't afford close-in neighborhoods. Rough-and-tumble public housing rimmed large parts of the city, conveniently out of the sight of the well off.

The workday started and ended late by American standards. Parisians routinely picked up fresh bread or stopped at a café for breakfast. Many offices closed for two hours at lunchtime. Paris emptied during the cherished vacation month of August. Work had its place, but the rhythm of the city reflected the high premium that Parisians put on maintaining their quality of life.

Washington had an altogether different ethos. The first U.S. president had picked neutral ground, not a center of power, as the seat for America's new federal government. Carving the diamond-shaped District of Columbia out of unsettled parts of Maryland and Virginia reflected the vision of a limited role for the nation's capital. The founding fathers wanted to create a carefully controlled enclave rather than a metropolis.

Washington did not emerge as an urban powerhouse until the twentieth century. The forces that reshaped the city included a wave of black migration from the South after World War I, the growth of federal programs that began during the Depression era, and the global engagement of the United States triggered by World War II. The expansion of the public sector fueled a strong local economy, a legion of government service providers, and an army of lobbyists. A large diplomatic corps, reinforced by the offices of the World Bank and International Monetary Fund, added cosmopolitan flair.

For the most part, however, Washington's movers and shakers didn't view the District of Columbia as home. Elected officials and high-ranking appointees came from somewhere else. Some lived on Capitol Hill or in the northwest quadrant of the city, but most of the area's higher-income skilled workforce settled in the mainly white suburbs. The American dream of home ownership, neighborhood schools, and mall shopping reversed the urban dynamic of Paris. The well off trekked to and from the District on overcrowded highways, leaving an under-resourced, predominantly black city with a litany of problems. Downtown Washington emptied at the end of every workday rather than for a month each year.

By the same token it was the political calendar—not lifestyle preferences—that made Washington tick. You could feel the beat of filled hotels, late-night meetings, and busy restaurants when Congress was in session. Presidential inaugurations took the city to a whole other level. Yet the pace could slow to a standstill during the summer and the campaign season. Politics ruled.

I thought Marion and I would be able handle the change of setting. A family friend helped line up a one-bedroom apartment in a new high-rise off Connecticut Avenue that looked like heaven. A gleaming kitchen, parquet floors, and a balcony overlooking the swimming pool at an affordable rent would have been far beyond our reach in Paris. The location was a stone's throw away from Rock Creek Park and solved the commuting problem.

Marion's teaching job at the French School of Washington promised to be a big plus. The French-speaking community in Washington numbered in the thousands, large enough to support an accredited lycée. She'd keep her French connection and work with colleagues who had made the adjustment to the States.

Washington itself had a lot to offer too. The city wasn't an intellectual mecca, but its museums and performing arts center were top tier. The government attracted plenty of interesting, well-educated people. Besides, Marion had cousins in the area to add to my family ties.

Marion's arrival in early August tested my optimism. Everything seemed fine at first. She liked the apartment, which we furnished with a few pieces of rented furniture. Her introductory meeting at the French School, where she would teach language arts to ten- and eleven-year-olds, went well. She charmed my parents, whom I asked to give us space while we settled in. We got together with her cousins and saw some of my grad school classmates. And we made the rounds of Washington's signature tourist sites.

As the blush of getting to know Washington wore off, however, Marion grew increasingly homesick. The French School didn't provide the base of support I had been counting on to ease her transition. She never talked about her colleagues at work and never suggested that we meet any of them. Her change of mood caught me off guard. Perhaps I should have anticipated the delayed impact of leaving her parents and surroundings. She was experiencing culture shock. For all her worldliness Marion had never had to fend for herself. She hadn't inherited the resilience forged by her family's wartime hardship. I missed the cues because I was so intent on making our transition to DC work.

Marion's longing for home threw us into our own personal Catch-22. The more stranded she felt, the more she found fault with all things American. The critique of the cultural wasteland that I had heard around her parents' table returned to ours. Americans lacked taste and sophistication. Americans dressed and ate badly. Americans had no sense of irony. The complaints she leveled weren't aimed at me personally. I took no comfort in being an exception.

I didn't hear Marion's cry for support. Her barbs struck me as a flat rejection of the future I wanted for us. A transatlantic marriage had to have a base. If I were going to be the principal breadwinner, the base that made the most sense was an American organization. Marion's outbursts left me burning inside. I saw a power play in which I was being forced to choose between my wife and my identity. She was shutting down on the United States to push me into a long-term commitment to France. In her eyes I would have no trouble finding something interesting to do in Paris, and her family would ensure our financial security. In my eyes I would be a kept man.

Our relationship unraveled by the day. Marion's feelings and mine ran so high that we weren't able to talk about any of the long-term issues that we should have discussed before getting married. I confided the gist of what was happening to my parents but insisted that they stay out of it. Instead,

I reached out to Dad's brother Leon, the well-known DC psychiatrist, who was sure to have had experience in these matters. Marion and I met several times with him, but his calm, reasoned voice didn't get through.

Marion and I hit the wall one winter day midway through the school year, when she flung her engagement ring out the window and looked ready to start throwing other things. I saw her desperate anger as a final act of repudiation. It was more than I could bear. Something in me snapped.

The next day I rented a month-to-month studio apartment within walking distance of Brookings. I moved my things out of the Van Ness apartment and would not return until after she left for France. I felt shattered. I had made the wrong choice by following my heart without knowing my partner well enough and without anticipating the compromises that we would both have to make. I was as much at fault as she was for failing to love wisely. And now we would both pay the emotional price for that mistake.

Marion and I never saw each other face-to-face again. Her cousin in Washington alerted me to her departure from DC when the spring semester at the French School ended. The family lawyer handled the civil divorce. Under Jewish law I had to initiate a religious divorce in France. My parents negotiated with Marion's to cover the cost and never told me how much it turned out to be.

Almost forty years later Marion reached out to me by email. She wrote in simple, elegant French that she was living in Paris and had a twenty-six-year-old daughter. She couldn't help but think how incredibly young and naive we had been. She wondered how I was doing. My communications skills deserted me. Worried about the feelings of my family, in English I declined further contact.

I threw myself into work to ease the pain. Brookings was too large and impersonal to provide much support. I had to make my own way in a ten-story building geared to individual research. The foreign policy program to which I was attached was smaller than the flagship economics and government studies programs. We never met as a group. Along with other one-year visitors, I sat apart from the permanent staff in a small cubby in the library. The respected Henry Owen, who had agreed to fund me for a year, didn't reach out. A colleague joked that Brookings was a collection of thoughtful people united by their interest in policy, publishing, and parking spaces.

The workplace had none of the feel of an ivory tower. Dress was coat and tie except during off-hours. Most of the brightest lights at Brookings had significant government experience. Many of the biggest names came out of the Johnson administration. They weren't much interested in theoretical issues. They wanted to understand and influence the debate over America's grand challenges. On the whole they were left-of-center moderates who valued analysis more than ideology.

I had no idea at the time that the Nixon White House was targeting Brookings as a hotbed of anti–Vietnam War protest. Former Department of Defense whiz kids Morton Halperin and Leslie Gelb were writing books about U.S. decision-making in Vietnam. The world learned later that Halperin's phones were being tapped and that President Nixon actually ordered a break-in that was never carried out. That's how far he was ready to go to retrieve an alleged record of President Johnson's bombing of North Vietnam.

As far as I was concerned, Brookings and its right-of-center counterpart, the American Enterprise Institute, were part of the infrastructure of high-level U.S. public service. They were places where talented people coming out of government could land, retool, and go back. I saw these in-and-outers every day. Heavyweight economists Charles Schultze and Alice Rivlin stood in the wings to become future Democratic presidential advisors. Their protégé Robert Reichauer would become director of the Congressional Budget Office. Conservative Herbert Stein was at Brookings before his 1972 appointment as chairman of the Council of Economic Advisers in the Nixon administration. I hadn't decided where I stood politically, but I could see myself moving back and forth from a research institution to a government post.

An out-of-the-blue invitation from the RAND Corporation to speak on U.S. troops in Europe boosted my spirits. A European security specialist at RAND, Horst Mendershausen, had found my article in the fall 1971 issue of *Orbis* helpful. Was I available to fly out to the West Coast to give an informal talk?

I jumped at the chance to visit the renowned think tank set up by the air force in Santa Monica, California. RAND, unlike Brookings, got its start during the early days of the Cold War as a dedicated Department of Defense resource. Its experts, shielded from the daily grind of Washington, analyzed the strategic environment facing the United States in every key dimension. RAND's large staff had the capacity to handle tasking in technology, strategy, economics, regional conflict, foreign area studies, and more. Whereas Brookings tried to reach a broad policy audience, RAND produced customized reports—a good share of them classified—for the defense community and other public sector clients.

The laid-back Los Angeles beach community that RAND called home brought me into a different world. Too excited to sleep much, my introduction to Southern California was an exhilarating 6:00 a.m. jog on a picture-perfect day. I had plenty of company on the freshly raked white sand between Santa Monica and Venice, the hippie community a few miles south. Runners, joggers, and walkers were out for their predawn exercise. Bikers sped along the ribbon of concrete that ran through the beach. A band of surfers paddled out, looking for the right wave. As I took the whole scene in, it felt awfully good to be away from Washington.

The session at RAND put me in front of about a dozen seasoned analysts. They greeted me warmly in their open shirts. After brief introductions they peppered me with questions on U.S. domestic politics. Congress was the wild card that could most affect U.S. security interests in Europe. They were looking for insights from inside the Beltway. Our discussion widened out to Alliance politics and East-West relations. When we broke after lunch, I left feeling that I'd have an open door at RAND in the future.

I returned from the West Coast with definite ideas about what to do next. First, I ought to move away from Washington as soon as the year at Brookings ended. The memories of a marriage gone wrong were too fresh to stay in DC. I needed a change of place. Second, I should build my academic credentials. Practically everyone around the table at RAND had a doctorate. A PhD degree would be especially valuable if I were going to aim for a career in and out of public service.

A solution fell into place over the next few months. The Woodrow Wilson School had decided to offer a doctorate in public affairs. My publication in *Orbis* and the work-in-progress at Brookings provided a good base on which to build. Professor Dick Ullman agreed to serve as my advisor. And my coauthor on the Monnet paper, Professor Bowie, found funding to support me at the Harvard Center for International Affairs starting in September 1972.

The race to get out of town pushed me to finish up a draft on NATO– Warsaw Pact force reductions. Luckily, I had little new material to review. My earlier work on U.S. troops in Europe had required sifting through a rich body of analysis on the costs, benefits, and risks of drawing down the American military presence. Negotiating with the Russians over the military balance added layers of complexity. The public record, however, was nearly blank on specifics. The master of negotiating frameworks in the Nixon administration, Henry Kissinger, had not fleshed out an approach. It looked like the administration and NATO were only making the case for negotiated force cuts to hold the line against unilateral action.

The use of force reduction talks simply as a domestic maneuver created an opening. Someone needed to look at the options if NATO really did engage the Warsaw Pact on mutual and balanced force reduction (MBFR). I was that someone. I didn't have the technical expertise to examine the hardware issues, but I did have the background to map out geopolitical alternatives and weigh their impact on U.S. interests. The MBFR paper that took shape in my mind was a think piece, not a research piece—the kind of analysis that a member of the National Security Council or State Department policy planning staff might be asked to provide.

My topic made it possible to set up meetings with people working on MBFR in the administration. I felt wide-eyed just seeing where they worked, passing through security, and going to their offices. Jim Thomson, a physicist who covered European arms control on Kissinger's staff, agreed to see me in the imposing Old Executive Office building next to the White House. Reginald Bartholomew, whose style was as brash as Thomson's was understated, met me at the Pentagon. Both of these rising stars—one a future president of RAND and the other a future ambassador to Italy—were much more interested in comparing notes on the Alliance politics of mutual force reduction than the U.S. position. I didn't care. It was huge to be able to trade ideas with real players and to see what the future might hold for me.

I came up with three MBFR scenarios. A Quick Fix would stabilize the U.S. military presence at a slightly lower level in exchange for token Soviet reductions, thereby disarming the proponents of unilateral withdrawal. An Ever-Present Balance, beginning with modest confidence-building measures, would seek significant cuts in NATO and Warsaw Pact weapons systems. The Protracted Parley would play for time, which could be used to shift the defense burden to European allies. These options needed elaboration. Coming up with a French-style framework, however, saved me from having to write off the entire year at Brookings.

Returning to the apartment off Connecticut Avenue as soon as Marion left, I replayed the failure of our marriage over and over. Each time I came to the same disappointing conclusion. I had spent ten years chasing after a fairy tale. There was no one to blame except myself for having made the wrong choice. This was the first really important failure in my life. It would take months to sink in and years to get over.

Self-absorbed, I looked for relief swimming laps and reading at the pool. One day I struck up a conversation with an attractive brunette. We exchanged personal stories—she was recently divorced—and started sitting next to each other every day. One late morning she asked if I'd like to come over for lunch. We went back to her place in our bathing suits. As she fixed sandwiches in her bikini, the possibilities scared me. I wasn't ready for any of this.

Bonnie's late-summer wedding to Paul Shechtman in the backyard of the family home in Chevy Chase punctuated my sense of lost time and direction. My nineteen-year-old sister, stunning in a simple wedding dress, was about to strike out on her own at the very age that I had met Marion. She hadn't looked for the exotic, falling in love with a scholar-athlete from Swarthmore whose background wasn't too different from her own. She would spend her senior year with Paul at Oxford as a newlywed rather than a girlfriend—in no small measure to meet Mom and Dad's expectations. The wedding put Bonnie on equal footing with me in terms of life experience. She was moving forward, and I had lost my way. Hopefully, I would be able to get my bearings in Cambridge, Massachusetts.

10 SWALLOWED

I drove up to Cambridge as a firestorm gathered around the Nixon presidency. The June 1972 break-in at the Watergate offices of the Democratic National Committee didn't prevent Nixon from winning reelection. The *Washington Post*, however, changed history in the spring of 1973 by breaking the story of a White House cover-up. The investigations that followed, culminating in a vote to impeach the president, forced him to resign in August 1974. Forty-eight officials who served under Nixon would be charged and convicted.

The nation was in crisis, and I felt more vulnerable than ever. I had to make my own way in a renowned university community, write a dissertation, reenter the dating scene, and rethink my professional future. Three rough years lay ahead.

Cambridge lived up to its billing as a distinctive, welcoming place to live. The fifth-largest city in Massachusetts, with a population just over one hundred thousand, stretched along the Charles River across from Boston. Harvard and MIT marked out opposite ends of Cambridge. The two great universities didn't put an academic stamp on the neighborhoods in between. Plentiful rent-controlled housing, a throwback to the city's industrial past, attracted a stable base of low-income families in the early 1970s. The lunch box defined the character of Cambridge as much as the book bag, giving the country's intellectual capital a down-to-earth feel.

I had no trouble finding a conveniently located, affordable one-bedroom apartment at 205 Walden Avenue. The plain, squared-off exterior concealed good floor plans and a scaled-back version of the amenities I had had in DC. Monthly rent of $220 included outdoor parking, utilities, and a small pool. My immediate neighbors were an elementary school teacher and a sales rep. Walden Park put me beyond the tumult of Harvard Square and a short drive away from Fresh Pond, a scenic reservoir perfect for jogging. I couldn't have asked for more.

I approached Harvard from an awkward position. The university offered clear degree paths for its own students and welcomed visitors from other institutions all the time. I didn't fit either category. Robert Bowie had stretched the rules to bring me aboard as a research fellow in the center he directed. His thank-you for helping him deliver for Monnet allowed me to be paid and treated as if I had a doctorate. In fact, I was still a degree candidate at the Woodrow Wilson School. The arrangement was generous but left me uneasy.

The Center for International Affairs, known then as CFIA, occupied a solid, three-story redbrick building at 6 Divinity Avenue near the Law School. CFIA didn't offer an undergraduate program. Its space was designed primarily for meetings—Harvard's platform for academic entrepreneurs to market their ideas and themselves.

My first visit to CFIA confirmed that I would have to fend mostly for myself. Mr. Bowie, with his shock of white hair and glasses, greeted me politely from behind his desk. Our get-to-know-you meeting only lasted a few minutes. He steered away from any talk of transatlantic relations or Monnet, who was his peer and not mine. I wondered how the two of them got along so well. I found it as difficult to connect with the distinguished American lawyer-diplomat as it had been easy to relate to his friend in Paris. The director of CFIA wasn't the type to take me, or perhaps anyone, under his wing.

Sally Cox, Bowie's administrative assistant, walked me around CFIA. She exuded energy and commitment. There wasn't room for me to have an office, but I would have a mailbox. In fact, I would find the mailbox full. Now that someone had come to the center with an interest in European security, she knew where to put all of the periodicals addressed to Henry Kissinger that had piled up on her desk. I was more than welcome to use the reading room. Naturally, I had a standing invitation to the CFIA speakers program as well as informal discussions.

I became friends with Cox, who matched my height and had the rough-hewn look of a horsewoman who loved the outdoors. She taught me the New England way of boiling lobsters and eating them over newspapers with drawn butter. Our conversations always circled back to CFIA, where she had devoted herself since its founding in 1958. She was close to her family, but she never said a word about her father, the independent-minded Watergate special prosecutor Archibald Cox, whom Nixon fired in October 1973. I thought the better of asking.

She filled me in discreetly on the politics of CFIA. The center had been targeted for bombing by antiwar activists in 1970 because several associates did work for the Defense Department on Vietnam. No one in Washington was more disliked on the Harvard campus than Henry Kissinger, the principal defender of U.S. bombing in Cambodia. He had been deputy director of CFIA, using the center as his stepping-stone into government. Cox doubted that he would ever return. With or without Kissinger, CFIA had intellectual firepower to burn.

Its two most original thinkers, Joseph Nye and Samuel Huntington, were coming into their own. They weren't working directly in my area, but I sought them out.

The personable, self-assured Nye broke new ground with his analysis of interdependence. He saw the growing links that cut across national boundaries, like the European security club, as game changers. The classic texts on international relations, which treated governments as unified actors, were off the mark. Years later Nye pushed his thinking further. Twenty-first century policy makers had to factor in "soft power"—the social, cultural, and institutional components of influence—along with "hard" military capabilities. The United States had a deep reservoir of soft power. Handwringers worried about America's decline needed to pay more attention to the intangibles that changed the equation.

The shy, introspective Huntington examined sources of conflict. In the 1960s he had challenged the long-held view that economic, social, and political development went hand in hand. Economic growth didn't necessarily translate into political stability, just as arms control didn't resolve underlying differences of ideology. After the collapse of communism, Huntington sketched out a more provocative vision of post–Cold War conflict. He predicted that the East-West ideological divide would be superseded by a clash of civilizations pitting the world's major cultures and religions against each other. The neoconservative Huntington saw international relations as an enduring struggle in which Western values would always be at risk.

The Government Department provided enough room for Nye and Huntington to coexist. They worked in apparent harmony under the same roof at CFIA. The concepts they developed, so fresh and so different from each other, didn't compete. Their example of mutual respect impressed me.

A more pointed debate was taking place a few blocks away from CFIA, at the Center for Russian Studies. The hardliners, led by Russian Studies director Richard Pipes, doubted the capacity of the Soviet system to change. The hopeful camp, led by Russian Studies associate director Marshall Shulman, believed that Soviet zeal had given way to grudging pragmatism.

The duel between these opposing views played out at the highest policy level, affecting the overall U.S. stance on arms control. Pipes aligned himself with influential hawks on Capitol Hill, chairing an official panel of outside experts who reviewed national intelligence estimates and challenged the U.S. negotiating position in strategic arms talks as too soft. Shulman threw his weight behind arms control as advisor on Soviet relations to Kissinger's successor, Cyrus Vance.

No battle lines ran through the newly established Center for European Studies, another of my haunts in Cambridge. *Europe* meant "Western Europe," where the success of U.S. foreign policy after World War II didn't stir much controversy. The fateful choices that led to European economic recovery, West German rearmament, and the creation of a Common Market had already been made. As a result, the future of Europe didn't hang in the balance.

The Austrian-born, French-educated founder of the Center for European Studies, Stanley Hoffmann had no interest in creating another flashpoint on campus. Renowned for his prodigious intellect and mastery of all things French, Hoffmann shunned comparison with his former colleague Kissinger. He loved teaching, related easily to students, and shared the misgivings of many in Cambridge over the White House role of "Henry the Great." The house that mattered to Hoffmann wasn't white. It stood around the corner from CFIA at 5 Bryant Street, where he had spent several years building a community of scholars who shared his passion for explaining Europe to Americans.

The rarified air of Harvard research pushed me to show what I could do. That meant publishing the work on MBFR that I had begun at Brookings. The questions that I posed weren't sweeping or theoretically significant, but they were timely and on target for policy makers. Force reduction talks provided a case study on striking the right balance between domestic politics, alliance commitments, and relations with adversaries.

I spent a full six months refining the five-thousand-word draft I had developed in Washington. That much effort might have been justified if I had had a big backlog of unread documents or a long list of interviews to conduct. My futuristic scenarios, however, were based almost entirely on references from a fragmentary public record. There were no documents to review. No one in Cambridge was in a position to know the thinking of the administration or U.S. allies. The only truly valuable resource I found was Bob Legvold, a protégé of Marshall Shulman in Russian studies, who had a remarkable grasp of the Soviet literature on European security.

As I added footnotes and tinkered with my Quick Fix, Ever-Present Balance, and Protracted Parley, I told myself that a well-done short paper would not only improve my standing at Harvard but also advance my dissertation. In fact, I was marking time because I found myself unable to push forward on the larger project.

The article that *Orbis* published in the spring of 1973, "MBFR: The Search for an American Approach," served its tactical purpose of giving me additional visibility within the Harvard community. Stanley Hoffmann invited me to try out (unsuccessfully) for an entry-level position in the Government Department. Paul Doty, a professor of biochemistry and active member of the informal U.S.-Soviet arms control group known as "Pugwash," also got in touch. He was about to establish a Center on Science and International Affairs across the street from CFIA. He liked my article and wondered if I would be interested in extending my research fellowship under his auspices. What a godsend!

These votes of confidence should have given me a lift. But I remained tied up inside, still replaying the breakup with Marion a year earlier. Just as I couldn't stop reviewing what I had already written, I kept going over the same emotional ground. Repetition and paralysis were two sides of the same coin.

I contacted my thesis advisor at Princeton over the summer. Instead of leveling with him about my writer's block, I proposed a project to start putting the East-West military balance into historical perspective. Two or three background chapters on the politics and diplomacy of the NATO–Warsaw Pact confrontation would tee up my recent work on U.S. troop stationing and MBFR. I would then meld the pieces into a finished product. Ullman, who had himself been trained as a historian, readily agreed.

The historical approach took me into a thicket from which I never emerged. The literature on the Cold War was overwhelming in volume. The story had been told many times. Researchers spent years poring over documents looking for something fresh to say. My advisor gave a mixed review to my first stab at an overview chapter on the post-1945 framework for European security. I had some potentially great insights that needed further development. But he scribbled in the margin that some of the material was "too well trodden to be of use in this form" and that some paragraphs were "more superficial than they need to be."

This effort to engage me had an effect that my advisor never intended. He surely expected me to turn the overview around in a few weeks and mail it back to him. I, however, raised the bar of expectations beyond my reach. I would write a concise, historically accurate, original introductory essay on European security—work of a quality that would prompt a Kissinger, a Hoffmann, or a George Kennan to take notice. I had felt the need to prove myself before but never at this level.

This scene setter would distill the paradox that the military standoff in Europe had protected and undermined the status quo at the same time. My typically French formulation—continuity and change—was the very same one I had used to analyze my junior year abroad. Now I had to apply it with clarity and simplicity to the division of Europe.

The task I set for myself was monumentally difficult—to simplify without oversimplifying, to cull the essential without losing sight of the peripheral. I spent hours mulling over how my ideas fit together and how they should be expressed. My routine interspersed walking and jogging, mostly around Fresh Pond, with typing and rewriting by hand. I internalized the challenge so completely that I didn't keep digging into the literature. I had always written in solitude but never isolation. It was utterly self-defeating to cut myself off from outside feedback and new sources of information. I still don't really understand why I did so. The project swallowed me up.

My painful, frustrating search for perfection lasted two years. The more I fell short, the more confidence I lost in areas in which I had never questioned my ability. A kind of panic set in, cutting my time on task. I looked for and found distractions—a teaching assistantship in Hoffmann's survey course on war, a six-week summer institute in Colorado Springs, a daily dose of Watergate hearings. By the time I produced sixty scene-setting pages, I had run out the clock in Cambridge.

In hindsight I can only shake my head at my inability to seek help. My advisor, Dick Ullman, would have been especially empathetic because he struggled with his own speech disability. Stanley Hoffmann would have provided support. Bob Legvold would have been more than willing to lend a hand. I was too proud and too ashamed to ask, withdrawing from Ullman and glossing over my lack of progress with those in Cambridge who might have intervened.

I didn't tell Mom and Dad much about my turmoil. They were part and parcel of it. This would be the first time that I had failed to measure up to their expectations. I dreaded disappointing them, while at the same time I yearned to be rid of the pressure. I had separated from my parents early in the physical sense. The process of standing more on my own emotionally and psychologically, which had begun during the hard times with Marion, had to continue.

Mom tried to lower the stakes as best she could. She never pried, but she couldn't stop herself from occasionally saying that she hoped I would get the "little piece of paper." Dad backed off entirely. He never asked point-blank how my dissertation was progressing. He and his associate were busy completing their book based on Dad's clinical work with hardened criminals. Instinctively, I ruled out any request for help. I had seen Dad go into his all-knowing therapist mode too often.

I didn't allow the writing problem to stop me from building a social life. Cambridge was full of interesting women, some studying and others working. They weren't as guarded as they would become a few years later, when AIDS hit. It was easy to strike up conversations after a lecture, in the laundry room of the apartment, or in a lunch place. Most of us depended on chance and fix-ups to meet people. The system worked. A slightly older research fellow who had lived in Europe and didn't go to bars or dance well could still get dates.

Still, socializing with married couples was easier. One couple with whom I became friends, Ron and Jane Stivers, helped me find the way forward. The Stivers worked as analysts in different parts of the CIA, he on the Soviet Union and she on Western Europe. His midcareer fellowship at Harvard took them out of their sterile offices in Langley, Virginia, for the first time in years. Pinned down by two young boys, they often set an extra place at dinner for me. The analytical side of the agency to which they were attached inhibited contact with foreigners. They kept current by reading, while I thrived on face-to-face relationships with people from different cultures and backgrounds. I sensed a twinge of regret on their part about a road not taken.

Ron Stivers provided the contact that gave me a fresh start in Washington. I told him about my writing struggle in the spring of 1975, when I faced reality. It was time to stop running in place and find a job. Stivers offered only encouragement, telling me that I had the tools to excel in the national security field. He called his one-time boss at the CIA Bill Hyland, who had served as Kissinger's principal White House advisor on Soviet affairs. Hyland was now playing the same role as assistant secretary of state for intelligence and research. He agreed to interview me as a possible outside hire. He had a large staff and could use a specialist on European security. Our short meeting in his big office went well. Hyland's trust in Stivers clinched a job offer. I owed the opportunity to an inside connection.

It took five months to get the top secret security clearance required of all State Department employees. The forms alone took several days to fill out. I had to account for all of my foreign travel as well as every change of address within the United States since college. Word filtered back from friends and former neighbors that FBI agents were checking me out in detail. The completion of the background investigation qualified me to be sworn in as a federal worker. If I didn't misbehave, I had the civil service equivalent of tenure.

As I left Cambridge, I replayed my first professional setback just as I had the failed marriage. In my heart of hearts I knew that I would be able to recover from the marriage. Time, distance, and experience were allies. The emotional scars would heal. The lack of a doctorate, on the other hand, would be an ongoing career disability. I would always have to outperform to be recognized in a policy world where credentials mattered. But I was going to a place, the Department of State, where merit counted. All I had to do was try harder.

11 RECOVERY

I returned to a different Washington in the fall of 1975. Nixon had resigned in disgrace. The war in Vietnam had ended in humiliation. The fury triggered by the killing of Martin Luther King Jr. had quieted down. A new president, Gerald Ford, was trying to steady the country. The first directly elected mayor of the District of Columbia, Walter Washington, was implementing home rule. The nation's capital was moving on, just like me.

The mere thought of working at the State Department gave me a jolt of self-confidence. The diplomatic corps had a lingering reputation for striped-pants elitism, but few agencies ranked as high in the federal pecking order. The secretary of state stood first in line for presidential succession within the cabinet. The influence of the department grew out of its lead role representing the U.S. government around the world. American ambassadors were the official emissaries of the president of the United States in every national capital and international organization.

The star power of Henry Kissinger added clout. Kissinger ran circles around State as national security advisor during the first Nixon administration. His appointment to become secretary in 1973 brought the department out of the cold and into the limelight. President Ford, who lacked international experience, relied even more than Nixon on Kissinger. To be hired by one of the secretary's lieutenants was a strong calling card.

With time on my hands, I thought about the new challenges facing Kissinger and his confidants. Congressional leaders were pushing hard to cut the imperial presidency down to size. They blamed Vietnam and Watergate on unchecked White House power. A strong congressional counterweight to the imperial presidency, they claimed, would restore the public's trust in government. Their demands for increased oversight and greater disclosure constrained the secret diplomacy on which Kissinger thrived. He would have to develop a broader base of support on Capitol Hill, a demand I saw through the lens of the troops-in-Europe debate.

The hobbling of the U.S. military marked another pivotal change. The chaotic evacuation of Saigon in the spring of 1975 highlighted a decade of colossal mistakes in the Pentagon. Among many other costs the conflict all but eliminated the U.S. capacity to project military power and the political will to use it. Kissinger had to offset the loss of a valuable diplomatic asset, the threat of armed intervention. Part of the solution would be closing ranks with allies—an opening for a NATO analyst who had something to say.

Kissinger would also have to pay heed to growing concern over U.S. economic vulnerability. The immediate threat stemmed from dependence on Middle East oil. Gas prices had tripled since the early 1970s. OPEC, an ominous-looking cartel of oil producers, threatened to keep supplies tight. There were trade problems as well. Foreign-made steel, textiles, and consumer electronics were gaining ground fast in the U.S. market. The world economy was proving to be a source of dislocation as well as opportunity for the United States. U.S. commercial interests had powerful backing and were bound to compete with my area, geopolitics, for high-level attention.

I didn't expect State to call on me right away to work on these problems. I'd have to prove myself on small tasks. But the direction of policy and diplomatic strategy was set in Washington. With luck I would be able to realize my dream of participating.

My high hopes hit reality on the day I reported to work. Dressed in a new charcoal suit and white shirt, I walked a bit uncertainly through the spacious C Street entrance of the department. There were no visible security safeguards outside or inside the main building, which covered almost seven acres between Twenty-First and Twenty-Third Streets just above the National Mall in northwest Washington. The open reception area and courtyard welcomed visitors. It was hard to imagine that more than six thousand people worked upstairs. I filled out papers and picked up the photo ID designating me as a foreign service reserve officer. A pay grade of 06, at a salary of $14,800, put me one step above professional entry level. The department couldn't go any higher because of the limit set by my previous $10,000 Harvard stipend.

Taking the elevator up to the fourth floor, I wended my way through the corridors until I found the open door marked OFFICE OF WESTERN EUROPE, BUREAU OF INTELLIGENCE AND RESEARCH. John Di Sciullo, the acting director, greeted me warmly. He and a half dozen veteran analysts were delighted to have their first new colleague in years. The whole office, except the incoming director, worked out of cubicles in a well-lit central space without a window. Mine, like theirs, had a standard issue desk and IBM electric typewriter. Welcome to the epicenter of U.S. foreign policy!

I quickly saw how much location counted. The seat of power was the seventh floor, where the Office of Secretary commanded a view of the Lincoln Memorial and Memorial Bridge. The regional bureaus that linked headquarters to embassies abroad occupied the next floors down. A fourth-floor location put Intelligence and Research (INR) on a lower rung than decision-making and operations. As a junior person assigned to a support bureau, I wouldn't be meeting too often with the secretary. In fact, I never saw him once while he was at the department.

The old-timers in my office explained that foreign service reserve officers stood at the bottom of a three-tier organization. State hired us to provide expertise and institutional memory in niche areas. A much larger cadre of foreign service officers (FSOS) ran the diplomatic corps. They entered the department via competitive exam, signing up for overseas duty and management responsibility. The culture of the department celebrated versatility, while we added depth. Presidential appointees made up the top tier. A handful filled key slots at main State, while several dozen held the choicest ambassadorships. The appointees were always a mixed bag, but their personal ties to the White House carried weight.

INR, which served as State's liaison to the intelligence community, employed more reserve officers than any other bureau. Piecing together evidence from covert and publicly available sources was tricky business. State had to have a stable of career experts to hold its own with the agencies that concentrated solely on intelligence. That's why the director of the bureau had been able to find a spot for me. His large fourth-floor staff monitored the day-to-day reporting of the CIA and represented the department when the White House asked for a net assessment of a potential threat to U.S. interests.

Western Europe drew much less attention in the world of intelligence than the Soviet Union and the Middle East. Upcoming parliamentary elections in Italy created one brief flurry of activity soon after I arrived. The National Security Council asked for a contingency study in case Italy's large Communist Party won enough votes to participate in government at the national level for the first time. The secretary kept his own counsel, but the bureaucracy might come up with a few good insights or provide a rationale for the course of action he planned to take anyway. My acting director Di Sciullo, one of State's foremost experts on Italy, took me with him on the blue shuttle bus to CIA headquarters to get my feet wet in the interagency discussion.

The process was much less formal than I expected. Taking turns, specialists from CIA, the Defense Intelligence Agency, and the National Security Agency presented their views orally. Then the hard work of drafting started. The carefully hedged assessment concluded that the Communists wouldn't pose a serious threat as junior partners in a government of the left. Once the analysis was completed, the office resumed its nine-to-five routine of clearing cables, responding to queries, and turning out occasional briefs.

A fresh face named Peter Tarnoff turned my backwater assignment into something much more. Personnel brought him back from a plum job as consul general in Lyon in early 1976 to breathe life into our office. Word got around before he arrived that the foreign service had picked one of its best. His chiseled features and razor-cut brown hair came out of central casting. He wore tailored European suits, folding a silk handkerchief into the breast pocket for flair. His perfect French gave him an authenticity that few others at State could match. Yet his style was casual and very American. He was quick, competent, and never combative. No one got on the fast track at State picking fights.

I clicked with Tarnoff right away. We were only five or six years apart in age. He tested my French, and I passed. As we got to know each other, he mentioned his New York Jewish background and a father who had dreamed of going to Hollywood. He wasn't an Ivy Leaguer but had earned his way into the more selective European cone of the diplomatic corps. I was the rookie with plenty of intellectual capital who didn't know my way around the building. He helped me climb that learning curve. In return I produced analysis that made his office look good.

My new boss became my first mentor, making a huge impact without exerting himself much. Deftly, he started with a writing tutorial. State lived by the written word. Missions overseas reported via cable. The staff at main State briefed superiors via memorandum. There were too many issues and too many layers of management to do otherwise.

Always stressing the positive, Tarnoff complimented my writing but said it needed a makeover. "It's time to start writing for a policy audience, John. Forget the academics," he said. The readership at State and elsewhere in government expected any issue—however complex—to be reduced to its essentials in a page or two without losing nuance. He tightened and polished everything I wrote. It didn't take long to acquire the skill he was looking for, which had more to do with disciplined thinking than facility with words.

Tarnoff gave me access to the senior careerists in the two bureaus that covered European security. The European Bureau had a NATO Affairs desk that managed Alliance diplomacy. The Politico-Military Bureau, or PM, handled global issues linked to military capabilities, including arms control, arms sales, and weapons procurement. The scope of responsibility of the two bureaus intersected. A recommendation from a well-liked colleague was enough to get me on the calendar of top people in both bureaus regardless of my rank.

PM put me to work. George Vest, the tall, easygoing director, and Jim Goodby, his thoughtful deputy, wanted to explore the costs and benefits of standardizing NATO armaments. From a strictly military standpoint, the forces of the Alliance would be more credible if they used the same weapons systems. Member states, however, had economic and political stakes in defense procurement that often cut the other way. As a result, NATO fielded an array of different aircraft, tanks, artillery, small arms, and communications equipment. The tradeoffs between military efficiency, commercial interests, and Alliance burden sharing were complicated. Freed from the daily grind of cable traffic, I had the time to help PM figure out where the Europeans were coming from and what the implications were for U.S. policy.

This assignment brought me out of my fourth-floor cubicle. I met with the Policy Planning Staff and NATO Affairs to gather input. The INR report I drafted was good enough to be circulated to all of the principals working on European security, including the secretary's influential counselor. That was the State Department equivalent of getting a journal article published. Other assignments followed, establishing me as a working-level player and earning me a year-end promotion.

I kept my eye on the seventh floor, rating Secretary Kissinger from below. I arrived at State poised to give him low grades as leader of the diplomatic corps. He might be a star outside the building, but I felt sure that his big ego and disdain for bureaucracy would lead him to ignore the organization he was supposed to run. The foreign service would follow orders but wouldn't embrace him.

Wrong. Kissinger had a strong following up and down the line. He commanded respect and struck fear. The backbiting stories that went around made him a larger-than-life figure who worked impossible hours and set the bar immeasurably high. My favorite concerned Kissinger's hazing of newcomers to his staff. He was said to have called one newcomer back into his office three times, each time returning the memorandum that the staffer had been asked to write with the same gruff question, "Is this the best you can do?" The third time around, after two rewrites, the terrified junior officer said, "Mr. Secretary, this is the best I can do." To which Kissinger replied, "Good. Now I'll read it."

Kissinger won over the careerists with apparent ease. He gave them the stature they longed for. His huge appetite for information allowed them to participate in the policy process even though he wasn't looking their way for strategic advice. He surrounded himself with the brightest midlevel foreign service officers around. Making the secretary's staff and sticking was widely recognized as a badge of honor—a reminder that the boss wouldn't settle for anything but the best.

The diplomatic corps didn't gripe about its limited role. Few FSOs saw themselves as foreign policy gurus, and few had take-charge personalities. Their rough edges were worn down by the imperative of maintaining relationships in Washington and abroad. An effective diplomat had to keep lines of communication open. An effective policy maker had to make choices and defend a course of action. Often the two didn't mix. Many talented foreign service officers viewed their main job as making sure that the diplomatic machine ran smoothly. They weren't itching to take on the Harvard professor who joked that he was a legend in his own mind.

The 1976 presidential election brought change at the top that got me off the fourth floor. President-elect Jimmy Carter campaigned for a clear break from the hard-nosed pragmatism of the Nixon-Kissinger years. U.S. diplomacy should stand for American ideals, not copy our adversaries. Carter named Cyrus Vance, a lawyer from the Eastern establishment, to succeed Kissinger. Vance had served as deputy secretary of defense in the Johnson administration before a change of heart over Vietnam led him to resign. His nomination signaled that the rule of law would take priority over power politics.

As the transition unfolded, I learned that my mentor had close ties to the new secretary. They had worked together in Paris on Vietnam peace talks in 1968. Tarnoff was going to move up to the seventh floor to direct the secretary's staff. He'd be at the top of the paper flow in the building as well as the point man for State in dealings with other agencies and the White House. Perhaps his return from France a year earlier hadn't been accidental. The career service knew how to position its people.

Before leaving INR, Tarnoff sent me to Europe for two weeks of fact-finding and orientation at major embassies. The trip marked a personal awakening of what it would be like to work at State long term. I traveled on per diem and felt the bite of hierarchy. The casual, first-name culture that applied inside the building didn't apply to dealings with outsiders. At NATO headquarters, where I had met with the ambassador as a lieutenant in 1970, I could only see the head of the political section. In Paris my control officer refused to book an office meeting with my high-ranking friend at the Quai d'Orsay. These weren't slights, just the realities of the track I was on.

The parting thank-you Tarnoff delivered led to a new job. He couldn't bring me along to a staff reserved for FSOs. Instead, he recommended me to Les Gelb, the incoming director of PM. Gelb had worked for Vance at Defense, where he commissioned the explosive study of U.S. involvement in Vietnam known as the "Pentagon Papers." I had met him briefly at Brookings and followed his byline at the *New York Times*, where he served as diplomatic correspondent during Kissinger's years at State. Yes, he would be glad to have me. I had my own ticket to the seventh floor.

My old and new bosses had little in common beyond their close ties to the secretary. Tall and solidly built, Gelb had no interest in dressing the part of a professional diplomat. He preferred showing the fancy pants at State that clothes don't make the man. He also shunned anything that smacked of Kissinger's image, downplaying his doctorate from Harvard and his important work on national security decision-making.

The role of tough, confident outsider suited Gelb. He outthought and outmaneuvered the careerists most of the time, prevailing with a rare combination of forcefulness on bureaucratic matters and moderation on policy issues. It helped to have a big brain, a terrific pen, a quick wit, and a taste for infighting. He knew how to listen and lead too. He was going to go far.

Unlike Tarnoff, Gelb had to make an impact quickly. He had just won Senate confirmation at the age of forty. He had a champion in Vance, whom he would support in the battle for the president's ear that was sure to shape up with Zbigniew Brzezinski, the hawkish national security advisor. He had no idea what would come next. "Once you make assistant secretary," he said, "anything else is a matter of luck." I wasn't going to be a favorite of the man on the move, but I could learn a lot just by watching.

When Gelb brought his newly formed team together, it was clear that he had scoured the building and his Rolodex for talent. He was following a basic rule of bureaucratic politics he had once written about: surround yourself with good people if you want to be effective.

Two of Gelb's best finds worked alongside me. Alexander Vershbow, a Russian-speaking junior foreign service officer, became a resource on all things Soviet. The thoughtful, hardworking Vershbow would parley his linguistic skills and low-key style into an outstanding career that included ambassadorships to Russia and NATO. My other new office mate, Arnold Kanter, was a razor-sharp, wisecracking academic whom Gelb knew from Brookings. A generalist, he served as a one-man rapid deployment force on any issue that needed brainpower. Kanter eventually left State for the RAND Corporation, only to come back in the early 1990s in the powerful position of undersecretary of state for political affairs.

To make my mark, I volunteered to take on one of the hardest emerging issues Gelb faced. President Carter had decided to set an ethical tone for his administration by cutting back on U.S. arms sales to the developing world. He was so deeply engaged that he wrote marginal notes on records of U.S. arms sales that filtered down to my level. The United States, he declared publicly, shouldn't be an arms merchant to the world. His administration would take action to shrink an exploding global market. Unilateral U.S. cuts represented a first step down that path. But what was to stop other arms suppliers from filling the gap? That was the problem that hit Gelb's inbox in the spring of 1977.

I came up with a framework paper that sorted out the question of U.S. leverage. A good piece of analysis introduced me to the sharp elbows of office politics. My ambitious office director changed a few words and substituted his name for mine on the drafting line. If the paper went forward to the secretary, he would get the credit. Should I confront him, complain to Gelb, or file this experience away as another reason to think twice before staying the course at State? I was in a no-win situation. Instead of raising hell and risking a bad performance review, I kept quiet.

A few months later Gelb asked me, as the working-level lead, to accompany him on a mission to Bonn. He was going to meet his British, French, and German counterparts. Jessica Tuchman Mathews, a member of the National Security Council whose portfolio included conventional arms sales, joined us. I wrote the strategy paper and talking points. Finally, I was on the front lines of diplomacy.

The trip brought another strong reminder that I was a junior officer. Gelb had the rank to sit in first-class on the flight to Cologne, while Mathews and I chatted in coach. He came back briefly to say hello and tell us about the great food up front. Then, after we took a car to Bonn, he waited expectantly for me to carry his briefcase into the hotel. Mathews and I exchanged glances. The White House staffer, who would later become president of the Carnegie Endowment for International Peace, graciously picked the briefcase up from the trunk of the car.

Gelb shined at the meeting. He played a weak hand with a master's touch, arguing for coordinated, unilateral restraint as the most practical way to contain the explosion of global arms exports. The Europeans listened and asked questions. None challenged him. The State Department had requested this discussion, not the allies. When we returned home, he wrote a sparkling memo to the secretary. He declared victory. U.S. arguments carried the day, although we had no evidence that any minds had been changed.

I compared Gelb with Tarnoff, the two role models that I had seen in action in two years at State. Neither one had been born with a silver spoon in his mouth. Both owed their big breaks to a cabinet-level backer. But their careers reflected different goals and strengths.

The FSO path that Tarnoff took rewarded collegiality. The members of the diplomatic corps cared more about representing American power abroad than wielding it back home. Careerists were used to ceding authority to political appointees. Competition within the foreign service was intense but governed by a code that frowned on advancing at the expense of others or taking partisan positions. Those who didn't wish to play by those rules resigned. Winners like Tarnoff had to invest deeply and continuously in working the closed system that meted out opportunities.

Gelb's entrepreneurial path rewarded individuality. He and others like him got places by putting their own names forward. They took sides all the time, competing in the no-holds-barred world of Washington politics. The end game for them was making policy. They invested in relationships with experts and power brokers rather than an organization. Foreign travel was a necessity, but life abroad was a distraction.

The best of both worlds would be to combine Gelb's freedom of action with Tarnoff's personal style. It would be hard to pull off. Maybe I was conjuring up mission impossible.

12 TRANSITIONS

Life changed before my reckoning at State. Dad suffered a fatal heart attack in November 1976. His seizure caught Mom, Bonnie, and me unprepared. We had already lived through gall bladder removal, a major coronary, chronic high blood pressure, and the onset of type 2 diabetes.

Work brought out the best in Dad until the very end. He left the house by 7:00 a.m. to beat the traffic downtown and across the Anacostia River to the country's oldest federally run psychiatric hospital. The redbrick buildings of St. Elizabeths filled 175 acres atop a commanding hill in a rundown neighborhood of southeast Washington. In its heyday the hospital housed eight thousand patients and employed a staff of four thousand.

Bonnie, who spent a summer in Dad's project office, saw his face brighten as soon as he walked in the door. "He was a different person, smiling, courteous, and thoughtful," she recalled. The small staff respected him. The criminals whom he spent hundreds of hours interviewing revered him. He took an hour-long walk in his cardigan sweater over the lunch hour, usually with a research subject. Returning home by 5:00 p.m., he decompressed in front of the television after dinner.

Taxpayers got their money's worth. Dad's young associate Stanton Samenow, who got equal billing, distilled some three hundred thousand pages of dictated notes and produced the first draft of a manuscript. Volume 1, *The Criminal Personality*, challenged the conventional wisdom that social ills caused criminal behavior. Yochelson and Samenow sketched a profile of criminals as master manipulators who blamed tough neighborhoods, broken homes, poverty, and racism for their actions. Change only began when criminals assumed responsibility for what they did.

The Criminal Personality made a splash in the spring of 1976. Dad's thesis gave conservatives a solid counter to the liberal argument that social welfare programs could solve the crime problem. His investigation showed that crimes represented individual acts that had to be addressed case by case. Skeptics of federally funded cure-alls, led by Harvard's respected James Q. Wilson, endorsed the thrust of Dad's thinking. The Yochelson-Samenow volumes, three in all, would be viewed as groundbreaking. Copies are still available on Amazon. Forty years after Dad's death, the long-running hit TV series *The Sopranos* used his portrait of the devious criminal mind in its final episode to resolve the relationship between a mob boss and his psychiatrist.

Dad wanted the limelight after sixteen years of civil service obscurity. He jumped at the first out-of-town invitation to come along, a talk in St. Louis. He insisted on going alone, though he accepted my offer to pick him up at the house. We played gin rummy while Mom fixed an early dinner. I dropped him off at National Airport in plenty of time to catch an early-evening flight. As we shook hands and I wished him well, he said: "I'm looking forward to speaking. It's about time."

Mom's urgent middle-of-the-night call to Bonnie and me brought the three of us to a motel room in St. Louis the next day. Dad had collapsed in the airport. He was unconscious and on a respirator in the intensive care unit of a nearby hospital. Bonnie's husband, Paul, joined us. We huddled silently in a motel for a few days, fearful that Dad would remain in a coma indefinitely. On the morning of the fourth day of our vigil, the doctor called to tell us that Dad had passed away during the night. He had never regained consciousness. The end, breaking the agony of waiting, came as a relief.

Dad's funeral in the Washington Hebrew Congregation drew a large crowd. Rabbi Haberman, who had started his career in Buffalo and knew my parents, delivered the eulogy in his take-charge voice. Neither Mom nor Bonnie nor I made comments. None of us were up to it. When the service ended, as we got into the limousine to drive to the cemetery a mile from Dad's office in Anacostia, the finality of his loss hit me. I broke down sobbing.

My emotions ran deep because they were so mixed. Dad had passed along his core values of hard work, personal responsibility, and helping others. They were mine too. Yet he hurt those closest to him deeply. He failed to acknowledge in volume 1 how much Mom had supported him, dedicating his life's work to the administrator of St. Elizabeths, whom he scarcely knew. I pictured him berating Mom, clamping down on Bonnie, and relishing his croquet win over eight-year-old me.

My way of honoring his memory expressed my ambivalence. I said Kaddish for him every Friday night or Saturday morning for a year, never missing a service. Dad deserved a perfect record of attendance. I went alone to Washington Hebrew Congregation, usually on Friday nights after work. This was a personal gesture. Yet I chose a ritual prayer that Dad had never bothered with when he lost his parents. I was aligning myself with his father, the kosher butcher whose face lit up as he hoisted me up on his shoulders. Grandpa would have followed tradition.

I would never get over my divided feelings. Dad's strengths awed me, but I also wanted to be his opposite. I'd watch my eating, stay in shape, support my wife's goals, attend my kids' games, embrace compromise, and remain flexible.

In contrast, Mom idealized Dad. Whatever his faults, he was the love of her life who had given her what she valued most—her children, financial security, and social standing. She looked back with absolute certainty on her choice of the brilliant, penniless grad student from Buffalo over the rich boy from New Haven. Despite her vitality and good looks at age seventy, she was always going to be Mrs. Samuel Yochelson. She kept the phone listed under his name and continued to use their joint checkbook. His suits remained hanging in the closet until she sold the house.

Mom made her priorities clear. She wanted to avoid becoming a burden on her children and to guard the legacy of Sam Yochelson. Settling Dad's estate, she found that his life insurance, government pension, and a paid-up home ought to see her through if she lived frugally. As for his legacy, she bristled at the prospect that Dad's coauthor would get undue credit. Mom saw the younger man as an intruder who had talked Dad into using the editorial *we* to assume a far greater role in the research than he deserved. I treaded lightly, reminding her that there would be no manuscript at all without him. In any case there was little any of us could do.

We took action to memorialize Dad's work at Yale. Mom and I joined forces with her brother David and Dad's brother Leon to endow the Yochelson lecture in forensic psychiatry. The Department of Psychiatry agreed to team up with the Law School to bring a prominent speaker to campus every year. This endorsement brought closure to Mom. She and Dad were making a mark where their life together began.

The loss of Dad coincided with a new beginning for me. He never set eyes on Diane Kamino, a petite blue-eyed blonde from upstate New York whom I started to date just before he died. He would have been struck by her beauty, wholesomeness, and interest in politics. He also would have recalled how fate brought him together with Mom on a blind date.

I met Diane by accident at a rooftop swimming pool in Foggy Bottom during the summer of 1976. Her girlfriend, visiting from New York, struck up a conversation with Bernard Gotlieb, a French diplomat, whom I had invited over. They flirted while we looked on. Eventually, the four of us pulled up chairs and introduced ourselves. Diane and I, the bystanders, lived in the adjoining apartment houses that shared the pool. She worked on the Senate Small Business Committee. Our talkative friends exchanged contact information. They didn't see each other until the following year at our wedding.

I was ready for a serious relationship when I asked Diane out to a performance of the Alvin Ailey dance troupe at George Washington University. I felt settled in Washington. Time had helped me let go of painful memories. I wanted to stop the revolving door of Cambridge days.

My date was six years younger than I was and barely reached my shoulder. She was incredibly good-looking. Her luminous eyes set off the high cheekbones on her heart-shaped face. She had a lovely smile and perfectly groomed hair, with bangs that fell softly across her forehead. There was nothing showy about her. I liked her demure, understated style. The gap in age didn't seem to make much difference. We were in the same place professionally—new to the neighborhood and to our jobs.

Diane came from the same East European Jewish stock that I did. She, too, grew up in upstate New York. Her father was a self-made success in retailing. Although she had a strong sense of family, she had a "stand-on-your-own" streak much like mine. She had moved from Syracuse to New York after college for a master's degree in education. She decided to try Washington when New York's plummeting finances dried up the market for entry-level teachers. After a stint as a receptionist at a real estate firm, she landed an interview for a secretarial position with the senior senator

1. My parents, Kathryn and Samuel Yochelson, with me at seven months, Camp Kilmer, New Jersey, 1944. Courtesy of Bonnie Yochelson.

2. (*Opposite top*) With my baby sister, Bonnie, at the beach, New Hampshire, 1953. Courtesy of Bonnie Yochelson.

3. (*Opposite bottom*) My mother attends my promotion to first lieutenant at headquarters, U.S. Army Europe, Heidelberg, Germany, 1969. Courtesy of Bonnie Yochelson.

4. (*Above*) Diane and I celebrate our wedding, Syracuse, New York, 1977. Courtesy of the author.

5. Our daughters, Lisa and Laura, Les Lecques, France, 2000.
Courtesy of the author.

To Ambassador Dave Abshire
Great leader of great causes
mentor ... to so many
including this devoted
admirer and friend.
Anne Armstrong

DAVID M. ABSHIRE
LECTURE
MARCH 18, 1983
Center for
Strategic and International Studies
Georgetown University

To my good friend Dave
with great appreciation for
your contributions to
Security. Sam Nunn

6. David Abshire, president of CSIS, flanked by Senator Sam Nunn (D-GA) and
leading Republican Anne Armstrong, Washington DC, 1983. Courtesy of the
Center for the Study of the Presidency and Congress.

7. (*Opposite top*) With former secretary of state Henry Kissinger at CSIS International Councillors meeting, Washington DC, 1988. Courtesy of the author.

8. (*Opposite bottom*) As a member of the President's Export Council, meeting President George H. W. Bush, 1991. Courtesy of the author.

9. (*Above*) European industrialist Carlo De Benedetti and *Washington Post* publisher Katharine Graham at the Council on Competitiveness, 1996. Courtesy of the Council on Competitiveness.

10. (*Above*) John Young, cofounder of CSIS, listens to Senator Joseph Lieberman (D-CT) on Capitol Hill, 1997. Courtesy of the Council on Competitiveness.

11. (*Opposite top*) Vice President Al Gore, keynote speaker, with me, Council on Competitiveness chairman Bill Hambrecht, and MIT president Charles Vest at the first national innovation summit, Cambridge, Massachusetts, 1998. Courtesy of the author.

12. (*Opposite bottom*) Professor Mike Porter, Harvard Business School, with Senators Jay Rockefeller (D-WV) and Bill Frist (R-TN) at a Council on Competitiveness briefing on innovation, Capitol Hill, 1998. Courtesy of the Council on Competitiveness.

13. (*Above*) Meeting First Lady Hillary Clinton on the DC circuit at a White House reception, 2000. Courtesy of the author.

14. (*Opposite top*) Mary Anne Fox, chancellor and BEST board member, hosts navy interns and mentors at a ceremony honoring female Nobel laureates, University of California San Diego, 2011. Courtesy of the University of California San Diego.

15. (*Opposite bottom*) Irwin Jacobs, cofounder of QUALCOMM and BEST chairman, addresses four thousand students at the USA STEM Symposium in Washington DC, 2015. Courtesy of the USA Science and Engineering Festival. Photograph by Mike Colella.

16. BEST vice president Karen Harper and I congratulate students from Ron Clark Academy, Atlanta, for winning the MATHCOUNTS Video Challenge, at Disney World, Orlando, Florida, 2014. Courtesy of the author.

from New York, Jacob Javits. She got hired, impressed her supervisor, and worked her way up to professional staff member.

What an appealing story, I thought. This beautiful, soft-spoken girl had a lot going for her. We found it easy and natural to spend time together. We went to Sarsfield's, a neighborhood restaurant, for half-price burgers on Monday nights. We walked to the Georgetown Sweet Shoppe for ice cream. She had me over for her specialty, chicken baked in onion soup with mushrooms. I had her over for spaghetti with doctored-up Ragu sauce.

I introduced Diane to jogging around the reflecting pool between the Lincoln and Washington monuments. Although we eventually worked up to two laps several times a week, we got off to a wobbly start. Catching her shorts on a fence, she tripped and burst into tears. The scrape didn't hurt. It was the painful memory of being pudgy and not good at sports as a child. My heart went out to her as she wiped her eyes. That moment marked the beginning of her lifelong commitment to fitness.

Other qualities drew me to Diane as we saw more of each other. She hadn't been scarred by a failed marriage the way I had. She had her share of experience with boys but had never been engaged. She didn't go into detail about her previous romances, nor did she drill down into my first marriage. Her reserve reflected definite ideas about what was proper in male-female relationships. Rehashing feelings and dissecting relationships crossed the line. Yearning for a fresh start, I welcomed her "Don't Tell, Don't Ask" approach.

Diane also didn't bear the same burden of parental expectations that I did. As the first in her family to go to college, her parents took immense pride in her undergraduate degree from Syracuse University and her graduate degree from New York University. The most rewarding moment of her college career had been arranging an invitation to her father to speak to her class in marketing. He had tears in his eyes, she told me, when she graduated. The Kaminos weren't trying to raise an Ivy League intellectual, nor was I looking for one. Her good organization balanced my penchant for big ideas. Theory meets practice.

My new girlfriend didn't feel the same calling to public service that I did. The scene on Capitol Hill attracted her more than the power or the policy issues. Her senator, a liberal Republican serving his third term, was known for the competence of his staff. He conducted the final interview of every new staff member himself, a rarity for a legislator of his influence. Diane had only occasional contact with Senator Javits, who knew her by face and called her "dear," as he did most of the other women in his office. Her well-connected boss, Jud Sommer, had managed Javits's 1974 reelection campaign. As minority counsel to the Small Business Committee, he taught her how to handle constituent inquiries and had her track issues of special interest to the senator.

Diane could do her job well without working long hours. She used her spare time to keep up longtime friendships, something I had never done. We saw some of her closest friends from Syracuse regularly. Her girlfriend from elementary school had recently been certified to teach deaf children. One of her sorority sisters was a buyer for Macy's, while another was an attorney for the Commerce Department. I coveted Diane's firm grounding. My skills and interests rewarded mobility, not stability. Her life was anchored in family and lasting friendships—things I wanted too.

Our courtship followed a familiar ritual. Diane's mother met mine in DC. Then Diane invited me to her brother's college graduation in Syracuse. The Kaminos lived large. They drove his and hers Mercedes. Their one-floor home and pool were set in the center of an estate-sized lot. The handcrafted kitchen, French reproductions, and quality antiques reflected the eye of a professional decorator. This home, with its Waterford crystal and Georg Jensen silver, looked like a candidate for *Architectural Digest*.

Yet Sidney and Lillian Kamino never forgot where they came from. The gregarious military policeman and the refined working girl with the perfect figure had met near the end of World War II in Boston. He delivered on his first-date promise to marry her. Sidney got a foothold in the new field of discount retailing and relocated his young family to Syracuse. There he built a regional chain of fifty bargain centers, KBC, in the smaller markets that Kmart and others overlooked. He took the company public and became president of a national conglomerate that included such luxury brands as Tiffany and Cross. After a forced buyout in the early seventies, he reacquired and ran one of his most profitable stores. Lillian, a woman of great style, filled her generational role as helpmate.

The Kaminos didn't let their hard-earned affluence go to their heads.

Sidney spent long days in his big-box store, KBC, which dominated downtown Fulton, New York. Diane wanted me to see the store, about an hour outside Syracuse, where she had worked the cash register during summers and holidays. When we dropped in, we saw her father in full command of ninety thousand square feet of merchandise. No detail escaped his attention as we walked down spotless aisles filled with everything from blue jeans to housewares to hand tools. He was going to teach Diane's brother, Rick, every facet of the business that Lillian called the "little gold mine."

Unlike my parents, who craved recognition more than money, the Kaminos worked hard to enjoy a lifestyle that they had dreamed of as poor kids growing up. They took real pleasure in playing golf at their club, owning a place in Florida, and eating at the best restaurants. We went to their favorite, Grimaldi's, which always had a ready table for Mr. and Mrs. K. We laughed a lot. Sidney bantered with Fritz the waiter. The chef-owner came out to say hello. We greeted other regulars before leaving. This was nothing like a meal out with the purposeful Yochelsons. The Kaminos just wanted to have a good time, and they knew how.

Rick's graduation party brought the Utica branch of the Kamino family to town. Grandma Jenny, the matriarch, had supported her family as a kosher caterer. Aunt Betty and her husband, Uncle Spike, came too, along with cousins Roxie and Warren and their spouses. Word spread that Diane's boyfriend from Washington worked for the CIA. When the party ended, the Kaminos didn't go their separate ways like the Yochelsons and the Merseys. They all lived upstate, tied together by the opportunities that Sidney's business created. I sensed the closeness and enjoyed the camaraderie.

When we returned to Washington, the next move was up to me. I found it difficult to express my feelings. I had been so deeply hurt when I had given free rein to my emotions. Instead of straightforwardly proposing marriage, I tiptoed up to the question by suggesting that Diane and I look at buying a condo. Sensing that I was scared, she coaxed the words out of me. Happily, we walked over to a deserted State Department around eight in the evening. There were no security barriers or metal detectors in those days. The guard at the reception desk waived us in when I showed my ID. We went up to the office and used the free Watts lines to call family.

Our engagement sent the Kaminos into action. Lillian didn't hire a wedding planner. This was her moment to shine. She and Diane had a hand-in-glove rapport. Daughter looked up to mother as the epitome of high style and good taste, while mother looked upon daughter as the young professional who could do it all. They took the lead, while the effervescent Sidney said yes to their suggestions, and I went along for the ride.

The plan jelled quickly. The venue would be the ballroom of the venerable Hotel Syracuse in the heart of downtown. The date would be early November before the snows. The time would be late afternoon. Dress would be formal. The guest list would be large enough to accommodate friends and family but not extravagantly so. Aunt Betty would throw a party for out-of-towners on Saturday night at the country club. The wedding would take place the following afternoon at the landmark hotel.

We combined engagement ring and wedding dress shopping in New York City one weekend. Diane and I stayed in separate rooms at the Warwick, the business hotel in Midtown where Sidney was a regular. He took me down to the garment district south of Forty-Second, while the girls went off on their own. He knew the neighborhood cold, having stocked his stores with soft goods from the showrooms here for years. He told me about doing business with the clothing manufacturers who had their offices here.

I told him about my uncle Lou, the trucking sales and service manager who had to do business over three-martini lunches with the Mafia bosses that controlled transportation in this part of the city. We had a brisket sandwich in the Herald Square deli next to the original Macy's on Thirty-Fourth Street and Sixth Avenue. My future father-in-law, I thought, felt reassured that a Yale snob wasn't going to marry his daughter. That evening the four of us went out for a celebratory dinner at the 21 Club.

On Sunday Diane and I hunted for a ring in the diamond district on Forty-Seventh Street. Hundreds of dealers jammed the block between Sixth and Seventh Avenues on the West Side, many dressed in the black suits and white shirts of the Hasidic community in Brooklyn. We found the address of Mr. Doppelt, the dealer that Sidney had arranged for us to see. Making our way up an elevator and rickety stairs, we rang the bell of an office at the back of the building near a fire escape.

A middle-aged man with thinning hair checked us out through a peephole, opened the door, and invited us in. Then he pulled diamonds in my price range out of a small felt bag, explaining how color, hardness, size, and cut factored into the value of a gem. Diane made her choice, and I completed the sale on a handshake with no deposit. Mr. Doppelt insisted that Diane try the ring for at least a week. This was how people who trusted each other did business.

The Kaminos were generous in extending invitations to the groom's family and friends. I invited my brother-in-law, Paul, to serve as best man, along with Rick Kamino and Bernard Gotlieb, the French diplomat who was with me when I met Diane. Mom's brothers Lou and David and her sister, Bea, attended, along with the widows of her brothers Henry and Paul. Uncle Leon flew up alone to represent Dad's side. This was the last joyous occasion for my extended family.

The wedding came off perfectly. Soft lights and flowers transformed the hotel ballroom into a fairyland. Diane looked radiant in a classic white gown. Mom beamed as she walked up the aisle on Leon's arm. Bonnie served as a bridesmaid. The Reform rabbi who had conducted Diane's Bat Mitzvah officiated, along with the cantor from the Conservative synagogue, where the Kaminos also belonged. After dinner Grandma Jenny took a turn at the mike to sing "You Are My Sunshine," the first song I ever learned. Then Sidney took over to sing Sinatra songs. We danced until after midnight. Driving to the airport the next morning for a short honeymoon in the Virgin Islands, I knew that my life was back on track.

13　CENTER OF THE ACTION

A carefree week of snorkeling primed me to get serious about the future. My wedding band glided to the bottom of the Caribbean on the first day. I wasn't going to let my new responsibility as a breadwinner slip away like that. It was time to decide whether to stay at the State Department or look elsewhere.

State commanded my respect but not my devotion. As an outside hire filling a Washington desk job, I never felt the pride of representing my country overseas that George Kennan described in his memoirs. I was actually taking a spot on the seventh floor that ought to go to an FSO. My future would be up for grabs after my champions Tarnoff and Gelb left.

Two years of experience took some of the gleam off government service. Although I worked with some terrific colleagues, I also saw bright people lose their edge and bureaucratic rivalries get in the way of good policy. The federal salary cap of $36,000 took a toll on high performers, whose only reward was getting a good next assignment. One colleague with four kids asked for help to break out. Little by little, the reality sank in that a career in government could involve more sacrifice than I was ready to make.

There were other reasons to move on. The military confrontation in Europe remained frozen. The reserve officer track at State would keep me plowing over the same material, while I was itching for something new. The gap between my pay and professional standing gnawed, especially because I did not want to be beholden to my in-laws. The department offered no shortcut to promotion. A weak evaluation report could take years to overcome. The surest way to begin making up lost ground was changing jobs.

Capitol Hill looked more promising than the executive branch. Congressional staffers had no job protection at all, but they could go places with the right boss. The career of Ted Sorensen, JFK's chief policy aide and speechwriter, showed what could happen. Sorensen had signed on with the junior senator from Massachusetts when he was first elected. They grew so close that the future president used to refer to Sorensen as his intellectual blood bank. The strongest members of Congress had their Sorensens, regardless of party.

I passed up a chance to interview for the open position of foreign policy advisor to Senator Ted Kennedy. Robert Hunter, a fellow Europeanist who had left that spot for the staff of the National Security Council offered to get me in the door. Kennedy's liberal politics gave me pause. I also knew that Dad's younger brother, the celebrity psychiatrist, was treating a member of the family. Uncle Leon, the soul of discretion, told me that the Kennedys attracted formidable staff. He added, however, that I might also be asked to pick up the laundry. That was all I needed to hear.

A more promising lead turned up in Les Aspin, an up-and-coming congressman from Wisconsin whom I got to know through the Woodrow Wilson School network. The rumpled, unpretentious Aspin would in time move up to chair the House Armed Services Committee and would later serve as Bill Clinton's first secretary of defense. He volunteered to help me jump to the Hill when positions opened up after the 1978 election.

Before Aspin could act, I got an unexpected offer from the Georgetown University Center for Strategic and International Studies (CSIS)—a well-connected, right-of-center think tank. Ken Myers, director of the European Studies Program at CSIS, had a knack for putting together good meetings. I participated in several of his sessions. He appreciated having an insider around the table, and I liked the exposure.

Myers made his pitch over onion soup at Jean Pierre, a pricey K Street restaurant near his office. He had just received a two-year grant to support a high-level CSIS conference in Brussels celebrating the thirtieth anniversary of NATO. There was enough funding to bring a senior fellow aboard. I would be a tremendous asset. There would be few set responsibilities. Unfortunately, he could do no better than $24,000 a year.

I delayed my acceptance for a day to avoid looking too hungry. What could be better than a $6,000 raise and a chance to reposition myself at the place where Henry Kissinger was writing his memoirs? According to the grapevine, CSIS had outcompeted Columbia, Oxford, and Yale to land Kissinger. His arrival turned a hardline policy research center into a hot property.

More than money, CSIS would free me of bureaucratic constraints. I recalled being frozen out of a working meeting at the White House mess that I had organized. There weren't enough places at the table because someone with a higher rank decided to attend at the last minute. That wouldn't happen anymore. Think tanks were outward-looking organizations on the prowl for funding, media coverage, and the attention of policy makers. With a career in government off the table, I craved the freedom to explore the Hill, the private sector, and nonprofits. Now I'd have it.

I left State without fanfare and checked into CSIS in September 1978. The center occupied up-to-date office space at 1800 K Street, connoting easy access to the White House and State Department. Most of the staff of eighty squeezed into the fifth floor, with additional offices, including a suite for Kissinger, scattered above. The International Club, a carryover from segregation days that didn't discriminate against any members of the diplomatic community, provided meeting rooms and a moderately priced dining room below.

CSIS made a vivid first impression. A lot of young interns reflected the center's connection to Georgetown University. Power photos featured congressional leaders participating at CSIS events. I spotted Senators Pete Domenici, Hubert Humphrey, Sam Nunn, and William Roth, along with a young-looking Congressman Gerald Ford. The report of a high-powered working group on energy and national security was on prominent display in the waiting area. CSIS sent an activist message. We have convening power, and we use it to tackle big strategic challenges.

What a contrast between the K Street upstart and the Brookings Institution, where I had spent 1972–73 as a visiting fellow. Brookings had its own building as well as the cushion of an $80 million endowment. CSIS paid rent and financed itself project by project. Brookings created a reflective setting in which scholar-practitioners produced carefully vetted publications. CSIS, always hopping, pursued a strategy of direct engagement in the policy process. Instead of relying primarily on individual scholarship, the center brought key players together to debate the issues and look for common ground.

David Abshire, a lean, six-foot-four Tennessean with thinning black hair, had invented the CSIS model. He had a lot going for him—a commission from West Point, social and political connections, a doctorate in history from Georgetown, and a self-effacing style that didn't threaten others. Beyond that he had a rare gift for making national security challenges come alive. He persuaded a renowned World War II naval hero, Admiral Arleigh Burke, to serve as founding chairman of the new center in 1962. Almost immediately, he leveraged Burke's credibility and a foundation grant to organize a star-studded conference on political, military, and economic strategies in the decade ahead. Hefty honoraria brought a Who's Who of postwar thinkers to the Georgetown campus.

Intuitively, Abshire grasped that outsiders with intellectual capital were eager for policy access and that insiders would benefit from their insights. His timing in the shadow of the Cuban Missile Crisis could not have been better. In one fell swoop his three-man operation brokered the outsider-insider dialogue. That move did much more than put CSIS on the map. It created a singular template that fueled the success of the center for years to come.

CSIS was a frontline presence in the think tank community by the time I got there. Abshire gained stature as assistant secretary of state for congressional affairs during the turbulent early 1970s. He impressed Kissinger and won praise as a Republican appointee who could work well with the Democrat-controlled House and Senate. When he returned in 1973, he pumped up a $700,000 per year enterprise to the $2 million level. Congressional study groups, expanded regional studies, an energy road show, and a transatlantic arms initiative put CSIS at the center of the action.

Abshire drew me into his orbit as the NATO thirtieth anniversary conference approached. He saw the Brussels event in early September 1979 as a venue to feature Kissinger and other notables under the aegis of CSIS. Abshire wanted to excite donors, make news, and throw a coming-out party. The scholarly publication that my boss Myers was editing was a sideshow.

I got my chance to help on the conference planning team. The suggestion I threw out went over well. Why not brief the key speakers instead of leaving their presentations to chance? A face-to-face review of the program would get them to focus. Abshire thought I'd be a natural for this role because I knew the issues and had a State Department credential.

Flying to Brussels two days early, I won my spurs as the center's advance man. Conference cochair Henri Simonet, the respected foreign minister of Belgium, reminisced in French about his early work with Monnet. François de Rose, a veteran French ambassador to NATO, laughed when reminded that I had addressed him as "Your Excellency" during an interview as an army lieutenant. Then came Viscount Étienne Davignon, vice chairman of the Commission of the European Communities, and Laurence Martin, director of Chatham House. All appreciated the extra attention.

Kissinger stole the show in the gilded Palais d'Egmont. Speaking from notes on the opening day, he questioned the U.S. nuclear guarantee to safeguard Europe. The French were right after all. An American president wouldn't risk Chicago to deter a Soviet attack on an allied capital. "It is absurd," he said, "to base the strategy of the West on the credibility of the threat of mutual suicide." Acknowledging that he contributed to the theory, he joked that he wasn't casting blame "because everyone here who knows me knows that the acceptance of blame is not what I will go down in history for." NATO needed more military options to get beyond the fantasy of mutual assured destruction.

Kissinger had published the same critique twenty years earlier as a little-known academic. When delivered by a celebrity, his warning made headlines and rattled nerves. It set the stage for a dramatic day two response from General Alexander Haig, Kissinger's former assistant in the White House and recently retired Supreme Allied Commander. Haig delivered the usual assurances regarding the U.S. security commitment without picking a fight with his former boss. The tempest in a teapot soon blew over but not without the media coverage that gave CSIS a win.

I returned to Washington with a sense of accomplishment and a foot out the door. A fast-growing consulting firm, Science Applications International Corporation (SAIC), made me an offer to help grow its government practice in European security and arms control. I felt close to getting a second offer from Bankers' Trust in New York, which was forming a unit in the emerging field of political and economic risk analysis in international markets.

I asked for a meeting to thank Abshire. He got out from behind his desk to sit across the coffee table in his office, a small but significant courtesy that I noted for future use. He listened as I outlined my plans, his agile mind racing. Then he peered over his reading glasses. "John," he said in his southern accent, pausing for effect, "hold on. You have talent. Your light was under a bushel basket around here for almost a year. Now I know what you can do."

Abshire laid it on thick as he sketched a third option. Without missing a beat, he continued: "You want to do international risk assessment. No firm can compete with the knowledge of our experts. They cover the globe, and they know U.S. policy too. Stay here and build a csis risk assessment practice. Suggest a title. We'll set you up in an office. I'm confident that I can get the Executive Committee to agree to a salary of $35,000. We need you."

There was no resisting the Abshire treatment. Many years later his son called him the "King of Compliments" in a heartfelt, joyful eulogy. He must have decided before our conversation that I was the right fit for csis, not as an expert but as a generalist who could handle the center's clientele. He was offering a bridge to the private sector at a competitive salary. Better yet, he was giving me a chance to move outside the box of U.S.-European relations.

That evening Diane smiled at my description of the Abshire meeting. She hadn't heard the homespun expression about lights being hidden under bushel baskets. "I guess I saw the light before he did," she quipped. We agreed that I should jump at the csis offer. I'd be able to expand my horizon beyond Europe, learn about global business strategy, build a relationship with Abshire, and raise my paycheck to a senior government level.

I moved to a window office and had business cards printed with the approved title, "Director of Business Planning." I also hired a capable secretary, Rose Marie Goncz, an army spouse whose skill at shorthand made her indispensable. Her job description reflected the workplace of the early 1980s: typing, filing, booking travel, and providing conference support.

We relied on a wondrous new office technology, the fax machine, to send and receive documents in real time.

Abshire took care to give the new venture a low profile internally. Although CSIS presented itself to the world as a single institution, it was really a collection of individuals running their own programs and projects. Abshire generated new ideas, played traffic cop, and managed relationships with big donors. He didn't want any of the senior people at the center to see me as a competitor. The nonprofit consulting operation was going to deepen ties with existing donors and attract new ones, not create an independent revenue stream.

My job had no political bent. I had the credential of a policy analyst, not an operative. To be successful, I had to grasp the needs of the center's corporate donors, make sure that my colleagues were prepared, and add value wherever I could. One of my favorites at CSIS, defense specialist Bill Taylor, liked making fun of my apolitical role. He always drew a laugh by introducing himself as a Republican, someone else as a Democrat, and me as an opportunist.

I dove into corporate outreach company by company. IBM, mindful of its financial exposure and reputation, wanted to stay as close as possible to rising antiapartheid sentiment inside and outside South Africa. Future assistant secretary of state for African affairs Chester Crocker knew that issue cold. Goldman Sachs, doing due diligence on government-backed securities, commissioned assessments of sovereign risk in Southeast Asia and Latin America. Tom Reckford, a skilled former CIA and corporate analyst, answered the call. Westinghouse, staggered by the Three Mile Island nuclear accident, used CSIS to help identify new market opportunities. I drew upon the CSIS stable of "formers" and "futures" to provide the background they were looking for.

U.S. policy stood out as a particular risk factor for the private sector as companies grappled with cascading economic change. National security and foreign policy often superseded the nation's commercial agenda. The Carter administration clamped agricultural sanctions on the Soviet Union over its invasion of Afghanistan. The Reagan White House vetoed the export of pipeline components to the Soviet bloc. Cold warriors didn't care much if the use of economic leverage turned U.S. companies into unreliable suppliers. They took American economic superiority for granted.

In response the business community pushed for a stronger handle on the levers of U.S. power. Corporate goals varied widely, but the determination to work the system remained a constant. CSIS was one channel among many to get an inside track to policy makers. Companies looked for lobbying help elsewhere. They used the center to gather information, build relationships, and connect their bottom lines to the high road of the national interest.

I saw how the link between think tanks and the corporate sector could play out soon after arriving at CSIS. One of the most able senior members on the staff, Mike Samuels, impressed the chairman of the U.S. Chamber of Commerce in a project on U.S. export policy. Before long Samuels found himself leading the international division of the chamber. A few years later he became a deputy U.S. trade negotiator. Perhaps I could be another Samuels.

Corporate demand for analysis was more limited than I had hoped. The best customers were companies making long-term investments. Dow Chemical asked me to arrange for Robert Neumann, a Middle East expert on tap to be named ambassador to Saudi Arabia, to meet with senior management. A corporate jet flew us up to headquarters in Midland, Michigan, for a working dinner. Dow was deciding whether to locate manufacturing plants next to petroleum supplies in the Persian Gulf. The CEO and his board peppered the ambassador-designate with tough questions on Saudi energy production, internal politics, and industrial development.

Requests like this one came infrequently. Most companies were looking for influence rather than analysis. They wanted policy outcomes that put the U.S. government on their side. Corporate wish lists seemed endless and often worked at cross-purposes—prying open foreign markets, loosening export controls, enforcing fair trade laws, and strengthening (or weakening) the dollar. The draw of CSIS was its capacity to bring policy makers to the table in a give-and-take setting.

On the whole the DC-based specialists who covered international issues lacked standing within their own companies. No matter how able they were, Washington reps were on the wrong side of the crucial divide that separated revenue producers from overhead staff. Midlevel recruits from government had little room for career development and were vulnerable to downsizing. IBM, still a bastion of white-shirted uniformity in those days, made a point of avoiding outside hires with policy experience. "Our culture rejects outsiders," an IBMer said bluntly, "the way the body sometimes rejects an organ transplant."

My corporate education took a fresh turn when Ronald Reagan won the presidential election of 1980. Abshire saw his victory as a one-time opening to start building an endowment. Donors would flock to CSIS if the center positioned itself as a ready resource for the incoming administration.

The master strategist seized the moment. First, he covered his political flank by offering an office to Jimmy Carter's outgoing national security advisor. "We'll keep Brzezinski and Kissinger on separate floors," he said, only half-joking. For good measure the center brought in Robert Hunter, another Democrat from the NSC, to run the European studies program.

Then Abshire, who had not taken sides during the presidential campaign, agreed to serve as deputy director for national security of President-elect Reagan's transition team. This was the ultimate insider assignment, which called for planning and executing the handover of power in some twenty-seven departments and agencies. Abshire culled his network for key people to vet papers and brief new political appointees. It was no accident that three CSIS colleagues found their way to senior positions within the administration.

Abshire didn't call on me until after he had played his political card successfully. CSIS was riding high. The outlook for endowed chairs in political economy and international business looked solid, but one prospect required special handling. He asked if I could carve out some time to write a proposal for a $1 million gift from Toyota Motor Company to endow a chair in Japan studies.

Why Toyota? Abshire had served for several years on the board of an international exchange program, Youth for Understanding, with Eiji Toyoda, the company chairman, whose family had founded the business. Toyota had grown too fast to keep a low profile in the U.S. market. Its surging exports had American automakers up in arms, triggering congressional demands for quotas. The company had to improve its image and operate more professionally in Washington. The clever fund-raiser at Youth for Understanding brokered a donation to csis.

The proposal was a formality. Toyota would never risk the loss of face by changing its mind. Still, csis had to put its best foot forward. It was easy to make the case for bringing aboard an internationally recognized Japan scholar, even though Japan was a total mystery to a Europeanist like me. U.S. policy makers needed real grounding on what the U.S. ambassador in Tokyo, former Senate majority leader Mike Mansfield, called "the most important bilateral relationship in the world."

The mechanics of the chair took more thought than spelling out its rationale. A limited term, allowing for chair holders with diverse interests and views, seemed wiser than an open-ended commitment to a single scholar. Toyota also had to be informed up front that the return on a principal of $1 million, even under my wildly optimistic assumption of a 10 percent return per year, would not support a full-fledged program. I reviewed every word with Mr. Moriya, the English-speaking vice president of the Washington office.

Abshire asked me to fly with him to present the proposal in person. His office scheduled four days of meetings to justify two days of travel. Abshire had high-level contacts growing out of a maritime dialogue that csis had facilitated between Congress and the Diet. He also knew Ambassador Mike Mansfield from Senate days. With little time to prepare, I joined him on the thirteen-hour Pan Am nonstop that left JFK at noon on a Saturday. My adrenaline flowed as we touched down on Tokyo's single-runway Narita Airport at 2:30 p.m. the following day. I had finally made it to Asia.

We were booked at the luxurious, understated Hotel Okura across the street from the U.S. embassy. It was widely known in Tokyo as the embassy's annex. The Okura had hosted American presidents. Visiting cabinet officers always stayed there. The softly colored wood paneling, thick carpets, and serene gardens reflected a Japanese sensibility. The Okura set a standard in cordial, efficient service that I had never seen.

In no time I saw that Japanese culture was far different from anything I had experienced in France. Whereas the French took immense pride in civilizing the world with their way of life, the Japanese were attached to their uniqueness. The separate strands of their language, spoken and written, took years to master. I would learn about this country mainly by interacting with a thin layer of cosmopolitan business executives, government officials, and intellectuals. It would be impossible to know how much they filtered. As I later found out, the Japanese referred to them as "barbarian handlers."

Abshire glided through our conversations with Japanese politicians with no concern for the communication issues that were on my mind. He didn't speak a foreign language and did not adjust his delivery for interpreters or English speakers. His natural likability, however, never failed to come across. He spoke earnestly, smiled often, and delivered his overview of the Reagan administration with a touch that went over well. From all indications the Japanese felt that they were getting privileged information from a staunch supporter of the U.S.-Japanese strategic alliance.

Ambassador Mansfield, esteemed in Japan for his seniority, took a gentle poke at Japanese tradition when we sat down in his corner office. He asked if we'd like a cup of American coffee, mixed the decaf himself, and served us. This quiet put-down of Japanese tea pouring by young girls reminded every visitor where he stood on the American style of doing business.

The seventy-eight-year-old Mansfield, his face deeply weathered, did most of the talking. We heard his set piece, complete with a map comparing Japan with his home state of Montana. The one-time champion of a U.S. military drawdown in Europe argued forcefully for Pacific engagement. Of course, Japan had to be pressed on the trade front. But the in-crowd in Washington needed to be reminded that too much was at stake to allow Japan bashing to define the relationship. He was preaching to the choir, but his sermon was convincing nonetheless.

We took the bullet train to Toyota headquarters in Nagoya for the most important meeting of the trip. The smooth 225-mile-per-hour ride to Japan's fourth-largest city showcased the strengths of an economic superpower. Chairman Toyoda's representative, Moriya, met us with a car and driver. We rode in a nondescript premium sedan, the Crown, through a large, drab industrial area to a 1960s vintage, four-story main building. Toyota definitely wasn't flaunting its power. Only the Cézanne that graced the wall of the conference room where we met made a statement.

Abshire and I sat across the long table from Chairman Toyoda and his nephew Shoichiro Toyoda, the head of manufacturing, who was being groomed to take over the company. Both men were short and stocky, one in his late sixties and the other in his midfifties. They relied on their trusted man in Washington rather than a professional interpreter, a puzzling choice that never would have been made if this were a business negotiation.

After presenting his well-honed brief on the Reagan administration, Abshire outlined the proposal. I jumped in briefly to make a few clarifying comments. The elder Toyoda spoke sparingly, and his nephew didn't say a word. Their faces brightened when Abshire asked about the Toyota philosophy of car making. Toyoda talked about daily improvements, a concept that had been shaped by visits during the 1950s to the Ford Motor Company. He offered beautifully wrapped presents as the conversation ended. Abshire presented the tokens he had brought from the States. The interpreter Moriya assured us on the way back to the station that the conversation had gone well.

By seating me at his side opposite the top two executives of Toyota, Abshire had given me the credibility to manage the relationship moving forward. The younger Toyoda always kept an open door for me, and we saw each other regularly. On a visit to Washington a few years later as chief executive of the company, he accepted an invitation to a catered reception at our home. This was a novelty because Japanese do their business entertaining at restaurants. A white stretch limo circled the neighborhood until 7:00 p.m. sharp. I winced at the showy vehicle, which seemed so ill suited to our guests but carried the whole entourage.

As the enjoyable evening with CSIS leadership wound down, Toyoda asked if he could walk around the first floor and basement. He tapped gently on the walls and examined the fixtures. His company was getting into the prefab housing business, and he felt comfortable enough with me to check out American construction. To reciprocate, his wife took Diane shopping for pearls on her one and only visit to Tokyo.

The success of our mission paved my way at CSIS. I would be the point man for building the CSIS presence in Japan. More important, Abshire and I bonded. Without the Internet to distract us, we spent hours together preparing for each meeting, comparing notes afterward, and trading personal stories. He talked about growing up in Chattanooga, his lackluster record at West Point, combat duty in Korea, and his love of history.

War intrigued Abshire. While I had an academic interest in the causes of conflict, he zeroed in on outcomes. His face lit up as he talked with deep knowledge about Napoleon, Washington, Lincoln, Roosevelt, Marshall, and Eisenhower. He saw the conduct of war as the ultimate test of leadership. He drew easy parallels from the past to the present. I took it all in, realizing that the subject area closest to his heart was also his surefire hook to engage the DC heavyweights and CEOs with whom he wanted to cultivate relationships.

Abshire never stopped thinking about how he could build CSIS, even with five kids and a wife who ran her own business. By the end of the trip I felt comfortable calling him Dave and knew that he would take my call day or night on anything that affected his life's work.

Although Abshire and I came from different worlds, his view of the way Washington worked shaped mine. Nothing of lasting importance, he stressed, ever got done on a partisan basis. To be effective, CSIS had to help decision-makers build consensus. In his day it was the principals who cut deals, not their staffs. Abshire knew a surprising number of them on a first name basis through work or social connections. He was the Republican who had the agility to build coalitions across party lines.

What Abshire was trying to do met my definition of public service. I might never operate at his level, but I was a coalition builder too. My business planning job didn't make me part of the mix yet, but I was going to get there. Once I did, I'd have a better chance to work on big policy challenges from outside rather than inside government. CSIS was the right place for me.

I became one of Abshire's half dozen younger protégés. He trusted youth, surrounding himself with people in their twenties and thirties. I was older than most. Some had political contacts. Some were backroom drafters. Some had showpiece credentials. The common thread was that we all had something important to contribute to CSIS. He confided in each of us but kept all of the relationships separate. He grounded his leadership in personal ties, not team building. I followed his example years later when I had a staff to direct.

My brighter prospects paled in comparison to the difference that Diane was making in our lives. When Senator Javits lost the Republican primary of 1978, she decided to try something new. Commercial real estate looked inviting. It was a fast-growing field that would allow her to study for a broker's license and get back to the workforce in less than a year.

A well-organized, attractive woman who wasn't pushy stood out in a competitive field dominated by men. Diane got good training in the DC office of a Chicago-based broker, Arthur Rubloff, whose offices were two blocks away from CSIS. She paid attention when her first boss told her that the only difference between a two-thousand-square-foot and twenty-thousand-square-foot transaction was the broker's commission. She had the patience and persistence to succeed at canvassing tenants, taking no for an answer much more often than she got a meeting. Soon my spouse was earning six figures moving trade associations, law firms, and a division of the World Bank.

Diane never compared our incomes. Because she didn't draw a salary, she gracefully insisted that I was the breadwinner whose monthly check covered the bills. Her earnings just accelerated the timetable for buying a house. In the meantime we enjoyed our two-bedroom rental in Foggy Bottom. We walked to work, jogged around the reflecting pool regularly, and combined CSIS travel with time in France. It pleased me that Diane enjoyed herself there. We rode bicycles through the fields around the Château de Chenonceau, and she drove a stick shift for the first time through the back roads of Burgundy.

We crossed a threshold from newlywed renters to homeowners in the spring of 1981. After months of hunting, we closed on a compact colonial on a quarter-acre lot in the Maryland suburbs. The choice reflected our middle-of-the-road tastes: a financial stretch but within our means, recently built but not new, stylish but not extravagant, relatively close-in but still a forty-minute commute in rush hour. Diane's mother came down with her decorator, whose recommendation to knock down a wall between the dining and living rooms gave a distinctive look to a standard subdivision model. What meant most to me was making the purchase entirely on our own.

Diane and I weren't the only ones making brick-and-mortar transitions. Mom sold the house on Greenvale Road at a good price. With Bonnie's help she found a spacious condominium near the National Cathedral, where she lived for the next twenty years. Bonnie and Paul, returning to Manhattan after his Supreme Court clerkship, used her inheritance from Dad as a down payment for an apartment on the West Side. The Kaminos bought a villa on a golf course in Del Ray Beach, where they planned to spend more time during the winter. Everyone seemed to be on the move.

14 THINK TANK ENTREPRENEUR

Dave Abshire liked to tell a story about having taken command of a platoon as a young officer during the Korean War. A grizzled sergeant took him aside when he reached his unit. "Lieutenant," the sergeant said, "this platoon is either going to get better or get worse. It isn't going to stay the same."

Abshire saw truth in the sergeant's advice for any organization. I viewed the insight in more personal terms. Either I was going to reposition myself at CSIS or fade. My corporate marketing portfolio was missing something essential: a specific content area that I could call my own. I needed to direct a program to make the center my first-ever career base. Otherwise, I would be merely a facilitator.

My break came when CSIS endowed the Dr. Scholl Chair in International Business and Economics. The Chicago-based Scholl family, which had a strong allegiance to Abshire and Georgetown University, came through with long-term support in the area closest to its global success in foot care products. The first choice to fill the chair, Thibault de St. Phalle, looked like a perfect fit. He had served on the board of directors of the Ex-Im Bank, the export finance arm of the U.S. government. He was also coming out with a book on trade, inflation, and the dollar, to be published by Oxford University Press.

The classy St. Phalle intended to take a star turn. The mixed reviews of his book, however, did not give him the recognition he and the center had anticipated. As a high-level executive, he wasn't about to roll up his sleeves to organize meetings, write proposals, or raise funds. But the center needed a workhorse, not a show horse.

I asked Abshire if he would consider splitting off the research and writing responsibilities of the Dr. Scholl Chair holder from the operational task of establishing an international business and economics program.

He hesitated for a few uncomfortable months, not wanting to embarrass St. Phalle. Then he came around. The growth opportunity for CSIS was too important to pass up.

The title of program director made me a think tank entrepreneur in Washington. Now I had the DC equivalent of a small business to run. The goal was affecting policy, not making money. It was up to me to figure out how. Hundreds of others were trying to do the same thing. My comparative advantage grew out of the power of the CSIS network, which I counted on to make up for a thin background in economics. I'd give the program a moderately conservative, free market tilt that appealed to business without slamming the door on labor. If the right opportunity came along, I might take a shot at a political appointment.

My new duties put me ahead of the game in making a connection to Kissinger. He chaired a high-powered group of chief executives, the CSIS International Councillors, who contributed a minimum of $50,000 per year to participate in two off-the-record sessions on the global business environment. Some of their funding covered Kissinger's suite and administrative support. None went to him personally. The format called for an opening dinner, a full day of discussions with guest speakers, and Kissinger's own finale. He attracted the CEOs of more than forty prominent global companies.

Pam Scholl, whose father headed the Dr. Scholl Foundation, managed the International Councillors. I admired her energy, dedication, and attention to detail. She had full command of logistics but approached me for help in choosing topics, lining up speakers, scripting Kissinger, and writing up notes for members who missed meetings. She worked with his staff and prepped him personally, while I provided a CSIS voice in the discussion. Sitting at the table gave me the credibility to work with the councillors. It couldn't get any better than that for someone who had read Kissinger's junk mail at Harvard and toiled anonymously under him at State.

Scholl and I worked well together. We livened up the semiannual meetings by moving every other one out of Washington. Councillors readily agreed to host the group on their own turf. The extra cost to CSIS was marginal, while a bit of competition among the members made for memorable events in Paris, Hong Kong, Tokyo, Mexico City, Marrakesh,

Stockholm, Venice, and New York. We always arrived early, allotting a full day to meet with the host, confirm meal arrangements, and check out the meeting space. We sweated every detail, especially which of the center's important donors would sit at Kissinger's table and where name tents would be placed for the discussion.

We had our trying moments. Kissinger blew his top in Paris when slow dinner service at the Hotel Bristol delayed his introduction of Mayor Jacques Chirac until 10:30 p.m. Scholl and her mother brought chicken soup to my room when I came down with the flu in Hong Kong. I filled in for her when she got food poisoning in Marrakesh. We celebrated a triumph in Mexico City, capped by the remarks of President Salinas on his economic reform agenda, only to see both the peso and his political career collapse within a year.

I had to make due with the outside view of Kissinger. He knew who I was, called on me at meetings, and thrilled Mom by speaking generously when she introduced herself to him in the elevator one day. Once we joked about what it had been like toiling for him on the fourth floor at State. I would like to have gotten closer, but he didn't have the bandwidth.

Kissinger projected a head-of-state aura. His two-man private security detail signaled that he had enemies. His entrances and exits created a quiet stir. His work uniform—a buttoned blue suit, white shirt, and conservative tie—never varied. Although Kissinger lacked physical bearing, his gravelly voice stilled any room. I only saw him strike a deferential tone once, in New York in the early 1990s, when introducing Richard Nixon at a councillors meeting. Kissinger left no doubt who had been the boss.

He used humor, often at his own expense, to connect with audiences. He mocked his heavy accent, suggesting it gave him a special affinity for southerners whenever they opened their mouths in Washington. He explained that his 1960s treatise on NATO, *The Troubled Partnership*, only sold well in the one bookstore that displayed it in the section on marriage counseling. He recalled the elegant woman who introduced herself at a cocktail party and asked him to fascinate her because everyone said he was fascinating.

Kissinger's *tour d'horizon* was the high point of every meeting. He gravitated toward hot topics in the parts of the world he knew best, providing his own unique perspective. Diplomatic crises were his bread and butter. His presentations rarely touched on personalities. Leaders came and went. National interests were the touchstone of his analysis. Invariably, he came back to the factors that shaped U.S. policy. Councillors never challenged him.

The brilliant performer put little effort into shaping the agenda or steering the discussion. Our suggested topics and high-ranking invitees sailed through his office without objection. Kissinger called on councillors in the order they raised their hand, posed an occasional question, and never tried to establish a sense of the group. It fell to me to pull the threads together and make every comment look good in summary notes for internal distribution only. The casual, off-the-record nature of the group was deliberate. Kissinger knew better than anyone how to command a premium.

There was more going on than met the eye. The councillors forum eased Kissinger's transition from government to the private sector. He absorbed the culture of business from high-powered CEOs without exposing his lack of experience with their world. Once he felt at home and had completed the second volume of his memoirs, he launched his own international consulting firm in 1982. Kissinger Associates tapped into a rich market for confidential assessments and access to government leaders around the world. The firm, with offices on Park Avenue, counted some of the councillors as important clients. Kissinger was converting fame into fortune while helping Abshire market CSIS.

I took full advantage of my seat at the table. The councillors were always willing to make time for me because I staffed their club. I never could have made these contacts if I had stayed in government. They could lead anywhere.

Akio Morita, the chairman of Sony, cut a dashing figure when I called on him in his New York headquarters. His shock of white hair, fluent English, and easy manner won him celebrity status as the public face of the world leader in consumer electronics. His business and lifestyle choices—living in New York for many years, flying a corporate jet, and appearing in an American Express television commercial—put him in a different league from other Japanese business leaders. He was exceptional, just like the Sony Walkman portable cassette that revolutionized the music industry in the 1980s.

When we met at his headquarters in Tokyo, however, Morita didn't want to stand out at all. He greeted me in the same Sony jacket that thousands of factory workers wore. His views on trade, investment, and exchange rates reflected the Japanese corporate mainstream. He later coauthored a book with a hardline politician, arguing that Japan should say no to U.S. pressure. Mastery of the American idiom didn't make him a change agent in his own country.

Another Asian councillor, C. H. Tung, also taught me not to judge a book by its cover. Tung ran a family-owned shipping empire out of Hong Kong. He spoke clipped Oxford English, wore a crew cut, and sent his kids to Princeton. He came across as a thoroughly Western businessman. He handled pressure under fire with great class, honoring his commitment to host the Kissinger group amid a 1980s oil glut that brought his fleet of tankers to its knees. Tung's pledge of personal property as collateral to save the business made headlines the day of our meeting. Flying back from a meeting with his bankers in Tokyo, he welcomed the councillors to his home as if nothing had happened.

An astonishing turn of fortune took place when Britain handed Hong Kong back to China in 1998. The Chinese picked the urbane shipping magnate to be their first chief executive. His Western polish overlay a deeper commitment to a much older civilization. We spoke briefly when he called me for advice on handling the American media when his name was being floated. A few days later C. H. Tung became Tung Chee Hwa, confirming how little I understood of Eastern ways.

Peter Wallenberg, a close friend of Kissinger, gave me a glimpse into a European dynasty. The Wallenbergs were the wealthiest family in Sweden. A celebrated cousin had saved tens of thousands of Jews in Nazi-occupied Hungary. The Wallenberg Group controlled a significant share of Swedish industry through its bank holding company. Wallenberg's jovial, unpretentious style told me that he could get along with the Socialists who ran the government.

When the councillors met in Stockholm, Wallenberg made a point of introducing me to his son Jacob and nephew Marcus. They were going to succeed him in a few years, and we weren't far apart in age. He wanted them to get an early start creating their own network. I stayed in touch with them. They included me in a weekend of outdoor activities for friends and associates from around the world.

Another regular, Othman Benjelloun, provided my first insight into the Arab world. The modest Moroccan billionaire had ties to his country's royal family that conferred valuable import and export licenses. We had lunch in French when he came to Washington, a break from English that he greatly enjoyed. Secure in his standing with a moderate, pro-American regime, he discreetly accumulated wealth while helping his country modernize.

When Benjelloun hosted the councillors in the opulent La Mamounia Hotel in Marrakesh in 1987, I got a foretaste of the looming clash between Islam and the secular West. Female guests sunbathed topless near the pool, while groundskeepers in traditional garb looked on from behind a fence. No one acknowledged the combustible mix in plain sight. I found it too sensitive an issue to raise with Benjelloun himself.

The only female councillor, Anne Armstrong, gave me a White House connection. The astute, beautiful Texan—a star in the Republican Party—chaired the President's Foreign Intelligence Advisory Board as well as the CSIS Board of Trustees. She counted Vice President George H. W. Bush and Reagan chief of staff James Baker as personal friends. She knew Kissinger from having served as ambassador to Great Britain for part of the time he was secretary of state. Her loyalty to CSIS was unlimited. The addition of her trusted personal assistant, Judy Harbaugh, to the center's support team sealed the link.

Armstrong liked the job I did raising funds and managing relations with VIPs. When Diane and I hosted Dr. Toyoda at our home, she could have just dropped by but, instead, stayed the whole time. She invited us to dinner with her husband, Tobin, when we ran into her at a resort in New Mexico. When Dave Abshire left to become ambassador to NATO, she called me regularly to keep tabs on how things were going. The former cochair of the National Republican Committee became my most influential backer without once asking me about my politics.

Hank Greenberg showed how assertive CEOs use nonprofits to promote their interests. Greenberg came out of the Middle West to transform the

American International Group, or AIG, into a goliath of the insurance industry. By all accounts he was the smartest, toughest executive in the business. A small man who dominated those around him, he saw AIG's long-standing relationships in Asia as its greatest asset. Thus, he invited Kissinger, whose credibility in China had no equal, to chair AIG's International Advisory Board. He supported CSIS generously to advance both his company's agenda and his own. Abshire reciprocated by sponsoring him in the Alfalfa Club, one of the most select groups of power players in the country.

Greenberg took notice when I moderated a U.S.-Thai business meeting in Bangkok that he promoted under CSIS auspices. The participation of several members of Congress and the recently retired chairman of the Joint Chiefs of Staff sent the required message that AIG had access at the highest level. I handled the long, hard names of the Thai participants well and kept everyone at the table engaged. I was too cerebral, however, and lacked the connections to impress a Wall Street mogul who coveted a cabinet post. Greenberg found a true political insider to work with on the CSIS staff, Wayne Berman, whose career soared.

My contacts with the councillors, limited though they were, counted in DC. The city measured status by where you worked, who your boss was, and the people you knew. The immediate payoff came on the diplomatic circuit, where ambassadors fought for insider contacts. They had cables to write, visitors to schedule, and a presence to maintain. Only a handful of embassies commanded real attention, but all of them entertained to stay in the loop. My value rose on the merry-go-round of working lunches, black-tie dinners, and receptions. I had Abshire to thank.

The Kissinger connection didn't provide a foundation, however, for a program that would put CSIS on the map in the international economic policy arena. I owed that opportunity to the revival of the CSIS Quadrangular conferences. These meetings brought together American, Canadian, European, and Japanese leaders. The Quad economies accounted for 60 percent of world output in the 1980s. They controlled the international financial institutions and set the multilateral trade agenda. As they went, so went the global economy. At this point China was barely a blip on the horizon.

CSIS had launched the Quad conferences in the wake of the oil shock of the early 1970s. It appeared then that the United States and its allies might be held hostage by oil-producing countries. Abshire turned to the Senate to mobilize a joint Western response. He paired the irrepressible Hubert Humphrey, reelected from Minnesota after serving as vice president, and his home state friend Bill Brock from Tennessee. The initiative lapsed when Humphrey died and Brock lost his Senate seat.

Now Brock was in the Reagan cabinet as U.S. trade representative (USTR). He welcomed a relaunch of the Quad dialogue to extend his reach beyond formal channels. He and Abshire, both from privileged families, went way back. Together they lined up impressive cochairs: the Canadian trade minister, the vice president of the Commission of the European Community, and the English-speaking former Japanese foreign minister. The born-again Quad, hosted by CSIS in September 1982, resurrected the goal of securing the future of the industrial democracies.

My small team took the lead in organizing the center's highest-profile event since the Palais d'Egmont NATO Conference. Two hundred business leaders packed into the CSIS conference room on the basement level of 1800 K Street to hear Kissinger's opening keynote. Members of Congress spoke at dinner on trade issues. Secretary of Defense Weinberger made remarks on economic sanctions. Instead of taking a back row seat, as I had in Brussels three years earlier, I moderated a panel on international economic problems featuring the CEO of Chase Manhattan and the former president of the Bundesbank.

Brock and his counterparts glowed afterward. They proposed making the Quad an annual forum. Their political interests dovetailed with my desire to establish a real economics and business program. They got to lead a private sector conversation timed to feed into the yearly G7 summits of Western leaders. These parleys included heads of state, finance ministers, and foreign ministers only. The Quad gave Brock and his counterparts a voice. CSIS, in turn, got to support a cabinet-level dialogue in which companies paid to play and experts eagerly contributed.

I didn't try to run the show myself. Each leg of the Quad would be backed by its own nonprofit. The forum would rotate between capitals, spreading the costs of hosting. But now I had a framework tied into the policy process on which to build.

Abshire soon took a three-year leave of absence to serve as ambassador to NATO. Before leaving, he agreed to my request for a promotion to vice president. If you don't ask, I realized, you stay put. The presidency went to Amos Jordan, a straight-arrow West Pointer who had come to CSIS from senior posts at Defense and State. A national security expert, he had his hands full minding Abshire's store. The Quad was the least of Jordan's challenges. He delegated it to me, and I vowed to make it a success.

Brock gave the new venture policy relevance, the most indispensable asset in the think tank world. The Republican insider, who knew Congress, had a mandate from President Reagan to chart the future course of U.S. trade policy. He had an open field to follow up the deep cuts in industrial tariffs made in the 1979 Tokyo Round of multilateral trade negotiations. He didn't want to yield his preparation of next steps exclusively to his own staff, other government stakeholders, or the lobbyists who trooped into his office. The American working group of the Quad served as a sounding board in a friendly setting, while the international meetings raised his profile abroad. He enjoyed the conversation so much that he stuck with it after moving over to become secretary of labor during Reagan's second term.

Brock's journey of inquiry gave me a funding draw, a network, and an education. Looking every inch the senator, he carried himself with self-assurance and set a tone of remarkable openness. Brock wasn't afraid to think out loud in front of others. He gave free rein to the creative trade strategist on the USTR staff, Geza Feketekuty. His personal engagement made it easy to assemble thirty top-tier private sector participants, many with high-level government experience. Its members included Brock's successor as USTR, Clayton Yeutter; a future national security advisor, Frank Carlucci; and the first woman to serve on the President's Council of Economic Advisers, Marina Whitman.

The discussion forced me to retool. My intellectual capital, coming mostly from geopolitics, had little bearing on U.S. international economic strategy. The role of government, so dominant in national security, sparked controversy in the economic sphere. The fast-changing and increasingly interdependent world economy posed difficult, unfamiliar challenges—the erosion of national sovereignty, the redistribution of economic power, and the loss of U.S. competitiveness. I drank from the fire hose and enjoyed every drop.

The Quad proved a hard sell to the media despite my enthusiasm. Journalists wanted to see sparks fly, while Brock was trying to thread the needle of economic diplomacy. Alan Murray, a future bureau chief of the *Wall Street Journal*, offered help. An old school tie to Abshire brought him regularly to csis. His ready smile and unassuming manner cut against type in an industry in which many people at his level were full of themselves.

The approachable Murray put me in touch with Helene Cooper, a go-getter who covered trade at the *Journal*. She treated me as a news source, picking up a lunch tab on her expense account. Cooper followed the nitty-gritty of negotiating issues much more closely than I did. A good reporter, I learned, couldn't get away with the broad strokes that worked at csis.

I found more in common with Bruce Stokes, who wrote for a different audience. He specialized in trade and competitiveness at the *National Journal*, a widely read weekly for DC insiders. Stokes had spent his junior year in Paris and shared my interest in Japan. He could always count on me for quotes, leads, and second opinions on his stories. It helped to have a friend with a following. A one-page profile with a picture got the word out that Yochelson was a player.

The road to trade expansion that Brock was exploring looked rocky. U.S. policy had to balance the strong and vulnerable sectors of the national economy. Agribusiness, high-tech exporters, and financial services clamored for access to foreign markets. They had a sympathetic ear in a White House deeply committed to free trade. Pacific Rim imports, however, were also battering U.S. manufacturers. The dislocations taking place in autos, capital goods, semiconductors, and other industries couldn't be overlooked. Many U.S. companies saw themselves as targets of mercantilism and cried for protection.

Brock and his staff threw up their hands over the soaring dollar. The Treasury liked high exchange rates that strengthened the position of banks and lowered the cost of imported consumer goods. From the USTR standpoint, however, the erosion of the nation's industrial base was bad news both economically and politically. A series of case studies that I commissioned, *Under Pressure: U.S. Industry and the Challenges of Structural Adjustment*, highlighted the pace of dislocation. Domestic production of industrial fasteners, almost a $1 billion business, went under in a decade.

The Quad exerted pressure to bring the dollar down. In March 1984 the *New York Times* cited our concern over "the severe and potentially enduring damage" that record trade deficits were doing to American manufacturing.

The advanced industrial economies remained badly out of kilter with each other in the mid-1980s. Europe suffered from slow job creation and low growth, a condition harshly called "Eurosclerosis." Japan was piling up huge trade surpluses that fanned the flames of U.S. and European protectionism. The American economy was soaking up global capital to finance its trade imbalance and supplement domestic investment.

Western governments paid lip service to tackling these problems in tandem. Each had a one-sentence solution. Europe had to revitalize by increasing the mobility of capital and labor. Japan had to shift away from export-led growth to more domestic consumption. The United States had to put its fiscal house in order. Politically, each of these tasks was the equivalent of climbing Mount Everest. That's why it was essential to make a private sector case for joint action that provided cover for all governments.

In March 1986, when the Japanese hosted the Quad before the G7 summit in Tokyo, they looked ready to play a larger role in the liberalization of world trade. Brock raised a glass to thank our hosts after a delicious steak dinner at the Hotel Okura, asking mischievously whether the generous portions had exhausted Japan's quota of U.S. beef imports. The Europeans, in a striking role reversal, seemed more insular than the Japanese. They made their top priority the creation of a unified internal market. Otherwise, they said, Europe's place in the global economy was a moot point.

The Quad convened in Washington in April 1987 against a background of impasse. In theory the wheels of global adjustment were turning. Treasury Secretary James Baker had negotiated the Plaza Accord to depreciate the dollar. The European Community had committed to create a single market by 1992. The Japanese government had accepted blue-ribbon recommendations to reorient its economy away from exports. In practice, however, a weaker dollar had not reduced the U.S. trade deficit with Asia. Japan had not taken action to increase consumption. Europe had pulled back from fiscal expansion despite record West German trade surpluses.

The grim outlook led to an exciting, well-attended meeting. A boyish Steve Jobs stood up dramatically at the opening dinner to declare that he came from Death Valley, not Silicon Valley. Japanese competition, he said bluntly, was killing U.S. computer chip makers. If that industry went the way of domestic steel and autos, the United States would mortgage its high-tech future to Japanese suppliers. The next day the Yale-trained CEO of Seiko Instruments turned the tables on Jobs. He laid out a litany of Japanese shortcomings based on his company's development of Epson printers.

Paul Volcker made remarks over lunch from a prepared text, mindful that any offhand comment could move markets. The former foreign minister of France, Jean François-Poncet, presented a masterful summation. CSIS published the Quad statement, *Breaking the Economic Impasse*, with my name on the cover.

I learned after the meeting that the position of assistant secretary of state for economic and business affairs was open. If I was ever going to have a chance at a political appointment, now was the time. There were two years left in the Reagan administration. I had influential Republican sponsors. I knew the issues, the State Department, and the interests of the private sector. I registered as a Republican and threw my hat in the ring.

Anyone going after a high-level policy job had to mount a campaign. Both White House personnel and the decision-maker at the Department of State, Deputy Secretary John Whitehead, needed to know the depth of my support. Anne Armstrong went all out on my behalf. Abshire, who had returned from NATO to help the White House weather the Iran-Contra arms scandal, weighed in as well. Two members of the cabinet and the national security advisor came through with notes and phone calls. Whitehead invited me over for an interview that went well. He had been a featured dinner speaker at the Quad. We touched lightly on the issues and made small talk about his former company, Goldman Sachs.

After pulling out all the stops, I learned that the White House had nominated someone else. Armstrong found out what happened. Her friend Jim Baker, who had his own eye on the State Department, had a candidate. He was a capable insider on the White House staff who could move into the job seamlessly. "I forgot to speak with Jimmy," Armstrong said, adding that it might not have helped if he really wanted his own person.

My professional disappointment was more than offset by the birth of Lisa Rachel Yochelson on May 15, 1987. She arrived a week late, induced after eight strenuous hours on a Monday afternoon at the George Washington University Hospital. Because this was birth by appointment, the Kaminos flew down and were overjoyed when I gave them the thumbs up after coming out of the delivery room. Diane was exhausted but thrilled. We took Lisa home to a newly purchased place in Bethesda that we had bought expressly for her arrival.

Adversity had taught Diane and me to put success at work in perspective. The first blow came when her mother, Lillian, was diagnosed with breast cancer a few years after we were married. The doctors warned us after the operation that they had not been able to remove the whole tumor. The disease spread slowly. Diane was able to take Lillian on a weeklong getaway to Paris—daughter treating mother—which gave both of them great joy. We visited Syracuse and Del Ray Beach every few months. We had no choice but to take things a day at a time.

Diane also ran into difficulty getting pregnant. She was determined to have kids, doggedly consulting with specialists in Washington and New York. Her courage amazed me. Three operations later—two for her and one for me—we were still trying. Finally, on the advice of Mom's internist, Ace Lipson, we tried a breakthrough procedure that worked. Diane glowed, enjoying every minute of pregnancy until the painful day of delivery.

Lisa changed my sleeping habits. She and I logged many hours up and down the stairs until she fell asleep against my chest. I loved every minute of it. Diane needed rest because she had decided to continue working. As the commissions flowed in, her firm named her a corporate vice president. Her earnings enabled us not only to buy a new house but also to sponsor a live-in nanny from Peru, Amparo Zevallos, who soon became part of the family.

Diane lost her mother a month after Lisa's first birthday. The family kept a vigil during the last months. We flew to Florida every other weekend, providing comfort as the cancer and the chemo took their toll. The end of the suffering brought a measure of relief but left a hole in Diane's heart.

After doing everything she could to support her father, Sidney, Diane agreed to take a week off with me in the South of France after Labor Day. We had a relaxing stay in Cannes, where Diane bought baby clothes for Lisa and we discovered the best bouillabaisse on the Côte d'Azur. Coming home, we tried Ace Lipson's procedure again. Miraculously, another baby was coming.

This time both the pregnancy and delivery went smoothly. I drove Diane down Canal Road along the Potomac River at 2:30 a.m. to the same hospital we had gone to two years earlier. We had to wait for a bed. Laura Susanne Yochelson came out just before 7:00 a.m., delivered by the same doctor who had brought Lisa into the world. I assisted again. Mom came to visit. Sidney arrived and soon noticed that Laura had Lillian's telling birthmark. The cycle of life had repeated itself.

15 TIME TO STEP UP

Parenthood changed priorities at home. Diane decided that she was ready to cut back at work. She felt as if she were shirking her duties when she saw Lisa's attachment to our nanny. She got such pleasure breastfeeding Laura. The real estate market was cooling anyway. It was time for her to take a break.

I wanted Diane to have the option of giving the girls full-time attention without changing our comfortable lifestyle. Our up-to-date four-thousand-square-foot colonial backed onto woods in a Bethesda neighborhood convenient to downtown. The pressure I put on myself to carry the whole financial burden came from inside. I was in my midforties. It was time to step up. I had to prove that it was possible to work as a policy wonk and live like a lawyer. That meant doubling my income.

I stuck to CSIS as my base. The center was in as strong a position as ever with the new administration of George H. W. Bush. Secretary of Defense Dick Cheney and Secretary of Commerce Bob Mosbacher had both been very active at the center. Kissinger protégé Brent Scowcroft took over as national security advisor. Anne Armstrong stayed on as chair of the President's Foreign Intelligence Advisory Board. I would be naive to give up the center's network. Instead, I would try to tap it while keeping a primary commitment to CSIS.

The culture of the center, much like academe, allowed for outside earnings. That was part of the appeal of the think tank world, in which salaries except at the very top stayed close to federal pay. Abshire served on the corporate boards of Proctor & Gamble and Ogden Corporation. The standards he set were clear. All outside relationships had to be disclosed. They couldn't take up more than half a workday a week. And they couldn't conflict with the interests of CSIS.

As I tried to decide where to begin, I found myself staring at a list of things to avoid. Don't do anything at the expense of the center. Don't undermine your credibility as an honest broker in the Quad Forum. Don't facilitate the lobbying of U.S. government officials or members of Congress. I had a narrow path to walk if I were going to respect my own code of conduct.

The immediate option I ruled out was working for Japanese interests. My travel to Tokyo ranked among the most rewarding growth opportunities csis offered. I spent almost six months there in one- to two-week increments during the 1980s. The visits were all business, mostly conducted within taxi range of the Hotel Okura. My affiliation with the center gave me high-level access to the Japanese corporate and government establishment. I was building support for csis, while my opposite numbers were looking for the lowdown on U.S. policy.

I found my counterparts hard to get to know and easy to respect. Their hospitality and courtesy knew no bounds. We spoke candidly about the strengths and weaknesses of the world's two largest economies, never touching the unspeakable subject of World War II. Not once, however, did I manage to break through on a personal level in spite of the skills I had picked up in France. I chalked up the missing rapport to cultures that were too far apart.

My conversations illuminated sharp contrasts. They were savers. We were consumers. They valued cohesion. We celebrated individualism. They managed from the bottom up. We led from the top down. They executed brilliantly. We led the world in innovation. I saw differences everywhere. How ironic that the Japanese credited an American management expert little known at home, W. Edwards Deming, with having produced the roadmap for the stunning performance of their export sector.

More than a decade of dialogue with Japanese colleagues affirmed Kissinger's classical view of international relations. The strong ties that bound our countries together grew out of national interests rather than shared experience. Japan had a vital stake in access to a vibrant American market. Washington had a reciprocal interest in a prosperous Japan that recycled its trade surplus into U.S. Treasury bonds. The security of Japan had an American anchor. The global economic leadership of the United

States had a Japanese anchor. At the highest level both sides wanted the bargain to hold despite intense friction over trade.

Nevertheless, I saw the U.S.-Japanese economic balance shifting before my eyes. The Japanese media ran stories in the late 1980s claiming that their Imperial Palace in the heart of Tokyo had more value than all of the real estate in California. The staff of Japan's leading business organization, the Keidanren, was calculating the year that the Japanese economy would overtake that of the United States. The provocative best seller by Harvard social scientist Ezra Vogel, *Japan as Number One*, seemed to be playing out.

The company I knew best, Toyota, typified the power shift. When Abshire and I traveled to Nagoya in 1981, all of the Toyotas sold in America were economy and midsized imports. By the end of the decade Toyota had a large U.S. manufacturing facility, a network of transplanted suppliers, and an upmarket Lexus that challenged German luxury cars. The Japanese automaker was far outperforming General Motors, the world's largest producer. An executive in Kentucky described the company mind-set in vivid language as we walked through the new facility there. "We don't think of this plant as a building," he said. "It's a living organism that learns and adapts every day."

Booming firms like Toyota found it easy to acquire talent to navigate in Washington. The revolving door of U.S. politics produced a supply of well-connected insiders ready to represent foreign interests. A corporate economist who participated in my program at CSIS, Pat Choate, wrote an exposé in 1990 accusing these lobbyists of selling their country out. Choate's inflammatory book, *Agents of Influence*, went overboard but gained him national attention.

I wasn't in Choate's camp. Who was I to sit in judgment of others who had a perfect right to market themselves? Still, it simply didn't feel right to go on a Japanese payroll. That would cost the high ground in U.S.-Japan relations that CSIS allowed me to take. My personal relations at Toyota could not have been stronger up and down the line, but I would never try to cash in on them.

I had no such qualms about approaching contacts in Europe. Europeans enjoyed their quality of life too much to threaten ours. Their companies were locked into benefits packages and constrained by labor restrictions.

They lagged in the information technology revolution. They were good customers for American products and services even though they protected their agricultural sector. U.S. and European multinationals were so heavily invested in each other's markets that nobody noticed. A European source of income wouldn't raise an eyebrow.

I sounded out a banker with a magic name, Baron Edmond de Rothschild, whom I knew through the Kissinger councillors. Rothschild had once described himself as French born, a resident of Switzerland, and a citizen of the world. He left Paris for Geneva as a teenager in 1940, when France stripped his father of citizenship for voting in the French Senate against the pro-Nazi Vichy regime. An only child, he learned the family business after the war and excelled without the customary family alliances. His investment bank in Paris backed high-flying ventures such as Club Med. His private bank in Geneva got a strong early foothold in wealth management. His affiliate in Tel Aviv financed much of Israel's energy infrastructure. He took control of the Union Bank of California and sold it at a handsome profit to Mitsubishi Bank. Only his English cousin Jacob matched his achievements in their generation of the dynasty.

Rothschild wasn't a joiner but made an exception for the Kissinger group. He identified with Kissinger's Jewish background and self-made success. They saw eye to eye on Middle East peace, the international issue that engaged Rothschild most. Still, Rothschild never pursued a personal relationship with Kissinger. His sporadic attendance at meetings gave me a pretext to offer briefings to provide some return on his $50,000 CSIS membership

To my delight, Rothschild accepted the standing offer to call on him from time to time. He always sent his car and driver to my hotel, an old-school courtesy that said more about his values than my standing. Usually, we had a working lunch in the offices of his Compagnie Financière in Paris on the fashionable Rue du Faubourg St.-Honoré. He dressed with the elegance of a trim, good-looking man who took his appearance seriously. He wasn't physically imposing—medium height, graying brown hair, small features, and a perfectly trimmed full mustache that made him stand out.

Rothschild had a take-charge personality in his own domain that contrasted with his subdued style in public. He spoke with a voice of intensity, conviction, and great natural charm. He did most of the talking in perfect English, learned in part from spending a year in New York, and shifted to French to give directions to his staff. He set a fast pace, changing subjects often and occasionally calling in a secretary to dictate a brief note. I saw him as a restless man of action who craved information, not theories.

What drew me magnetically to Rothschild was his family narrative. When he talked about his grandfather, also named Edmond, I sensed he had a deeper purpose. The elder Edmond, also a successful banker, had made history by acquiring land to help impoverished East European Jews settle in Palestine at the turn of the twentieth century. The grandson was a link in the same unbroken chain. He was writing the latest chapter of a 250-year-old history of striving. I knew little of the pressures, rewards, or price the Rothschilds paid. I knew something about striving, however, and wanted to learn more.

I asked Rothschild if I could provide any part-time support and explained why. He answered yes on the spot. He had a project in mind at a stipend that brought me halfway to my extra earnings goal. I would be a consultant to his charitable foundation in New York. I should follow up with his longtime lawyer, George Shapiro, who wore a second hat as its president.

Only later did I come to see how much time Rothschild spent saying no to requests like mine. Anyone who knew him eventually asked for something. My yes was one in a thousand.

The consulting assignment drew upon skills that I already had. The Rothschild Group was going to sponsor a weekend seminar for selected customers and prospects at a luxury, family-owned ski resort in eastern France. The focus would be business opportunities for midsized businesses in Europe in light of the breakup of the Soviet bloc and the movement of the European Union toward creating a single internal market. The discussion would be in English. I would help line up speakers, advise on logistics, serve as moderator, and produce a summary of proceedings. Pepperdine University, where Rothschild's son had studied, would also collaborate.

The event came off well. A magnificent setting and sumptuous food didn't hurt. The banks turned out well-informed chief executives from a dozen countries. The likable dean of the Pepperdine School of Business,

Jim Wilburn, delivered a high-ranking Russian and Richard Riordan, the future mayor of Los Angeles. I landed the European commissioner with small and medium-sized businesses in his portfolio. The minister of economics of Hungary also came to make a pitch for foreign direct investment. Rothschild hosted graciously, taking over the microphone throughout the seminar to make remarks that were longer on sentiment than substance. The printed summary, with his bold signature on a navy blue and gold-embossed cover, had class. He complained afterward about the cost of clearing the hotel for three nights during peak season, but he chalked the seminar up as a success.

Soon afterward, the ailing Shapiro announced his retirement from Rothschild's law firm, Proskauer & Rose. His departure left the presidency of the New York Foundation open. Rothschild decided to offer me the position. He wanted to split off the confidential legal work that Proskauer did from the task of serving as his representative for philanthropy. I was thrilled with the title, which carried no authority but called for me to sign off on a long list of charitable contributions. I would meet Rothschild several times a year at his principal residence, the Château de Pregny near Geneva, and follow up at his direction with recipients.

I kept perspective on my new insider status. Rothschild entrusted the details of his personal life and fortune to a very small circle. I wasn't going to be part of it. He and I called each other by our first names, but I was still a hired hand. The swirl of his relationship with Baroness Nadine de Rothschild, a former actress and author of a best seller on married life, passed me by. I saw more of their only son, Benjamin, whom Rothschild was grooming to inherit the keys to the kingdom. Nevertheless, helping Rothschild in one priority area gave me a privileged look at the balance sheet that intrigued me most: the benefits and burdens of carrying on the family tradition.

The past weighed unevenly on him. The world expected a successful Rothschild to make millions and live big. The financial challenge set his gray-blue eyes sparkling. He loved the chase. He surrounded himself with good people, pushed them hard, and returned their loyalty. He and his two most senior associates used the familiar *tu* instead of the formal *vous*, an act of closeness that astonished me. Rothschild needed the intimacy of family in a workplace that was so much an extension of himself.

The high life, on the other hand, wore him down. We were having lunch near the Olympic-size swimming pool at the château when he allowed himself to let go. "You have no idea," he said, "what it takes to run this place ... the grounds, the furnishings, the cleaning, the fresh flowers in every room every day. I have seven residences, a hunting lodge, and a yacht, all staffed and ready to go. It can be unbearable." But these material possessions were part and parcel of being a Rothschild. What you owned defined who you were.

The first property Rothschild sent me to visit, the Château Clarke vineyard in Bordeaux, had a special place in his heart. Great wineries ran in the family. Two of the most famous, Château Lafite and Château Mouton, were located in the region. The parcel he had bought in the 1970s, however, lacked the premium classification that the wine authorities of Bordeaux sparingly dole out. No matter. He vowed to create a classic by starting from scratch with the finest grapes, latest technology, and most expert winemaker.

Outstanding results went largely unrecognized. The rigid classification system based on soil quality and location rated Château Clarke as "bourgeois" rather than the coveted "first growth." Neither a superior product nor the Rothschild name could overcome the power of old ways. "This wouldn't happen in California," he remarked when I returned from my two-day mission. "You live in a country of endless possibilities. France is not a country like that."

Rothschild got more satisfaction giving money away. He took his cues from family priorities. Support for the indigent, especially orphans and displaced persons, figured prominently among dozens of annual gifts. His largest contribution in Europe went to a clinic and research center in ophthalmology named in 1905 in honor of a great cousin, Adolphe. He asked me to visit the impressive facility on his behalf. He also asked me to show the flag at the dedication of a new wing that he had donated to the International School in Geneva.

These good works failed to energize Rothschild the way another of his foundations did. The Rothschild Caesarea Foundation north of Tel Aviv had a different mission from its New York counterpart, serving as a catalyst for economic development rather than a funding channel. Caesarea had a formal structure that grew out of Rothschild's transfer of the largest privately held tract of land in the country, some 7,400 acres, to the State of Israel during the 1950s. Even so, the U.S.- and Israeli-based foundations both fell under the broad category of nonprofits. They were also financially linked.

My canny employer had a plan for me all along. I was going to serve as American point man to fill a high-tech industrial park on the very soil his legendary grandfather had purchased to help create a Jewish homeland. If successful, the project would create a Rothschild legacy for the twenty-first century.

I returned to Israel for the first time in more than thirty years to visit Caesarea. The precarious kibbutz-based country I had idealized was no more. Immigration, education, and entrepreneurship had transformed it into a vibrant economic power, while the search for security threatened to turn it into a garrison state. Driving north from Ben Gurion Airport, I marveled at the wondrous changes and asked myself if I would feel the anxiety.

My destination on the coastal plain between Tel Aviv and Haifa seemed a world away from the front lines of Palestinian resistance. Caesarea was one of the most exclusive small towns in Israel, an archaeological treasure and a residential oasis with a golf course. It was here that Rothschild hoped to co-locate companies that would drive Israeli prosperity.

My short orientation left me concerned. I expected to find a small team with a vision and a strategy for economic development. Experienced U.S. companies were going to ask tough questions and base their decisions on analysis, not personal relationships. The manager-in-charge at Caesarea, a contemporary of Rothschild from an old-line Israeli family, struck me as a nuts-and-bolts operator. He knew everyone who counted in his own country and no one who counted outside. The sophisticated marketing plan I was looking for wasn't there.

A follow-up visit led by Rothschild confirmed my fears. He had larger personal issues at stake than the industrial park. He was determined to engage Benjamin in the Caesarea foundation, which was the family's only link to its Jewish roots. Support of Israel was the surrogate for religious practice for the assimilated Rothschilds. I felt the tension between an overbearing father and a handsome, polite son who showed more interest in skydiving, hunting, and women than studies or work. Every Jew present prayed silently for the father. Meanwhile, the manager of economic development had a free hand to go after commissions from Israeli firms moving up from Tel Aviv.

I decided to play my ace in the hole. I was working closely in Washington with the head of President Bush's Export Council, Heinz Prechter, an influential niche player in the global auto industry. Would Prechter be interested in meeting Rothschild at a mutually convenient time in New York? Would he consider coming to Caesarea?

Prechter, a bootstrap millionaire who had emigrated from Germany in the 1960s, liked the idea. Diane and I hosted dinner at 21 Club, Rothschild's favorite haunt, and it went well. Prechter flew to Caesarea from Detroit on his corporate jet piloted by two Israeli air force veterans. He sketched out an ambitious scenario to jump-start automobile manufacturing in Israel, visited Jerusalem, and took off for Japan. I don't think he was ever serious, but he met a Rothschild and gave me credibility.

The dream of populating the industrial park with global brand names and agile start-ups never materialized. Rothschild wasn't prepared to make the management changes required to give that option a chance. Physically, he started to go downhill after an unsuccessful cataract operation. The foundation in Caesarea drained him as it became increasingly ensnared in legal disputes over land development.

A visibly weakened Rothschild informed me in the spring of 1994 that he would not need a representative for philanthropy anymore. His Hebrew-speaking lawyer in New York would assume the presidency of the U.S. foundation. He thanked me for my service and offered a generous severance. Two years later, catching a draft after another eye operation, he died of emphysema at age seventy-one. His life ended in personal isolation and uncertainty over a heritage he had fought hard to pass on. Within a few months Baron Benjamin de Rothschild had swept out his father's closest associates in Paris and Geneva. He was going to carry on the family name his own way.

I looked up to another European benefactor, Carlo De Benedetti, as a Renaissance man. The Italian media called him "The Engineer," the problem solver who had transformed an iconic typewriter company, Olivetti, into a force in the European personal computer market. De Benedetti had built a multibillion-dollar holding company around Olivetti that spanned manufacturing, publishing, and finance. A target of terrorists during the 1970s, he reemerged as one of Italian industry's most visible and influential leaders. His moderate center-left views made enemies at home, but he commanded attention in Brussels and wide recognition across the U.S. private sector.

I got to know De Benedetti through the Kissinger councillors. He stood out as one the most engaged and substantive members. The Engineer listened attentively. His brief comments were always on target. He seemed equally at ease talking politics, economics, technology, or diplomacy. He had the good looks and polish of a man of culture. Perhaps I could find a way to assist him.

De Benedetti didn't need help on the business side. Olivetti repackaged U.S. technology, making the company a key customer of Intel microprocessors and the Microsoft operating system. He knew all the big names in computing and seemed just as well connected on Wall Street. He didn't know Washington, however, in spite of Olivetti's reliance on U.S.-based companies. He might be looking for a window there. I had a link to him through his trusted advisor Paolo Mancinelli, who had done graduate work in international studies at Johns Hopkins. It was essential to have an in-house advocate to get through to a CEO at De Benedetti's level.

Mancinelli put out a feeler on my behalf. Yes, De Benedetti was interested in additional insight on the Washington political scene. As publisher of Italy's leading newsweekly, *L'Expresso*, he liked having an independent resource. De Benedetti and Rothschild were close, perhaps even distantly related. Olivetti would bring me on at the same consulting fee as the Rothschild foundation. To economize, I'd combine my European travel to stop in Italy as well as Switzerland or France.

I faxed monthly briefs to De Benedetti. Most focused on how the United States was adjusting to massive changes in the global economy. International financial pressures, I observed, were likely to force the Bush administration and Congress to address the U.S. budget deficit. The United States would have to get its red ink under control to finance its trade imbalance regardless of the president's campaign pledge of no new taxes. De Benedetti saw a parallel in Italy. His country was counting on the creation of a single European currency to impose much-needed fiscal discipline. "Italy is practically ungovernable," he told me. "We have to rely on the external force of a European treaty to do the right thing."

My assessment of Bill Clinton, who broke the twelve-year Republican hold on the presidency in 1992, also struck home. I alerted De Benedetti that Clinton would not turn his back on the global economy. He had defeated the incumbent Bush by claiming the middle ground in American politics. One of the ways he did so was by championing globalization, which meant expanding trade and investment. He was so committed to that principle that he'd be willing to risk part of his base of support within the Democratic Party.

As it happened, Clinton took on organized labor to win congressional approval of the North American Free Trade Agreement and the Uruguay Round of trade negotiations on the strength of Republican votes. His core political challenge was finding a path between the center he believed in and the left he needed. De Benedetti saw himself in a comparable position in Italian domestic politics, a Social Democrat who sometimes had to make common cause with Socialists. But he also had to take on the left as a cofounder of the European Roundtable of Industrialists.

De Benedetti suggested that I look for an American outlet for my commentaries, as long as he got the first look. The economics correspondent of the *Christian Science Monitor* in Washington, Amy Kaslow, recommended me to her editorial page editor. The *Monitor* didn't try to compete for big names with the *New York Times*, *Washington Post*, and *Wall Street Journal*. It had room for short pieces that offered more analysis than advocacy. As a result, my slightly revised memoranda to De Benedetti became a steady stream of op-eds in a newspaper with a national voice.

I felt the pull of history during my working visits to Olivetti headquarters. Ivrea, the bustling town north of Turin from which the company drew much of its workforce, traced its origins to Roman times. I stayed in a simple hotel in the surrounding five lakes region, a wooded area of breathtaking beauty on the route to the Alps. De Benedetti's advisor Mancinelli invited me to restaurants off the beaten path. His dynamic lead executive on information technology policy, Bruno Lamborghini, took me on weekend hikes throughout the region. I bonded with both men easily as I learned that the ungovernable Italians had a great way of life.

De Benedetti's attempt to bring a typewriter company into the computer age didn't survive the relentless march of global competition. Olivetti had a brand and a distribution channel, but the company could not add enough value to its U.S. components to command a premium price. U.S., Japanese, and Taiwanese computer makers moved into the European market with lower-cost products of comparable quality. The business setback coincided with a politically motivated effort to drag De Benedetti through the courts over his brief membership on the board of a failed bank in the early 1980s.

He responded with ingenuity and determination. De Benedetti reshaped Olivetti into a holding company for a valuable telecommunications franchise. He stayed the course in the Italian justice system and was acquitted. Throughout the ordeal I found myself trying to give him support rather than the other way around. Like many other successful people, he regrouped and found a new way forward. In the meantime he remained a member of CSIS and kept me on the payroll.

My step up on earnings had larger consequences than I had expected. Together, my CSIS and outside commitments kept me out of the country six weeks a year for as long as ten days at a time. My attempt to give Diane the option of spending more time with the girls left her no choice but to stay home because I wasn't around to pick up the slack.

Six weeks away didn't seem excessive, measured against the demands of the private sector or the travel of U.S. trade negotiators. Many of the people I knew through CSIS made much bigger sacrifices. When I wasn't on the road, I used Sunday mornings as quiet time in the office for writing commentaries and attending to Rothschild foundation business. I dropped one or both girls at Mom's to do activities and have lunch, a weekly ritual they looked forward to.

Lisa and Laura didn't see it my way. The treats that I brought back from Geneva airport, especially the chocolate gold coins and the European version of M&Ms, were always a hit. It was awfully hard, however, to explain what I did when I traveled or when I was at the office. Even though I never missed major events and spent a great deal more time with them than Dad had spent with me, they formed an early impression that I was a part-time parent.

Diane knew exactly what I was doing, and why, but she, too, drew a conclusion that I hadn't anticipated. Because I was going all out to provide for the family, she decided to assume the entire burden of managing the household. My help was welcome but not required. Her first love wasn't homemaking, but in her eyes this division of labor was a matter of equity. It was a selfless act on her part that was never discussed. It just happened.

My success reinforced Mom's view that her son could do no wrong. She missed the distinction between being a subordinate and a peer. I was working with the Rothschilds, and that's what counted. She welcomed seeing Diane assume the kind of support role that she had always played herself. My sister, on the other hand, greatly admired Diane's achievements in real estate and had a hard time understanding why she had stepped back. Bonnie was of a generation that felt a woman had to do it all. Like it or not, my good intentions put a new family dynamic in motion.

16 TOPPED OUT

My unsuccessful bid for a big job in the State Department near the end of the Reagan years set the stage for a consolation prize under his successor. The White House of George H. W. Bush notified me in the spring of 1989 that I had been nominated for the President's Export Council, the principal national advisory body on international trade.

I owed this plum to CSIS. My center colleague Wayne Berman, the shrewd political strategist whom Secretary of Commerce Mosbacher had brought in as his counselor, orchestrated the move. After recommending two of his closest allies for subcabinet positions, he put my name forward for a group whose important-sounding title far exceeded its influence. Berman scored points with Abshire for extending the reach of CSIS while doing me a favor.

The outgoing and incoming Export Councils looked different. Reagan's council included the CEOs of some of the nation's largest exporters. Companies like Boeing, Cargill, Caterpillar, DuPont, Fluor, and Westinghouse had decades of experience cracking international markets. The chairman, Eastman Kodak CEO Colby Chandler, had the rank to sit at the head of the table with that crowd.

The Bush council had its share of big names but looked thin on trade expertise. The list included Johnson & Johnson heir Robert Wood Johnson IV, private equity investor Henry Kravis, Home Depot cofounder Ken Langone, Enron CEO Ken Lay, and PepsiCo chief Michael Jordan. The lineup of global manufacturing firms looked weaker than Reagan's. Council chairman Heinz Prechter, a personal favorite of Bush, ran a midsized, privately held business in Detroit that customized sunroofs for automakers around the world.

Prechter had been Bush's top fund-raiser in 1988. He headed up the

Republican Eagles, each of whom bundled a minimum of six figures in contributions. The Eagles were well represented on the Export Council. They didn't need detailed knowledge of U.S. trade policy. The staff of the Department of Commerce covered that base.

The opportunity for me was helping the likable Prechter, who had no Washington office and little familiarity with trade policy. A short, stocky man with brown hair and blue eyes, he had an immigrant-makes-good life story that put him in a different category from a Fortune 100 CEO. Coming from a small town near Nuremberg, Germany, Prechter got his start installing sunroofs as an exchange student in San Francisco in the early 1960s. Then he spent his life savings, about $800, on tools to open a workshop in Los Angeles. There he applied his metal-bending skills to making one-of-a-kind cars for collectors in the film industry. Henry Ford II saw his work, urged him to move to Detroit, and introduced him to civic leader Max Fisher.

Their support helped Prechter grow the American Sunroof Company into an enterprise that employed five thousand people in sixty facilities worldwide. Along the way he added real estate, a local newspaper chain, and a large cattle ranch in Texas. His political mentor Fisher, a Republican force, introduced him to fund-raising. What made Prechter unusual, and must have endeared him to the Bush family, was his lack of a special-interest agenda. He believed in free enterprise and saw the Republican Party as its most reliable advocate. He never played up his political connections or lost the common touch.

Prechter absorbed my briefings on U.S. trade with Asia and Europe. Together with Patricia Harrison, another DC-based Export Council member, we gamed out his remarks in the set-piece meetings, where he sat beside Mosbacher in the secretary's large conference room. We brainstormed a personal recommendation that Prechter could deliver to Mosbacher and Bush, a presidentially led commercial delegation to Asia. The White House followed through on this trade mission, whose positive results were marred by the misfortune of the president throwing up at a state dinner in Tokyo.

The high point on the Export Council calendar was a meeting with Bush as he geared up for reelection. He knew so many of the members personally that the occasion had more of a social than a business flavor.

Nonetheless, I felt honored to be part of the line that formed afterward for handshakes and official photos. The Export Council marked a step up the Washington ladder and was a résumé builder.

The appointment enabled me to come to Abshire's rescue when a bleeding intestine hospitalized him in Hawaii on his way to Tokyo. A midnight call from his poised Japanese-speaking assistant, Jay Collins, put me on the first flight to Honolulu to stand in for him with a VIP audience. I wouldn't have gotten the call without the political credential. Although my PowerPoint went over well, status sometimes counted more than competence in the game of influence that CSIS played. Abshire insisted on going on to Japan, where Collins's language ability saved his life when he was stricken a second time.

Prechter appreciated my support. He flew me to Detroit to tour his company, introduced me to his friend Governor John Engler, and agreed to become a member of CSIS. He accepted my invitation to meet Rothschild. Never once did we talk about fund-raising. We kept in regular touch until 2001, when I heard the stunning news of his suicide at the age of fifty-nine. The Prechter family attributed his death to a lifelong battle with bipolar disorder that he hid from all but his nearest and dearest.

My brush with power politics on the Export Council reconfirmed that I wasn't cut out for it. If I were, I'd have tried harder to glad-hand the heavyweight Republican donors on my own behalf and not just for CSIS. I quickly saw, however, that they didn't share my passion for figuring out how to advance the national interest in the new global economy. They were much more comfortable than I was taking partisan positions, writing checks, and working the boundary between money and government decisions.

I saw the window closing on my kind of centrism in the Republican Party during the 1992 presidential campaign. Bush paid heavily for having compromised with the Democrats two years into his term on a budget deal that raised revenues in exchange for deeper cuts in spending. Hardline Republicans lost faith in him for breaking the read-my-lips-no-new-taxes pledge he had made when accepting the presidential nomination in 1988. The primary challenge of journalist and former Reagan speechwriter Pat Buchanan revealed Bush's vulnerability. Buchanan's jingoism turned me off, while I respected Bush for making a pragmatic move to start capping Reagan-era deficits. Doing the right thing for the country probably cost him the election. If the Republicans were headed Buchanan's way, there wouldn't be much room for me.

I found my comfort zone in the relationship that CSIS enabled me to strike up with Paul Volcker. He agreed to chair the center's advisory board soon after stepping down from two terms as chairman of the Federal Reserve in June 1987. Many wondered how much effort the Reagan administration had made to keep an independent-minded Democrat, even though the president and world leaders heaped praise on him for wringing inflation out of the U.S. economy.

Volcker, who hadn't earned a private sector salary since the 1960s, accepted a Wall Street offer when he left government. He became chairman of a boutique investment company in New York founded by financier James Wolfensohn. An affiliation with CSIS brought him back to Washington occasionally and gave him access to the conservative camp. And I got to work with a living legend.

I did my homework before calling on Volcker. Based on sheer expertise in monetary policy, he had served both the Kennedy and Nixon administrations in subcabinet positions. As undersecretary of the Treasury under Nixon, he had participated in the historic closing of the U.S. gold window at $35 per ounce in 1971. Then he negotiated the pivotal transition from fixed to floating exchange rates. From there he assumed the presidency of the New York Federal Reserve until Jimmy Carter named him Fed chairman in 1979.

The battle Volcker waged against inflation drove the prime interest rate above 20 percent initially. I remembered how lucky Diane and I had felt to get our first home mortgage at a mere 13.25 percent in 1981. The Fed's tight money policy undercut Carter's reelection and led to tense face-offs with the Reagan White House. Volcker resisted political pressure and got results. Interest rates came down and stabilized, changing the trajectory of the U.S. economy for years to come. He was the most celebrated career public official of his generation.

I met with Volcker in the expensively low-key offices of James D. Wolfensohn Inc. in Midtown Manhattan. He had a physical presence that made me think of Charles de Gaulle, so broad and so tall that, at six feet two, I didn't reach much above his shoulder. The resemblance ended there. Volcker had a down-to-earth New York accent and a cheerful demeanor. He started off a bit formally and warmed up when he learned of our shared connection to the Woodrow Wilson School, where he was teaching a course on the global economy. We talked Japan and Europe, the two parts of the world that commanded most of his attention as a central banker.

When I asked Volcker whether he had someone on staff in New York to help him with research, he said no. Wolfensohn had approved a research assistant, but Volcker dropped the idea when he saw that the position would be charged to overhead. The company abhorred overhead, which cut into year-end bonuses. As incoming chairman, he had to respect the culture of his new employer.

Reading between the lines, I guessed that Volcker missed policy even if he didn't miss Washington. A macroeconomic giant used to dealing with heads of government now found himself advising on company transactions. Wolfensohn's firm was one of the most sought-after small players in mergers and acquisitions. No one expected a former Fed chairman to get into the fine points of deals. His on-call availability was an immeasurable asset that left him with time on his hands to be a statesman. He needed support to play that role.

I pitched CSIS as his go-to resource for regional insights. Did we have anyone working on Mexico? he asked. You bet, I said, recalling that the near-default of Mexico in the early 1980s had threatened to break the back of the six largest American banks. I would be glad to put him in touch with my colleague Delal Baer, who had her finger on the pulse of Mexican politics. I was his man at CSIS. All he had to do was pick up the phone.

Volcker became my only six-foot-seven-inch customer. He asked me to comment on a keynote he was going to deliver in Geneva marking the fortieth anniversary of the multilateral trade regime known then as GATT, the General Agreement on Tariffs and Trade. Unlike Kissinger, who often spoke extemporaneously, he prepared a speech for the record. His draft stressed that large trade imbalances threatened the trade and finance systems. The surplus economies, Japan and Germany, had to assume greater responsibility for the framework as a whole. Like Kissinger,

Volcker was a systems thinker. I called in a few questions to his charming administrative assistant, Anke Dening, and made a few suggestions that he found helpful.

Other requests followed. He got regular input from CSIS on Mexico, China, and post-Soviet Russia. He asked me to speak to his class at the Woodrow Wilson School about the impact of the European Community's single-market initiative, EC 92, on U.S. economic interests. I argued, and he agreed, that a stronger, more economically integrated Europe was more likely to be a good global partner of the United States than a weak one. On the ride back to New York, he asked me what I thought about the Japanese gobbling up prime American real estate. A few days later I read about the sale of Rockefeller Center to Mitsubishi at a record-breaking price. Volcker had advised the Rockefellers.

My most revealing conversations with Volcker took place in his New York office. I dropped by every few months to keep him posted on the Washington scene. Sometimes Wolfensohn came in and sat down for a few minutes. He had his own agenda in DC, as I learned when Bill Clinton nominated him to be president of the World Bank.

When Volcker spoke his mind informally, his values struck me more than anything else. One was his commitment to public service. He worried about polls that showed the declining trust of Americans in government. A democracy couldn't function if people didn't believe in the public sector. The facile critique that government was part of the problem, not the solution, made federal careers a harder sell. He could see the impact at Treasury, which had its pick of the crop of university graduates when he worked there.

Twenty-five years after he left the Fed, Volcker told a Washington audience how the nation's capital had changed. Whenever he came back, he felt the power of money. The Washington he had known as a federal employee wasn't a place where people got rich. Now it was. Many of the most able people coming to the city viewed government work as a stepping-stone, not a career goal. The lobbying money powered a multibillion-dollar industry that never stopped growing. Idealists looked elsewhere to make a difference. The nation's capital had indeed become part of the problem for anyone who wanted to improve the performance of the public sector. When Volcker launched a national initiative to do that at the age of eighty-seven, he based it in New York.

The other value that defined Volcker in my eyes was his distrust of privilege. He was a public school kid from New Jersey who had made good at Princeton. He wore his lack of social polish as a badge of honor. The renowned central banker actually felt a lot closer to Main Street than Wall Street. He was troubled by a financial sector that skimmed talent from the rest of the economy and took high risks with other people's money. His views came to light after the financial meltdown of 2008, but I had heard many of them years earlier. When we caught up after he returned to the limelight with a proposal to limit bank risk, his concern with the distortions created by Wall Street was greater than ever. "John, we need more real engineers, not the financial kind," he said.

Inevitably, I compared Volcker and Kissinger. The country owed them both a lot, but they drew different lines between public service and personal gain. One lived simply on the East Side. The other had one of the most exclusive addresses in Manhattan and an elegant country home in a Connecticut enclave. One made a point of flying commercial. The other flew private whenever he could. One was not interested in cultivating a power image, and the other was. I stood with Volcker's choices.

Two others stars, James Schlesinger and Zbigniew Brzezinski, had offices at CSIS. Schlesinger had tangled with Kissinger and lost as secretary of defense in the Nixon administration. He returned as the first secretary of energy under Carter. A tall, imposing pipe smoker and an economist by training, he had a powerful mind of extraordinary range. I never met anyone equally at home with technical detail and big ideas.

Schlesinger excelled as a conference speaker. On one memorable occasion in Vermont, he contrasted the grand strategies of the Soviet Union and the United States. The Soviets followed a go-it-alone approach in economic development, defense, and science. The United States positioned itself at the center of global networks in each of these domains. It came out on top by embracing interdependence. That kind of engagement should be America's touchstone in a changing world. I wished Schlesinger would put his many rich insights into writing, but he never did.

I hit it off well personally with him. He lived as quiet a life as a father of eight could. There was no Schlesinger, Inc. He advised Lehman Brothers, chaired the board of an important DoD think tank, and served on a few corporate boards. He seldom talked about his cabinet jobs, a telling indicator that they may have been more bruising than fulfilling. When I left CSIS, he gave me a book of letters he had edited from a self-made nineteenth-century merchant to his son. The warm inscription, with a friendly barb about giving advice as well as taking it, brought a smile.

I had less contact with Brzezinski, who had competed with Kissinger on equal footing in academe. The Polish-born Sovietologist and German-born historian were two of the brightest lights in the European Security Club. Brzezinski's stint as national security advisor to President Carter, however, failed to match the government record of his rival. He resumed his scholarly career afterward, radiating intellectual energy at CSIS and the Johns Hopkins School for Advanced International Studies.

I didn't always agree with Brzezinski's views but found him a strikingly authentic person. He kept current on primary resources, wrote books on U.S. geopolitical strategy, and retained his remarkable way with words. I recalled how harried he looked during his White House days, when he pushed his chest out macho style walking into the Department of State. Out of office, like Volcker, he seemed comfortable in his own skin.

My CSIS portfolio expanded in 1991. Abshire came up with the idea of establishing a commission to address U.S. domestic vulnerabilities in the post–Cold War era. The decline of the Soviet military threat, the rise of Asia, and the momentum of European integration called for a revitalized American economy. At my suggestion we named the initiative the "Strengthening of America Commission."

Abshire lined up Senate Armed Services chairman Sam Nunn, his closest friend on Capitol Hill, to cochair the effort. Nunn had damaged himself politically by opposing the use of U.S. military force to free Kuwait after the Iraqi invasion of 1990. Until then, he had looked like a prime contender for the Democratic nomination for president in 1992. The crushing of Saddam Hussein's troops in the first Gulf War, a triumph for the Bush administration, eliminated Nunn's chances. Abshire convinced him that an ambitious out-of-area project would help restore his leadership credentials. Nunn enlisted Pete Domenici, ranking member of the Senate Budget Committee, to serve as Republican cochair.

The commission required a full-time director with strong academic and policy skills. Debra Miller, a Harvard PhD with Commerce Department experience, fit the bill. Abshire and I empowered her to lead the effort, while we took part as well. Nunn and Domenici attracted a diverse A-list of fifty-five participants from industry, organized labor, education, and government. Some of the biggest names were Alcoa CEO Paul O'Neill, Motorola chairman Bob Galvin, American Federation of Teachers president Al Shanker, National Academy of Sciences president Frank Press, *U.S. News and World Report* editor-at-large David Gergen, and future UN ambassador Andrew Young.

The behind-the-scenes work of Nunn and Domenici reflected the best of a bygone political era. The senior senators from Georgia and New Mexico, respectively, trusted each other. They were personal friends whose families socialized because both maintained their principal residences in the Washington area. Politically, they were pragmatists known for their command of the issues. Nunn knew as much as anyone in Congress about defense policy. His capable staff raced to keep up with him. Domenici had comparable depth on the budget process. Both men, bookishly handsome in their large-lensed glasses, were at the top of their game.

The real brainstorming never took place during the plenary sessions of the commission in the Capitol. The cochairs brought together their key staffers and the CSIS team of Abshire, Miller, and me. Gergen sat in to supply political advice. We usually met around the conference table in Nunn's office, fortified by a bowl of fresh popcorn—no salt or butter—that never stayed empty long.

Nunn and Domenici feared for the future. The red ink on the trade account showed that the United States was consuming more from the rest of the world than it was producing. Likewise, the projected growth of the federal deficit meant that Washington was living increasingly beyond its means. National saving was at an all-time low, depleting the pool of resources available for research and development as well as plants and equipment. Piecemeal responses weren't the answer. The commission needed to come up with a long-term plan for renewal that balanced the budget and increased productive capacity.

Swinging for the fences, the cochairs hit upon restructuring the tax code as a possible game changer. Budget deficit reduction had turned into the no-man's-land of American politics. Perhaps the commission could make it safer by linking it to the national interest in boosting saving. Nunn and Domenici reasoned that the existing income tax was not only complex and unpopular but also biased toward consumption. They bet on a sweeping tax reform proposal that rewarded individuals for saving and companies for investing. They took the gamble even though neither one had made his reputation in the tax area.

Nunn and Domenici looked to the economists on the commission to crunch the budget numbers and produce a package of new revenues and significantly deeper spending cuts that would pass muster politically with centrist Democrats and Republicans. The key players were former congressional budget directors Alice Rivlin, a Democrat, and her successor Rudy Penner, a Republican. They came up with a ten-year blueprint to reduce the federal budget by $2 trillion, three-quarters through spending reductions and one-quarter through increased revenue. The package included a sweetener for Democrats—$160 billion in additional federal investments in education, R&D, and technology.

Skillfully, Nunn and Domenici didn't ask the members of the commission to sign onto every recommendation. All agreed to be listed as participants in the process who agreed at the most general level with the overall thrust of the Strengthening of America initiative. Miller drafted a clear, concise report for release one month before the 1992 presidential election.

The proposals of the commission failed to gain traction in spite of a flurry of front-page news coverage and praise from Washington pundits. The incoming Clinton administration adopted a more partisan deficit reduction strategy than Nunn and Domenici advocated. The White House decided to raise revenue by increasing taxes on high earners. The Deficit Reduction Act of 1993 squeaked through the House of Representatives by a single vote, with no Republicans signing on. Clinton won his bet that financial markets would be reassured, ushering in six years of growth that brought the country temporarily out of the financial hole. The Clinton increase, however, drove a wedge between Democrats and Republicans over fiscal policy that undermined the middle ground for the next twenty years.

I took stock of my future as CSIS moved on from the commission. There was plenty to keep me busy. The Quadrangular Forum had legs. Kissinger never seemed to lose a step. The interplay of regional and multilateral trade needed to be explored. The challenges of globalization looked more daunting than ever as China, India, and Russia transitioned into market-based economies.

Still, I realized that I had hit my limit after fifteen years at the center. Despite carrying a title of senior vice president, I lacked the academic or political credentials to succeed Abshire. I had reaped the full benefit of the CSIS network by submerging my own voice within that of the organization. I developed into an impresario of national and international meetings—learning the issues, making the conversation flow, and distilling the essentials. This was a valuable skill set but not one that translated into a reputation for leadership or policy expertise.

Aside from op-eds my collected works consisted of group-signed position papers, issue briefs, and edited volumes. My sole appearance on network television, a *Today Show* segment on U.S.-Japan auto issues, went well but never led to an encore. I presented at the high-flying conference in Davos, Switzerland, once but never got asked back. Only those with whom I worked knew my substantive strengths.

The organization man role used up all of my bandwidth. I spent about ten hours a day in the office when I was not traveling. I applied Abshire's management techniques of cheerfulness, praise, and sharing information to good effect. My long-lasting secretaries looked after my calendar, correspondence, and event support. The executive assistants, who never stayed longer than two years, backed me up on research, center politics, and operating in Washington. It was a demanding, rewarding routine— and I had it down.

As I approached fifty, I asked myself whether my career had topped out. The president of the United States was younger than I was. David Marchick, the gifted twenty-five-year-old assistant who had made me throw out my typewriter and buy a computer, was working in the White House. He looked to me as a mentor, but I saw him as mine too. Perhaps I ought to face the fact that time had passed me by. I could always stay put, but the striver in me wasn't ready to settle.

Diane said that she would back any decision I made. She had recast herself as a suburban mom, taking on all the weekday tasks except the occasional after-dinner pick-up from a play date. Suddenly the onset of her father's lung cancer hit her. She spent every other weekend in Florida for ten months, until he died in October 1994. An ugly battle over his estate with his aggressive second wife followed. The one-two punch of losing both parents within six years made it the roughest period in Diane's life. She endured the pain without shedding any of her workload at home.

I did my best to help, dedicating Saturdays and most of Sundays to Lisa and Laura. We found our own rituals, walking the banks of the stream behind the house and shooting baskets in the driveway. I started taking two weeks off every summer, allowing the four of us to drive up to Cape May, New Jersey, to rent a condo in a building with a swimming pool. We rode bikes down the boardwalk every morning, stopped for fresh blueberry muffins on the way back, and took late-afternoon walks on the beach. Those lazy days, however, hardly offset the price of my work schedule.

I heard about a good opening during the summer of 1995. Barry Rogstad, a friend who headed up an association of midsized businesses, alerted me that the Council on Competitiveness was looking for a new president. Would I be interested if he threw my name in the ring?

The council was a small nonprofit with an elite membership that dated from the Reagan era. Its quietly competent president, Kent Hughes, had served on the Strengthening of America Commission. Once he had invited me to a council dinner at the Phillips Collection, the elegant gallery near Dupont Circle that was Mom's favorite. I found myself seated next to *Washington Post* publisher Katharine Graham. The most influential woman in Washington gave me her full attention. She spoke her mind freely from a position so far above the fray that she could care less about being quoted. She liked what the council stood for but feared that it would become just one more self-perpetuating nonprofit. Despite her reservations, she was staying on the board. I had never forgotten that powerful endorsement. Yes, it would be great if Rogstad put my name forward.

The key decision-maker was Paul Allaire, the CEO of Xerox. Luckily, I had a good relationship with Michael Farren, the director of his DC office, who had served as undersecretary of commerce when I was on the Export Council. Farren said a lot of people were applying. Because I really wanted the job, I phoned Volcker for advice and support. Another stroke of luck—Volcker knew Allaire and volunteered to call him on my behalf.

Weeks passed before I got a thirty-minute interview with Allaire, an outgoing New Englander with a technical background. Later I learned that he had also spoken with three other finalists. He followed up by phone a few days after the interview, placing the call himself. I was so eager that I accepted the offer without asking about the salary. The pay didn't match my combined earnings at csis, but so what? This opportunity couldn't be measured in dollars, and it would relieve me of foreign travel.

After sharing the good news with Diane, I went to see Abshire. He congratulated me warmly, taking my new job as a validation of csis rather than a loss. As my departure neared, he hosted a send-off reception at the fancy Metropolitan Club. The astonishing turnout reflected more of a tribute to him than to me. Many nice letters followed, most of which found their way into Mom's scrapbook. The good wishes that meant most came from Anne Armstrong and Paul Volcker, who scribbled a postscript: "John, your efforts were really above and beyond the call of duty, as I am sure they will be in the new position."

17 TURNAROUND

I learned as much as I could about the Council on Competitiveness before starting work. Its founder, John Young, had succeeded William Hewlett and David Packard as CEO of the most celebrated company in Silicon Valley. A few years after he took over, the Reagan White House asked him to chair a presidential commission on industrial competitiveness. Many top U.S. firms, including his, were struggling to respond to the unstoppable Japanese. The Young Commission spent eighteen months gathering testimony, assembling data, and writing its report.

A divided Reagan administration didn't get behind the activist recommendations Young delivered to the president in 1985. Free market purists opposed his call for tighter policy coordination and a robust federal role in basic research, education, and workforce development. When Young was thanked and ignored, he decided to take matters into his own hands. He invited commission members and others to form a nonprofit in Washington to put their message across. The group included CEOs, university presidents, and labor leaders. They gave themselves three years to get the policy side of U.S. competitiveness on track.

Ironically, an agenda that grew out of a Republican mandate got its most receptive hearing from Bill Clinton and Al Gore during the 1992 presidential campaign. They ridiculed Republican ideologues for not caring whether the country made computer chips or potato chips. Candidate Clinton gained access to contributors with deep pockets in Northern California by defining himself as a high-tech champion. President Clinton named Young, who had retired as CEO of Hewlett-Packard, the private sector cochair of the President's Council of Advisors on Science and Technology.

I wondered whether the council had already served its purpose as I walked into 1401 H Street in December 1995. My initial conversation with my new colleagues wasn't uplifting. A dozen glum faces looked at me from around the conference table. They had reason to feel down. My immediate predecessor had departed six months earlier. A major initiative on the future of U.S. R&D had stalled. There was nothing else in the pipeline. A White House seal of approval looked like it had taken the wind out of the council's sails. The bank account told me I had a year to turn the situation around. I knew what to do, having watched Abshire deal with much worse than this.

Getting a handle on the business model came first. Young and his successor, George Fisher of Motorola, funded the council by recruiting members peer to peer. My chairman, Allaire, didn't want to spend personal capital growing a membership that had already reached 120. That tricky area fell to me. The council was a CEO club whose benefits weren't equal. The select group of thirty that made up the executive committee met three times a year, taking the lead on projects and meeting informally with top policy makers. Some of them, like Katharine Graham, invited me over to keep current and listen to any good political gossip that came my way. The members of the executive committee, however, set their dues on the same sliding scale, from $5,000 to $20,000 per year, as the general members who met once a year. The imbalance made for a difficult sales pitch.

I quickly decided that the financial future of the council lay in its work program, not its dues income. We the staff needed to propose projects that attracted supplemental support and gave general members a chance to participate. Coming up with good fund-raising pegs and doing quality work had to be my top priorities. Success there would make or break my tenure.

A closer look at the council's in-house resources didn't turn up a thought partner with whom to share the workload. Former National Science Foundation director Erich Bloch and former assistant secretary of commerce Deborah Wince-Smith were great assets but too heavily committed outside to do much heavy lifting. Vice President Suzy Tichenor had valuable corporate experience but a specialized focus on information technology.

A colleague at CSIS, Debbie Van Opstal, had exactly the right skills. She was a generalist like me who produced fresh, conceptually interesting work on the development of military and civilian technologies. She had the depth to manage projects and the creativity to develop original insights. csis allowed her to juggle her career while raising four kids but not on very generous terms. I offered her a big boost in salary, a vice presidency, and flextime. She accepted. Bringing her aboard was the best personnel decision I made.

Meanwhile, I had to win the confidence of the powers that be. Young invited me to dinner with several members of the executive committee before I was formally introduced to the leadership. We met at a good Italian restaurant, Primi Piatti, on Pennsylvania Avenue across from the World Bank. Young was there when I arrived, chatting with Charles (Chuck) Vest, the president of mit. Tom Everhart, president of Caltech and university vice chairman of the council, joined us. Bill Hambrecht, a pioneer venture capitalist from San Francisco, rounded out the table.

These incredibly accomplished men, all around sixty and over six feet, shared something important. Each had reached the heights of his profession on merit. Young, a cerebral outdoorsman with a strong jaw, had climbed the corporate ladder from little-known Oregon State. Vest, a jogger with a boyish smile and close-cropped hair, came from a modest family of West Virginia educators. Everhart, bespectacled and down-to-earth, was the first in his heartland family to attend college as well as the first engineer to be named president of Caltech. Hambrecht, whose unassuming manner hid his daring, had moved to California to strike out on his own after graduating Princeton and serving in the navy. I didn't see a shred of pretense in any of them.

My dinner partners were steeped in a world of engineering that I knew little about. Three held engineering degrees. The fourth, Hambrecht, invested in start-ups conceived by engineers and felt that the country could never produce too many of them. My liberal arts education focused on ideas. Engineering students applied math and science to solve real-world problems. The same curiosity that led me to abstraction led engineers to invention.

Young and company weren't looking for one of their own. We found common ground discussing the state of U.S. competitiveness and the future of the council. They left reassured that I knew the issues and could operate in Washington. I found them as impressive a group as I had ever met.

My opening conversation with the labor vice chairman of the council, Jack Sheinkman, went smoothly. Organized labor was the weakest leg of the council triad, comprising less than a tenth of the membership. Industrial unions saw their ranks being decimated by the diffusion of technology and outsourcing of production. Most labor leaders viewed globalization as a lethal threat, while most of the council's corporate members saw access to global markets as their greatest opportunity.

Sheinkman, who had just stepped down as president of the Amalgamated Clothing Workers, wasn't strident. His eyes lit up when I told him that I had worked with his predecessor, Murray Finley, at csis. Their union saw no alternative but to adopt advanced manufacturing technology to resist the tide of low-wage competition. Sheinkman, a lawyer and a died-in-the-wool New Yorker, liked Allaire. He stood by his record as a reasonable union leader.

A snowstorm prevented me from flying to Boston to meet Professor Michael Porter, the biggest name in the study of competitiveness. Porter, who taught corporate strategy at Harvard Business School, had an immense following in business circles. He had been one of the most influential voices on the Young Commission, contributing a definition of national competitiveness that affirmed the crucial link between winning in the marketplace and increasing the standard of living of all Americans.

Porter stood out as the most powerful weapon in the council's arsenal. He had served on the executive committee from day one. We talked for more than an hour on the phone, his animated voice conveying a passion like no other for U.S. performance in the global economy. I asked him what he thought about developing a net ten-year assessment of U.S. competitiveness in time for the presidential election. Yes, that sounded interesting and doable. The council remained his outlet of choice. My goal was to keep it that way.

An immediate piece of unfinished business remained. The council had spent a year gathering input on the U.S. r&d enterprise from noted scientists and engineers with varied backgrounds. Their insights made a forceful case for the $80 billion federal investment in basic research. Companies built off that foundational knowledge to create innovative products and services. The division of labor between the public and private sectors accounted for a large part of U.S. technological leadership. Bloch, the crusty and farsighted distinguished fellow at the council, knew both sides of this story. He had inspired the project, but a visiting congressional staffer who was supposed to direct the work had left it incomplete.

The Bloch report had to be finished pronto. Support for federal spending on R&D held the organization together. My council colleague Wince-Smith warned of language in the report that spelled trouble. She pointed out a passage that rated university-based research a better federal investment than the national laboratories, such as Los Alamos and Lawrence Livermore. Pitting universities against labs would alienate staunch congressional supporters of federal R&D. I followed Wince-Smith's advice, inserted balanced wording, and polished the rest of the draft.

The release of *Endless Frontier, Limited Resources: U.S. R&D Policy for Competitiveness* in April 1996 raised spirits in the office and gave Allaire a major win. He hosted a news conference at the National Press Club. Tom Everhart did the honors on the West Coast with Intel cofounder and Caltech trustee Gordon Moore. Senator Domenici, whose state of New Mexico had two labs, held an event on the Hill. The turnaround of the council had begun.

Porter followed up with the *Competitiveness Index 1996*, which charted ten-year global economic trends as well as U.S. performance. His strategic assessment covered saving, investment, GDP growth, employment, income distribution, productivity, and trade. As always, the balance sheet highlighted a mix of immediate gains and long-term vulnerabilities. Commentaries from Volcker and a half dozen council members added weight to the volume. Porter aced the media presentation in a blue suit and yellow tie, downing Diet Cokes to keep the adrenaline flowing.

As the council picked up speed, Allaire informed me that he was ready to move on. The chairmanship rotated every few years, and now he could leave on a high note. He asked me to find a successor because the council didn't have an active industry vice chairman.

I settled on Bill Hambrecht as the best candidate after checking the availability of several Fortune 100 CEOs. He was truly engaged in the council. Although he lacked a big-company operating base, he had world-class connections and a stellar reputation in Silicon Valley. I flew to San Francisco and asked on my own behalf, pending Allaire's concurrence. My timing was good. Merrill Lynch was about to acquire his firm, Hambrecht & Quist, freeing him up until he launched another venture.

Allaire didn't jump for joy. He had business issues with Hambrecht stemming from the commercialization of research done at his company's storied Palo Alto Research Center. Hambrecht had funded Internet winners like Adobe that Xerox never brought to market. "I used to stand outside the gate of Xerox PARC with my checkbook," he cracked. Nevertheless, Allaire wanted out and had no ready alternative. Both men were all smiles when the handoff took place early in 1997. Chuck Vest of MIT succeeded his friend Tom Everhart as university vice chair at the same time.

Hambrecht and Vest matched up well despite being a study in contrasts. My new chairman, an avowed Democrat, had no business interest in Washington. My vice chair had to defend an MIT stake worth hundreds of millions of dollars in federal grants that required support from both parties. Hambrecht valued room to maneuver to do deals. Vest was booked months in advance. Still, they liked and respected each other, and they both trusted me. Together we put the council into high gear.

The driver proved to be an ambitious project on U.S. corporate R&D strategy directed by my vice president Van Opstal. She questioned the conventional wisdom that American companies would limit their foreign investment to production capacity and keep their R&D crown jewels at home. If R&D were up for grabs, too, the innovation paradigm was shifting from national to global.

The council formed a large advisory committee to dig into the issues. Bill Steere, the quiet and highly successful CEO of Pfizer, took the lead, along with Hambrecht and Bill Brody, the triple-threat president of Johns Hopkins—an engineer, medical doctor, and former CEO. Chief technical officers representing $70 billion in U.S. R&D investment came to the table. Their participation provided a depth of knowledge and a multiplier that the council never had before.

The aha moment when the members of the advisory committee compared notes. All were allocating an increasing share of research budgets to R&D facilities outside the United States. U.S. locations would have to compete for the first time for the high-end investments of U.S.-based companies. Billions of dollars and thousands of high-paying jobs were at stake.

Working groups looked at innovation strategy company by company in five major industry sectors. All of the U.S.-based firms faced a new wave of competitors and a rapid acceleration of product cycle times. All were aggressively looking beyond their home market to locate investment, access talent, and meet demand. The same fundamentals mattered in every industry: people, capital, research, partnerships, regulatory and legal frameworks, and manufacturing capacity.

The report Van Opstal drafted, *Going Global: The New Shape of American Innovation*, reframed the competitive challenge as a race to innovate. Her overview captured the new reality: "The United States remains the world's innovation powerhouse, bringing a unique combination of strengths to the table. Yet globalization is leveling the playing field, changing the rules of international competition, and collapsing the margins of technological leadership. Our members are not convinced that the United States is preparing for success in a world in which many more countries will acquire the capacity to innovate." This statement rings as true today as it did then.

Hambrecht and Vest agreed that the best way to give the innovation agenda visibility in Washington was taking it outside the Beltway. Vest committed to a National Innovation Summit at MIT in the spring of 1998. To set the stage, we invited research university presidents in the Midwest, South, and West to host half-day regional summits. The presidents of Purdue and Georgia Tech as well as the chancellor of the University of California San Diego accepted enthusiastically. Each delivered the governor of his state, along with corporate leaders, economic development officials, and colleagues from other universities. Each regional gathering stressed the indispensability of federal support for basic research in an increasingly knowledge-based economy. I promised to carry the message forward.

The heaviest burden fell on Vest. Many would deem the National Innovation Summit at MIT a flop unless the president or vice president spoke. Vest's high profile in Washington fueled expectations. No university president worked the corridors of power more effectively. My pre-summit contact with him gave me a taste of the workload of the head of an elite institution. I never saw anyone juggle so much with such competence and apparent lack of strain. At a minimum his laptop must have had folders for faculty, trustees, donors, students, policy, corporate boards, associations, and the council. His emails could come from anywhere, day or night. I negotiated time on his calendar with his executive assistant, Laura Mersky, whom I called "cousin" because she had Mom's last name.

I gave Vest a timely cyber assist as the summit approached. We were shooting for Vice President Gore as the keynoter and couldn't get an answer. The vice president's staff leveled with me. They were sitting on the invitation because Gore was going to be in California the night before and had to be in Florida the afternoon of the summit. Tipper Gore adamantly opposed an East Coast stop in between. I pleaded for the vice president's private email and got it. Vest followed up with a respectful, beautifully written message. Bingo.

Hambrecht nailed down William Perry, the much-respected former secretary of defense. He also convinced a rising star in the Democratic congressional delegation, Nancy Pelosi, to attend. We balanced her with the Republican chairman of the House Science Committee, James Sensenbrenner. Senators Domenici and Kennedy committed, along with the governors of Florida, Massachusetts, and Michigan.

The program alone ensured success. Gore arrived on time and made gracious remarks before veering into a discussion of space-based technology applications. Perry delivered a tour de force on the role of defense R&D in the development of computer chips, wide-bodied aircraft, and the Internet. The council leadership rose to the occasion, stressing that the United States would have to compete on high-end products and services to support a high standard of living. The summit drew page 1 coverage in the *Wall Street Journal*. As we hoped, the council reached a national audience. I thanked my leadership, knowing that Hambrecht was likely to step down within a year, while Vest would stay to build on our momentum.

The summit opened a door to Congress. Vest and I called on Jay Rockefeller of West Virginia, his home state senator and ranking member of the Commerce Committee. Rockefeller advised going after staff instead of trying to reach members directly through a caucus on innovation. There were no legislative assistants for technology on the Hill. That's where the council could help. Rockefeller offered to speak with his Republican colleague Bill Frist of Tennessee, a widely respected and well-liked heart surgeon. Together they could organize a council forum on the policy debates surrounding important but opaque technical issues.

Rockefeller's dynamic chief of staff, Tamera Luzzatto, provided additional advice. "Innovation" sounded too complicated to fly as a title. Keep it simple, she said. Use a widely understood term like *technology*. To be credible, the council needed to present both sides of an issue as evenhandedly as possible. And remember that Senate and House staffers care about current legislation, not grand designs.

I consulted further with Bill Bonvillian, the thoughtful chief counsel of Senator Lieberman. He recommended Peter Rooney, a physicist finishing up a postdoctoral fellowship in Lieberman's office, to run the forum. Bonvillian underscored the need for full disclosure of sponsors. No funding source with a political angle would be acceptable. I approached the Sloan Foundation, the most prominent mainline funder of science and technology. Ralph Gomory, the brilliant and prickly ex-IBMer who ran Sloan, agreed to help. The senators and their staffs bought in.

The Congressional Tech Forum showed that civility had not been altogether lost on the Hill. The two patricians, Rockefeller and Frist, used their weight to attract headliners such as Intel CEO Andy Grove and neoconservative Richard Perle to debate export controls. Topics ran the gamut from digital recording to biotechnology regulation to taxing stock options. The lunchtime sessions, which usually took place in the Capitol, drew a crowd. The senators alternated as hosts, introducing the speakers and turning protocol upside down by deferring to the staffers during Q&A. Rooney, who had an advanced degree in political networking along with his doctorate in physics, excelled as executive director of the forum. The council established a presence on the Hill that lasted into the next administration.

The success at MIT laid down another marker on improving education and workforce development. A thin layer of scientists and engineers couldn't sustain U.S. leadership in innovation. The current generation of workers and the students coming up behind them faced a relentless global test. A council report on upgrading worker capabilities, *Winning the Skills Race*, hit the street soon after the summit. The nation needed a wake-up call to the skills shortage that lay behind the record job growth of the 1990s.

Amy Kaslow, the talented economics correspondent whom I knew at CSIS, joined the council as a senior fellow to lead the effort. Putting on her journalist hat, she combed the country for exemplars and extracted principles of best practice. Her search for excellence made a compelling point. None of the stakeholders—employers, workers, educators, or public officials—met the training challenge successfully on his or her own. Collaboration defined best in class. An expert task force cochaired by the presidents of Ameritech, the United Steelworkers, and the Stevens Institute of Technology endorsed Kaslow's findings.

A punchy presentation loaded with on-the-ground insight won praise but failed to energize the council membership. Research universities showed little interest in worker training, for which scrappy community colleges often had more to offer. Council CEOs paid less attention to the skills gap than to potential R&D breakthroughs. Unions that were losing members took scant comfort in the training they negotiated for their remaining jobholders. A call to action from Washington on a grassroots problem didn't resonate in the short run.

A few years later, however, the core idea of *Winning the Skills Race* caught on. The Department of Labor launched a multiyear program of workforce partnerships to help communities develop the right skills for new industries. Kaslow's first report had just been a little ahead of its time.

Al Berkeley, the president of the NASDAQ, suggested a different tack. His tech-heavy companies were under fire for hiring so many foreign nationals. The council should do something concrete to expand the pool of homegrown talent by raising the achievement of American students in math. On average American youngsters scored high in fourth grade in international comparisons. Then they lost ground as they moved up the education ladder. They ranked below the middle of the pack by the time they finished high school.

Why not create a website that enabled students to a see how they measured up to their counterparts in other countries? The Third International Math and Science Study, known as TIMSS, provided a pool of questions as well as data on country performance. Wince-Smith identified a scientist at Sandia National Laboratory, Marshall Berman, to direct the project. Sandia lent him to the council as a visiting fellow. NASA jumped in with additional support. Berman developed more than a website. His learning tool won acclaim from educational researchers for providing animated hints to students who had missed the TIMSS questions. Eventually, the National Association of Manufacturers took the site over.

The main boost coming out of MIT went to the council's signature work on innovation. Porter took center stage. I marveled at his routine. He started with an important, conceptually difficult problem—quantifying the national capacity to innovate. Then he found an associate, Scott Stern of MIT, capable of carrying out the analysis. They designed the approach together. After that Porter monitored the execution of the coauthored study, synthesized its findings, and put his stamp on it. Everybody won.

The Innovation Index constructed by Porter and Stern compared the capacities of countries to produce high-value, one-of-a-kind products and services. The index found that the pace of U.S. innovation was slowing in relative terms. The capabilities of the advanced economies were converging, while new centers of innovation were emerging in East Asia and Israel. For the first time the council made a data-driven case for a national innovation strategy.

Porter suggested going a step further. His most original work showed that innovation takes place in geographically clustered industry sectors. The United States had many such clusters, but only a few beyond Silicon Valley and Route 128 Boston had ever been studied. Instead of looking solely at the national factors that drive innovation, the council should provide the analysis to turbo-charge U.S. innovation in a half dozen metro regions around the country. Porter couldn't conduct the study himself, but he could oversee a team of consultants familiar with his framework of cluster analysis.

The new chairman of the council, Ray Gilmartin of Merck, threw his full support behind a Porter-led innovation project. The pharmaceutical industry invested more money in R&D as a share of revenues than any other. Merck had a record of in-house product development that was second to none. Gilmartin, who had majored in physics as an undergraduate, had a thirty-year relationship with Porter dating back to his days at Harvard Business School. We weren't going to lose our marquee resource.

The shift in leadership from an entrepreneur to a big-company chairman completed the turnaround of the council. No one had to talk Gilmartin into taking the chairmanship in the spring of 1999. He pursued it. Another Fortune 50 CEO, Duane Ackerman of BellSouth, waited in the wings. The president of the American Federation of Teachers, Sandra Feldman, solidified labor membership. A much-improved financial position allowed me to sign a ten-year lease for new office space. I had to manage for growth, not survival, moving forward.

All in all the council emerged as a true thought leader on my watch. We shined fresh light on the risks of globalization. Then we proposed a response based on a novel theory of innovative capacity. *Innovation* became a buzzword in policy circles. The principle of geographic clustering formed the basis for the next generation of economic development strategy. Van Opstal chided me years later for being too modest about my contribution.

Far from basking in the council's success, I began to ask how long I should stay. There was nothing left to do on my checklist. I proved that I could run a small, influential organization at a high level. A year-old conversation with John Young, whose opinion I valued more than anyone, kept haunting me. As he gently but firmly turned down my request that he remain on the executive committee, he said: "The council has to learn to live without me. The cause counts more than the founder. It's worth giving everything you've got for four or five years. Then it's time to pass the baton to someone else to do the same."

I had no desire to climb another rung or two up the Washington ladder. Lobbying turned me off. A political appointment would mean crushing hours and a pay cut. I'd have to swallow hard and stay put or rethink my career.

Despite my uneasiness, I played the Washington game by joining the Council on Foreign Relations. CFR brought together a cross-section of prominent people interested in the U.S. role in the world. Its roster of several thousand national members read like a Who's Who of foreign policy. I had yearned for blueblood recognition since college days. At last I had the title and connections to be considered by a group founded by the

Rockefellers. By luck my State Department mentor Tarnoff headed up CFR when I applied. Gelb, my other boss at State, made the world smaller still by succeeding him. I smiled inside at finally becoming part of an in-crowd.

The home front, however, prodded me to look for a new direction. Diane asked softly about leaving the area. She felt judged by Mom, the girls were a handful, and she was suffering from a painful loss of circulation in the fingertips that improved in warmer weather. I told her that I'd try my best to create some options. I wasn't wedded to Washington by any means. Politics had become a blood sport fed by lobbyists, ideologues, and election consultants. Yet we had to be realistic. I had specialized skills, a good salary, and a driver's license that read fifty-five years old.

The warm-weather location that appealed most to me was San Diego, which also billed itself as technology's perfect climate. I had an easy rapport with Irwin Jacobs, the cofounder of the region's highest-flying company, Qualcomm, who had joined the executive committee through the good offices of Vest. The chancellor of UC San Diego, Bob Dynes, was an active member. I worked closely with Julie Meier Wright, the president of the Economic Development Corporation. Diane's brother, Rick, who had created his own successful pet product business, lived two hours away, in Palm Desert. We had vacationed briefly there and liked it. It was too late to start over without connections.

Fate struck in September 2000, when Bloch, the gray eminence of the council, asked me to join him in a meeting with Rita Colwell, the director of the National Science Foundation (NSF). I had a cordial relationship with Colwell, a highly regarded biologist whose $5 billion agency was the largest federal investor in basic research outside the life sciences.

Colwell wanted to sound me out on an issue close to her heart. A congressional Commission on Diversity supported by NSF had recommended the creation of a body to broaden the participation of historically underrepresented groups in science and technology. She had firsthand experience with the problem, having once been denied a graduate fellowship on the grounds that, as a woman, she was undoubtedly going to get married and start a family. A generation later her daughter earned a doctorate in the biosciences and faced a comparably hostile environment. The situation was just as bad for African Americans, Latinos, American

Indians, and persons with disabilities. NSF planned to raise $2 million in seed funding from a coalition of federal agencies. She wasn't making any promises but hoped the council would consider submitting an unsolicited proposal.

In a split second I saw my exit strategy. Taking a career risk worthy of Dad, I fired back questions that must have stunned Colwell and Bloch. Did the new body have to be based in Washington, or could it be located in San Diego? Was it acceptable for a white male to lead the initiative? If so, would I be a viable candidate? I, too, was passionate about opening the doors of opportunity through education because that was my own family's defining experience. I cited Diane's health issue as my motivation, gliding over my own readiness to pick up stakes.

Colwell didn't flinch. She knew the strength of the council, having met with the executive committee and sent a representative to the MIT summit. Yes, California was fine. The NSF had a conference facility just north of San Diego, at Irvine. I was well qualified because the new entity would have to raise significant private sector resources. Due process had to be respected. The agencies providing start-up funds would review a council proposal.

A jumble of thoughts went through my mind as I left the meeting. Could I get an early commitment to leverage a federal grant? How would I handle this plan with my leadership? What about Mom, who was in good health and about to celebrate her ninety-third birthday? I asked Bloch to keep my confidence as we drove back to the council.

Irwin Jacobs of Qualcomm held the key. The explosive growth of his company, which designed microchips for cell phones, made him the most respected CEO in San Diego. He was also its most generous philanthropist. The tall, soft-spoken former professor of engineering wanted to give back to the community in which he had become a billionaire. The education of underserved kids ranked high among his priorities. I explained the situation in an email. Would Qualcomm consider a $1 million match of potential federal support in order to base a major diversity initiative in San Diego? The answer came back yes.

The next six months went by like a blur as pieces fell into place. I got the blessing of my leadership to submit a Council on Competitiveness proposal to NSF spinning off Building Engineering & Science Talent, or

BEST. Federal agencies pooled $2 million in grant funding. Qualcomm formally signaled its readiness to add another million, clinching approval. Two of the strongest members of my executive committee, university president Shirley Ann Jackson and business leader Al Berkeley, agreed to serve with Jacobs as founding board members. Bonnie lined up an apartment for Mom in a brand-new senior residence near her in lower Manhattan. We sold our home in Bethesda and put down a deposit for one on the drawing board in the sought-after San Dieguito school district.

Fittingly, the last big council event on my watch took place at UC San Diego in March 2001. Porter presented the preliminary findings of his cluster study to a standing-room-only audience of civic leaders. I felt honored to introduce him. Afterward I let the staff know that I'd be leaving at the end of July, taking a month of leave to move before beginning my new assignment. At a lovely reception my colleagues presented me with a leather-bound volume of the work we had produced together—my proudest career achievement. The Yochelsons said good-bye to Washington and rolled the dice on a fresh start across the country.

18 STRESS

I felt upbeat as we got our bearings in San Diego. While Diane's gentle pressure had prompted our move, I breathed a sigh of relief to be out of the trench warfare of Washington politics with salary intact. The incoming George W. Bush administration preferred to work with true-blue Republicans. It would have been hard to distance myself from Clinton-Gore.

We relocated to a beautiful corner of the country. San Diego County stretched seventy miles north from the Mexican border. A population of three million spread out over ten cities and eighteen military installations. Three hundred sunny days a year attracted tourists and transplants alike. Many incoming professionals worked twenty miles north of downtown, where an expanding circle of research-based biotech and communications firms flourished. Diane picked a four-bedroom model in a residential development going up in nearby Camel Valley. We lived three miles from the ocean, with a choice view of the mountains to the east.

Building Engineering & Science Talent had a mission worth fighting for. The problems confronting women and people of color had a personal dimension not found at the ten-thousand-foot level of competitiveness. Everyone had a story, many of which gave me goose bumps. My founding board member Shirley Ann Jackson had attended segregated schools in DC and endured unbelievable slights as a freshman at MIT in the 1960s. She ate alone in the cafeteria and wasn't invited to join student study groups. Her advisor told her not to major in physics because "colored girls should learn a trade." Jackson became the first African American woman to earn a doctorate from MIT, doing so in theoretical elementary particle physics. Later she chaired the U.S. Nuclear Regulatory Commission, before taking the reins as president of Rensselaer Polytechnic Institute. BEST was going to help create the next generation of Shirley Ann Jacksons.

The shift into a new field excited me. Intellectually, I was about to hit diminishing returns at the Council on Competitiveness, just as I had at the State Department. It felt good to make another jump rather than stay in the same groove. I wasn't going to meet a Kissinger or a Volcker. U.S. public education was too decentralized for anyone to make that kind of mark. Federal resources accounted for less than 10 percent of the $600 billion K–12 enterprise in which states and localities played key roles. But education remained the nation's engine of upward mobility and workforce development. I wasn't trading down in this career change by any means.

Mom was in good hands. My sister, Bonnie, by now an established art historian, devoted increasing time to her before we left Washington. She reworked Mom's memoir on collecting Israeli art into *Golden Threads*, a lovely illustrated volume. She negotiated the donation of the collection and Mom's papers to Yeshiva University. Then, to free me, she took charge of packing, moving, and finding a place for Mom to live independently. The Hallmark residence adjacent to the World Trade Center offered full service for seniors. The seventh-floor view from Mom's cozy apartment looked out on the Statue of Liberty. She loved it.

The destruction of the Twin Towers on 9/11, a month after we arrived in San Diego, signaled that much would not turn out as planned. I saw the first tower fall on TV while walking on a treadmill before 6:00 a.m. Pacific Time. Rushing to the phone, I reached Bonnie a few minutes before the lines jammed. She and Paul and my two nieces, Emily and Anna, were okay. They walked across Brooklyn Bridge that night to stay with friends. The Hallmark staff evacuated Mom and all of the other residents to a facility in Yonkers. Bonnie smuggled Mom back through the barricades, taking her in for several months. The stench of burned wires still lingered when I visited in December.

The change of scene that Diane was counting on to make life better created a transportation nightmare for her. Our dream house lay outside the perimeter of school bus transportation. We couldn't find a carpool in the neighborhood. She ferried the girls to separate schools. The nearest shopping was three miles away. Before long she was logging forty thousand miles a year on the car. I hit fifty a day myself driving downtown, having ruled out any office location for BEST in affluent North County. Our cuddly new puppy, Rocky, didn't relieve the strain of car-bound living.

We failed to anticipate the impact of the move on Lisa and Laura. Lisa made friends easily with high-performing girls. Her desire to fit in sensitized her to the needs of others. Her social networking skills were off the chart long before Facebook appeared. Lisa got good grades, mainly on the strength of her remarkable memory, but she was easily distracted. My last-minute interventions to help her meet deadlines backfired, increasing her self-doubt rather than creating a bond. Perceptively, she recognized that she was caught in the middle between the stars and the problem students at competitive Torrey Pines High School.

Lisa felt slighted at home for not shining in school. She worried about keeping her weight down. I saw her defensiveness as aggression toward her sister and mother. It brought out the tough cop in me, a role I had played for years. A nasty flare-up at the end of her junior year prompted me to seek counseling at Diane's urging.

Laura had more confidence in her academic ability. She had a rare capacity to concentrate and brought home As in every subject. She had a particular flair for writing. Her artful kids' movie reviews appeared regularly in the *San Diego Union Tribune*, together with her photo. But Laura dropped out of team sports, pressing herself to the limit in cross-country and later triathlons. She withdrew socially, despite the many friends she had had in Maryland.

Diane and I didn't pick up the symptoms until Laura was caught in the full grip of anorexia nervosa. I watched helplessly as she punished herself, mistaking occasional remission for healing. Wrongly, I believed she would get better if she were in the right professional hands.

The minefield of diversity in science and engineering piled on the stress. No issue held a candle to the complexity or sensitivity of broadening the participation of historically underrepresented groups. Women and underrepresented minorities stood united on the touchiest question. They agreed that innate talent had nothing whatsoever to do with their small share of the U.S. science and engineering workforce. White and Asian American men weren't born smarter. There was plenty of room for debate, but genetics had no place in the conversation.

I saw Harvard president Lawrence Summers trip the explosives at a small conference on women in science in Cambridge. He didn't know his mostly female audience. A revered MIT life scientist whom he didn't seem to recognize, Nancy Hopkins, sat a few seats away from him on the outside of the hollow square table. She walked out when he suggested that lack of natural aptitude accounted in part for the low numbers of tenured female faculty at top-tier research universities. Summers's remarks hit the media a day or two later. He never recovered. The explosion cost him his position and possibly the chairmanship of the Federal Reserve years later.

Differences pulled the underrepresented in many directions. Affluent white girls and low-income minorities had little in common. African Americans, Hispanics, and Native Americans couldn't be lumped together. Women of color, balancing their gender and racial allegiances, belonged in a category all their own. The subtle dynamic within and between groups was easy to miss. A misstep invited a disparaging look or worse. The message was harsh: "You simply don't get it."

Fortunately, NSF sent Wanda Ward, one of its most able careerists, to get BEST off on the right foot. The foundation, headquartered in an eight-story high-rise in suburban Arlington, Virginia, had a congressionally mandated diversity mission. Its Education and Human Resources Directorate funded tens of millions of dollars in scholarships, fellowships, and educational research to broaden participation. Its Behavioral Sciences Division kept official tab of changes in science and engineering degree production. NSF director Colwell had coined the acronym STEM—science, technology, engineering, and mathematics—the shorthand that replaced the less-elegant-sounding SMET.

My senior advisor Ward had blazed a trail herself as the first African American admitted to a high society girls' school in Atlanta. She earned an undergraduate degree at Princeton and a doctorate in psychology at Stanford. A tall, strong woman with a resonant public voice and a low-key manner in private, she framed the work program with me. BEST would establish its bona fides by conducting a national search for effective programs from preschool into the workplace. Then BEST would translate its findings into grassroots action.

The incoming George W. Bush administration was especially interested in what worked. With strong credentials as a two-term governor of Texas, the new president made K–12 education his first order of business with Congress. He reached out to Democrats and negotiated the last significant bipartisan agreement in the domestic policy arena. The No Child Left Behind Act (NCLB) leveraged the relatively modest federal investment in K–12 education to the hilt, demanding system-wide accountability for the performance of all students.

NCLB set an unreachable goal, a mistake that politicians of every stripe seemed prone to make in education. Every student in American public schools was to perform at grade level in core subjects by 2014. States were to measure progress every year, breaking out results by gender, race, and disability. Schools failing to make sufficient yearly progress across all subgroups faced progressive sanctions, leading to school reorganization. The act targeted the same low-income minority students whom BEST was trying to reach.

Ward used her network to identify more than one hundred expert researchers and practitioners to find the country's most effective programs. I tapped my Council on Competitiveness contacts to ensure that high-tech employers were part of the mix. We assembled three blue-ribbon panels and designated a dozen project integrators with free rein to participate wherever they wished. I had much to learn from the extraordinary people who agreed to take part in the search for excellence.

Dan Arvizu, who chaired the workforce panel, had shined shoes in the store where his father worked on the Mexican border as a youngster. He got noticed in community college by Bell Laboratories, the research and development arm of AT&T known for its half dozen Nobel laureates. The support of Bell Labs made all the difference for him, leading to a Stanford doctorate in mechanical engineering and a rapid career rise afterward. Arvizu became the first Hispanic director of a national laboratory as well as chairman of the National Science Board. Every success like his involved a life-changing intervention.

Mary Catherine Swanson, a high school English teacher in San Diego, bucked the tide of changing demographics in the late 1970s. She devised an elective program, AVID, that challenged at-risk students to take advanced placement courses. AVID supplied study skills, motivation, and student tutors. The positive results stunned local educators, some of whom thought the AVID students must be cheating. Swanson developed a business model that eventually grew the program into a national force reaching seven hundred thousand students in forty-six states. It took the energy and tenacity of individuals like her to change the odds for low-income minority students.

Two graduates of historically black colleges and universities (HBCUs) provided an insight into the changing landscape of minority-serving institutions. Carl Person, a studious, low-key NASA program manager, welcomed his daughter doing premed at his alma mater, Clark Atlanta University. His fraternity brothers made her a part of their families. HBCUs offered a level of security and support that couldn't be matched. Yet Bill Washington, a hard-driving Lockheed Martin executive, confided that his engineering degree from a historically black institution hadn't prepared him to compete with graduates of big-time programs. That's why he went into business development. He encouraged his talented son to go to Georgia Tech, a school that became the nation's top producer of African American engineers forty years after desegregation.

The small team I formed to coordinate the national search got off to a bumpy start. The vice president who came on board, distracted by personal issues, did not work out. The workload overtook the single mom with young children I brought on for administrative support. But our versatile director of communications, Brenda Sullivan, proved to be a gem. She had DC experience and roots in Southern California. Her local contacts were as valuable as her skills. Sullivan and I made up the core team, along with a solid research associate, Rob Henderson, and an experienced executive assistant, Janice Medina.

Board members contributed decisively in the early going. NASDAQ president Al Berkeley engaged the Bush administration, which held strong views on program effectiveness. Only programs with scientific evidence made the cut to be eligible for federal support. Some in the research community found the administration's definition of scientific evidence gathering so strict that it could marginalize our search before we got started. Berkeley, who cochaired the K–12 panel, invited an NCLB insider, researcher Doug

Carnine, to the table. Carnine pushed the White House view, which had to be taken into account.

Shirley Ann Jackson gave national visibility to BEST's agenda. She saw a looming gap in the nation's science and engineering workforce. The country couldn't close it without developing the talent of women and minorities. This underrepresented majority comprised two-thirds of the total U.S. workforce but only one-quarter of the technical talent pool. Jackson came up with a powerful image, the Quiet Crisis, to frame an urgent challenge that never made headlines. Her gifted speechwriter worked with Ward and me to strengthen the case. BEST published "The Quiet Crisis" as its first monograph. Jackson would present the analysis to dozens of influential audiences, moving a peripheral issue into one of central concern.

Everything came together at a BEST briefing in the White House Conference Center in January 2003. NSF director Colwell invited the seven federal agencies that had provided seed funding to participate. Arvizu, Berkeley, Jackson, and other leaders presented well. The Defense Department, in particular, applauded our efforts. A reception on the Hill followed in which our congressional champions took turns at the microphone. Jackson responded to House Science Committee chairman Sherwood Boehlert, Republican congresswoman Connie Morella, and Democrat Eddie Bernice Johnson on behalf of BEST. She referred to me as an Energizer Bunny, a high compliment from someone who kept a replica on her desk. We were rolling forward.

Our momentum didn't last. I checked into the hospital for open-heart surgery in April 2003. The cardiologist had called after an annual treadmill test with news that my arteries weren't delivering enough blood. An angiogram verified that I had Yochelson genes. Quadruple bypass followed as soon as I had cleared my calendar. The procedure kept me in the hospital for a week and at home for six more. I asked the surgeon during a follow-up visit if he recalled anything special. He answered reassuringly that he'd done so many bypasses since mine that he would have to refer to his notes.

The operation drained my physical confidence. The incision running down the center of my chest ached. The pulling of our puppy hurt when I tried to take him around the block. The medical team, however, pushed me to resume activity. I started slowly on the trails near our house, increasing the length of my walks every day. As I bounced back, five-mile hikes became part of a routine that I have kept up ever since. The doctors counseled me to keep fifteen pounds off, improve my eating, exercise six days a week, and start taking yoga to relieve stress. I embraced these changes, becoming a regular at the Scripps Fitness Center after I finished my rehabilitation there.

Although the health scare sank in, I couldn't change BEST's commitments. We had to deliver our findings to the House Science Committee no later than mid-2004. Funds were running low. This wasn't the time to slow down.

Another cycle of success and setback followed. BEST met its search deadline. We produced three quality reports that grounded me on the issues and gave credibility to the initiative. The handsomely presented analysis, filled with data and footnotes, took its place in the literature on STEM diversity.

The hotly debated quest for pre-K–12 exemplars took the most effort. A panel meeting in San Diego featuring college-bound at-risk students broke a long deadlock over research criteria to rate programs. Hearing from a Mexican American youngster heading to MIT spurred the experts to closure. Only seven out of two hundred nominated programs had sufficient research evidence to earn individual write-ups. The thin pickings confirmed that the country was spending billions of dollars on math and science education without a sufficient knowledge base.

The BEST pre-K–12 report, "What It Takes," distilled the common features of the seven rated programs. Linda Rosen, the savvy former mathematics counselor to the secretary of education, suggested the apt term *design principles*. Rosen and Carlos Rodriguez, a first-rate program evaluator at the highly regarded American Institutes for Research, teamed up with me to flesh out the principles. Putting them in perspective, we flagged the gap between program-level and system-wide STEM gains. Many educational reformers geared their thinking to entire student populations. They favored lifting all boats in whole districts to boost the underrepresented in STEM. In contrast, the BEST exemplars targeted specific groups. Such programs rarely reached enough students to bend the overall curve. The country needed both approaches to work.

The blue-ribbon panel on higher education reached consensus with relative ease. Diversity challenges arose every step of the way, from admission through graduate degree completion. The most serious was undergraduate attrition in science and engineering, an accepted part of the higher education culture that hit women and underrepresented minorities hardest. The panelists knew where documented progress was being made.

The exemplars profiled in their report, "A Bridge for All," fell far short of system-wide solutions. Most owed their success to charismatic leaders. Freeman Hrabowski, the dynamic president of the University of Maryland–Baltimore County, fit the mold. The Meyerhoff program he pioneered prepared underrepresented minorities—mostly African American males—for some of the nation's most selective medical schools and graduate science programs. The first words out of his mouth when we sat down in his office were "Our goal is to graduate the first African American Nobel laureate." Higher education celebrated Hrabowski for his one-of-a-kind achievement. NSF would spend millions trying to replicate his success at other research-intensive universities.

The workforce panel reinforced lessons learned at the Council on Competitiveness. U.S. multinationals looked at diversity in global rather than national terms. Their growing reliance on foreign-born and international workers made my friend Rodriguez and others seethe. Many of the same companies that lobbied for H-1B visas, however, were also allies. They had every interest in building innovation capacity at home, maintaining political support for U.S. R&D, and fielding a workforce that looked like their American customer base. Corporate recruiters often applied more pressure on universities than the federal government to diversify their applicant pool. The workforce report, "The Talent Imperative," highlighted the risks of inaction and defined best practices.

According to plan, the end of the search was supposed to lead to several years of community-based action. BEST had the intellectual capital and know-how to create full STEM development pathways. I foresaw a half dozen metro areas working in parallel from elementary school through career entry. Together they would point the way to success for all. BEST would coordinate the initiative. Large foundations would provide financial support; after all, they were already invested in local education. How could they say no to capitalizing on the NSF-funded assets that were in place?

I began knocking on foundation doors early, concentrating on those with major education programs. I had good personal contacts at Carnegie, Ford, Gates, and Kellogg. Calling on senior people in their main offices, I brought a concept paper and a long list of candidate metro areas recommended by a working group of community engagement specialists. The more leeway foundations had to select locales, the better.

My business model for sustaining BEST through foundation funding fell apart in the fall of 2003. Every prospect came back with the same answer. This is a wonderful idea, but professionally managed foundations have very little discretionary money. The question isn't about what BEST wants to do. It's about whether your proposal gibes with our commitments. We aren't doing anything in the field of STEM education at this time.

The rejections reminded me forcefully how far removed the cause of educational equity was from my earlier nonprofit work. I had the backing of the establishment at CSIS and the Council on Competitiveness. Money followed power, stacking the deck in my favor when I raised funds. Now the tables were turned, regardless of my Rolodex or proposal-writing skill. The underrepresented had numbers but lacked influence. Their long journey to an advanced degree in science or engineering made it very difficult to build a compelling near-term business case. NSF provided long-term support, but much of the rest was episodic.

The norm for all of the organizations in the STEM diversity space was getting by on a shoestring. A few business models were viable. Awards ceremonies, job fairs, and student groups produced sponsorship revenues. Professional societies generated dues income. Corporate donors founded a national action council to distribute scholarships. The enterprising Hispanic engineering awards conference HENAAC formed an educational arm, Great Minds in STEM, which delivered effective bilingual activities to its supporters. But the passionate advocates who filled the diversity community all operated close to the edge.

I had to scramble like everyone else. There was a chance BEST could fold before we had even delivered our reports to Congress. We had intellectual capital and an expert network of high quality. It was time to stop chasing the vision of community engagement and start looking for business wherever we could find it.

A happenstance dinner table conversation led to our first assignment. A board member, San Diego Community College chancellor Augie Gallego, invited me to attend a national forum of university presidents and corporate leaders. There I sat next to the chief of naval research, Rear Admiral Jay Cohen, who quizzed me on workforce diversity. As we talked, he was surprised to learn that universities in Puerto Rico were leading suppliers of Hispanic engineers. "You sound like an expert," he said, "and my office needs an expert review of the STEM education programs we fund. Send me a proposal."

The wheels of the navy bureaucracy turned too slowly. BEST needed a cash infusion before the contract for the Office of Naval Research started in the spring of 2004. I asked for help from a Kissinger councillor who had also joined the Council on Competitiveness. He turned me down flat over breakfast in the cafeteria of his Los Angeles–based insurance company. Who was I kidding if I thought I could maintain a DC salary working in the field of education? Only the superintendents of large school districts in the country made that kind of money. His lecture made me as angry as the freshman year advisor who had stuck it to me at Yale. We never spoke again.

The Hewlett Foundation in Silicon Valley threw me a lifeline. Marshall Smith, director of its education program and former deputy secretary of education, served on the K–12 panel. A former navy officer with heart issues like mine, he found $100,000 in end-of-year funds. My CSIS mentor Abshire, who chaired the smaller Richard Lounsbery Foundation, came through with an additional $60,000 in bridge funding.

One six-month job led to another. The U.S. Army, impressed with BEST's work for the navy, requested an independent look at its education outreach program. The community-based San Diego Foundation commissioned a study of effective STEM programs in the local area. That "what works" guide attracted the attention of the Ewing Marion Kauffman Foundation, which asked for a map of the STEM assets of the state of Missouri for a governor's summit. Kauffman, headquartered in Kansas City, then tasked BEST with providing similar analysis for the Kansas legislature.

These short-term projects paid off. The work for the military services helped solidify the Department of Defense as a future champion. The

San Diego assignment introduced BEST to our home county of forty-two school districts. Local philanthropists took note of multiple options that the BEST guide highlighted as ways to improve STEM education during the school day, after school, and through the teacher corps. The Missouri and Kansas reports demonstrated the value of our national expertise to state leaders. To my surprise, the midwesterners trusted outsiders to be more objective than in-state specialists who might have an ax to grind.

The BEST board backed my change of course. Berkeley and Jackson departed after the release of the reports to Congress, leaving San Diegans Jacobs, Gallego, and newly appointed UC San Diego chancellor Marye Anne Fox. Anne Petersen, a former deputy director of the NSF, rounded out my leadership. I didn't ask any of them for financial support. This was my challenge.

BEST reinvented itself as a virtual organization as I pieced projects together. Sullivan suggested working from home as a consultant, given that communications needs were limited. My executive assistant abruptly took a more secure full-time job. I ended up the sole employee, bringing on consultants as needed to accomplish the work at hand. BEST moved from its high-rent downtown offices to a one-desk sublet. The cash crunch forced me to skip every other paycheck for months at a time, but finances worked out at the end of every year.

I didn't tell Mom about the rough going. Her relocation to New York was going too well to spoil. I made sure to stay with her at the Hallmark three times a year in my crisscrossed travel. I loved seeing how much she enjoyed life thanks to the day-in and day-out support of my sister. She loved to reminisce. We walked in Battery Park. She introduced me to her cronies in the dining room. The staff treated her well. I never saw anyone age as gracefully as Mom did.

Diane bore the full brunt of BEST's struggles. They compounded the hardships that she felt at home. She blamed herself for everything that went wrong, even though much of it lay beyond her control. Laura's sickness, my blowups with Lisa, and the departure of her only close friend from San Diego left her running on empty. I saw how much she missed the support system she had left back East.

Diane sounded me out in the spring of 2007 about using part of her inheritance to buy a condominium in Bethesda. Laura was about to graduate high school. Lisa was finishing her sophomore year at the University of Redlands, a small liberal arts school east of Los Angeles, where she was doing well. Diane wasn't asking me to go back. She needed to get out of a place that was bringing her down. She wasn't sure how much time she would spend in San Diego, but I was building a solid relationship with the Office of the Secretary of Defense that looked as if it could bring me to DC frequently.

I supported Diane's decision but stayed resolute on keeping BEST afloat from its San Diego base. For me recovery from heart surgery and the survival of the nonprofit were intertwined. My cardiologist and beach walks went together with my colleagues and board. As concerned as I was about Diane and both girls, I couldn't write off the move to Southern California as a complete failure. Part of me felt proud of having overcome more than my fair share of adversity. The trials and tribulations attached me to San Diego. I still had a lot to prove and contribute. My definition of failure was a full-time return to Washington with my tail between my legs.

It was a turning point moment. My first marriage had dissolved over geography. Never would I have expected a similar issue to arise thirty-five years later and with a lot more at stake. I thought about family, trying to imagine what Mom might have said. She had died with a full heart at the age of ninety-nine in February 2006, a few weeks after a fall. She had outlived all of her friends in Washington. Diane arranged for our rabbi to conduct a graveside funeral. Bonnie hosted a memorial service a few weeks later in New York, where dozens of her friends who knew Mom paid respects. If Mom knew where things stood, she would have told me to put myself first. In life, like Diane, she never did that.

We sold the house with a view in Carmel Valley near the top of California's sizzling real estate market in August 2007. In its place we bought a three-bedroom, centrally located townhouse, where I created a home office. Laura decided to pass up Berkeley for American University in DC, the right choice as far as all of us were concerned. Lisa prepared for her junior year as an international business major at Redlands, looking forward to a semester abroad. The Yochelsons were going bicoastal.

19 COAST TO COAST

I should have seen that the road to viability for BEST led back to Washington. Perhaps the irony had caused me to overlook the logic. When NSF passed the hat to get us off the ground, the federal agencies that employed thousands of scientists and engineers were quick to do their part. NASA, the Department of Energy, and DoD only hired U.S. citizens with security clearances. They had jobs to fill and concerns about their future workforce.

An early signal of DoD interest came when my board first briefed federal officials in 2003. A tall, scholarly African American stood up when Shirley Ann Jackson left the podium. Visibly moved, he wanted everyone in the room to hear what he had to say. In a voice just as commanding as hers, he announced, "I'm John Hopps, deputy undersecretary of defense for basic research. We believe in the mission of BEST. The department is going to support this organization."

I followed up on my next trip to DC. Hopps suggested a late dinner at McCormick & Schmick's on K Street. He worked long hours during the week because he was commuting home to Atlanta on the weekends. He had served there as provost of his alma mater, Morehouse College, the highly regarded all-male HBCU. He had sterling credentials—a PhD degree in physics from Brandeis, research at MIT, a faculty position at Ohio State, and program management at NSF. His former student, astronaut Ron Sega, had brought him out of retirement to take a political appointment overseeing the DoD R&D enterprise.

The gentlemanly Hopps wanted to make DoD a force in the world of education. Defense was deemed to be a mission agency with a large stake in the supply of talent but no seat at the table on matters of policy. A few months at the Pentagon, however, had convinced Hopps that the department had much-needed assets to deploy in schools. DoD employed more scientists and engineers than any other federal agency. Forty thousand of them worked in its research laboratories across the country. They could make America's science teachers much more effective by working with them to deliver classroom lessons that lit the spark.

Hopps had a particular program in mind, one he knew from NSF. Materials World Modules, or MWM, immersed middle and high school students in the study of everyday materials. They explored the properties of each by doing a hands-on activity—mixing concrete, creating composites, and testing polymers. Then they worked on designing a new feature. The developer, Professor Robert Chang of Northwestern University, had reams of positive research data showing that students from all backgrounds benefited. He never succeeded, however, in ramping up his boutique program. The DoD delivery system was going to take care of that. Hopps had the ear of higher-ups. He said that the support of BEST would be invaluable in taking MWM national once DoD secured a congressional mandate.

Hopps had me sit down with his special assistant, who lived up to his billing as bright, capable, and strategic. Tim McClees, a tall, broad-shouldered former lacrosse player in his midthirties, had a military background and a passion for technology. He explained why education was a difficult sell inside DoD. The mission statement of the department made no mention of the word. Skeptics always trotted out the same argument. DoD should stick to war fighting and let the U.S. Department of Education do its job.

Nevertheless, Hopps and his superiors wanted to resurrect the National Defense Education Act of 1958, through which DoD had galvanized the U.S. response to Sputnik. The nation faced a comparable science and engineering challenge almost a half century later. Student achievement and interest in STEM were declining. Gaps in critical skills were opening up. The National Academy of Sciences described the state of U.S. STEM education as a "gathering storm."

Hopps died of a heart attack before Congress decided what role DoD would play in STEM education. I heard the shock in McClees's hushed voice when he called on a Sunday afternoon from Atlanta to alert me. His father-son relationship with Hopps was closer than mine with Abshire. A full auditorium attended the memorial service in the Pentagon's Hall of Heroes.

Congress pared down the DoD request from a stand-alone act to a five-year, $1 million a year National Defense Education Program—NDEP for short. Most of the resources went into postsecondary scholarships and research grants for junior faculty. Still, DoD received a funding line for K–12 education that was slated to grow to $20 million annually. The Office of the Secretary of Defense would be able to demonstrate the value of MWM.

Keeping Hopps's promise, McClees secured $500,000 to support BEST. We were charged with laying groundwork for the launch of the K–12 program in 2007. We worked with a satellite office of the Pentagon in Arlington, Virginia, and a program manager at the army's Picatinny Arsenal in New Jersey. This was how the DoD did business. Political appointees and senior career executives fought the battle for funding. Then they delegated implementation.

BEST was going to be a contractor in the middle of the food chain, notwithstanding Hopps's interest in using our national network. DoD employed the equivalent of seven hundred thousand full-time contractors, almost as many as the number of civilians who worked for the department. A strong culture of hierarchy prevailed. Political appointees attempting to make their mark set policy direction. Careerists playing it safe ran the vast support machine that never stopped. Contractors trying to stay on the payroll made up a large share of the worker bees.

BEST made do. I told myself that public service didn't have to be limited to high policy. We followed the same rules as every other service provider, taking direction from tenured federal employees. We offered support, not advice. Twenty-five years of casual name-dropping stopped. The influence game was over. BEST couldn't make a difference on the front lines of STEM outreach unless we accepted the working-level realities of the largest federal agency.

We got off to a strong start. The Pentagon point man in charge of implementing the K–12 program needed help. With the Department of Education looking over his shoulder, he worried about investing in MWM without independent research evidence. He had funding for a summer institute at two-year Garrett College in western Maryland, but he didn't have an evaluation plan.

I lined up a qualified researcher to join forces with the hardworking educators, Nancy and Steve Prislac, who ran the institute. They selected a demographic cross-section of eighty students from across the state for the four-week residential course. Every student that completed the program got a stipend. Only one dropped out. The responsibility of looking after the youngsters twenty-four hours a day was immense. Two nurses were hired to dispense prescription drugs.

The evaluation compared students who took MWM with a similar group who didn't. The two didn't realize until the last few days which was "treatment" and which was "control." While all students made gains, those of the treatment group were significantly greater. Top-notch filmmakers captured highlights. DoD ended the summer with evidence of effectiveness and a lively visual record. We laid the foundation to pilot MWM in Maryland and roll it out in nine states.

Then a change of leadership prompted a wholesale shake-up. William Rees, a new deputy undersecretary for research, reeled management back to headquarters, moved away from MWM, and rewrote the scale-up plan. He wanted to run the program himself instead of delegating its management to the army. He also didn't want to put all of DoD's eggs into the MWM basket. He gave labs in the field the discretion to offer other hands-on activities. A menu of options supported by DoD scientists and engineers would be disseminated in twenty states by 2010. The new appointee was cleaning house and putting his own stamp on things. BEST looked vulnerable.

I learned Contractor Survival 101. Taking a risk, I jumped the chain of command and got a meeting with the new boss through my contacts at the Council on Competitiveness. Sullivan and our filmmakers followed up with a winning communications proposal. They suggested a collection of short videos on DoD research for weekly online distribution. It would be called "LabTV," a digital age version of the *Weekly Reader* that sparked our top man's early interest in chemistry. He directed the filming of thirty webisodes for release during the 2008–9 school year. BEST got a new lease on life.

The program that emerged resembled a hub and spokes. The Pentagon served as the hub, deciding how resources would be distributed and funding a website, LabTV, training, evaluation, and partnerships. Laboratories used their allocations of about $250,000 to reach out to students and teachers in their communities. The hub created a DoD brand, while the spokes adapted their activities to local needs.

The hub and spoke structure fit my coast-to-coast shuttle exactly. Once Diane moved back to Maryland in mid-2007, I alternated three-week chunks of time between home offices in Bethesda and San Diego. One was a metro ride away from the Pentagon and the other a twenty-minute drive from the large navy lab on Point Loma.

It didn't take long to find a rhythm with my family on one side of the country, BEST's team on the other, and customers in both places. I spent holidays in the East. Bonnie came out West to visit once a year. San Diego afforded time for reflection, writing, and my own Jewish renewal. Bethesda kept the family together and kept me in the loop for work. The art of compromise led me to exercise at two gyms, become active in two Reform congregations, and balance beach walks with dog walks. What a difference a laptop and a Southwest nonstop made.

BEST set up the communications infrastructure that gave NDEP an identity. Sullivan coordinated the development of a sharp-looking website. She subcontracted LabTV to Vanderpool Films, which hit the mark by putting a warm, content-rich face on DoD research. The filmmakers won the confidence of labs everywhere they shot. Army, navy, and air force sites lined up to show off their cool projects. Videos on topics like tracking the flu, repairing the Hubble telescope, and printing skin went viral as soon as we started low-key Internet promotion.

Headquarters also funded partnerships with several nationally recognized nonprofits through our grant. One put me back in touch with Dean Kamen, a former member of the Council on Competitiveness. He used to annoy me to no end by soliciting members at council meetings to support his robotics competition FIRST. Now I saw the full measure of Kamen's contribution—a network of sponsors and volunteers who celebrated teamwork and hands-on problem solving for more than 150,000 kids across the country.

Another partner, the much-praised middle school math program MATH-COUNTS, opened my eyes to the brainpower of the Asian American youngsters who walked off with top prizes year after year. Its executive director,

Lou DiGioia, worked with DoD to widen the circle of students engaged in after-school math by ramping up a less competitive club program and creating a video challenge.

BEST supported a research experience at MIT for gifted and talented high school students, the Research Summer Institute, founded by the legendary father of the U.S. nuclear submarine, Admiral Hyman Rickover. Rickover's one-time assistant Joann DiGennaro built the program into a national treasure. She invited me to graduation every year, where I shared pizza with young DoD scholars and saw how they bonded with other teens in the STEM stratosphere.

I quickly became attached to all three partnerships as well as Los Angeles–based HENAAC, the Hispanic engineers group. Each of these nonprofits was going against the grain of popular culture to develop talent. Their leaders worked relentlessly. I understood why when I saw the high-fives of competing robotics teams, the glow of proud parents at MATHCOUNTS, the knock-out research talks made at MIT, and the joyful faces of Latino winners at the annual HENAAC awards conference.

The capable navy engineer who managed NDEP for three years, Bob McGahern, ran with the chance to build a program. His fifteen years of lab experience were a vital asset. As funding flowed to the field, he formed a community of local DoD STEM coordinators. His Irish wit and infectious enthusiasm held the group together on monthly phone calls. McGahern leaned heavily on BEST as a source of advice as well as a funding channel. A three-year competitively awarded grant made our virtual team, with its single-digit overhead, one of the smallest prime contractors at DoD.

The navy lab in San Diego viewed BEST in a different context. Perched on prime real estate that jutted into San Diego Bay, the large systems center had no history of community engagement around K–12 education. Its mostly civilian workforce of 2,500 scientists and engineers supported navy communications and ocean surveillance. They competed for projects like a consulting firm, working in the same world-within-a-world that I remembered from army days. Only NDEP funding made it possible for a senior researcher to dedicate full-time hours to get a STEM outreach program going.

Jim Rohr, a laid-back expert in hydrodynamics, drew the start-up assignment. He had a passion for developing talent and a rare knack for getting along with people. His PhD degree in engineering physics didn't hurt either. Still, the self-effacing Rohr had to win the backing of his leadership, recruit volunteers, partner with schools, and allocate his limited resources in a county of five hundred thousand students. In his eyes I was the STEM education guru who introduced him to many of the right local players. He seldom made a move without BEST's input.

My tale of two cities told a story of churn at the Pentagon and change in San Diego. Despite its promising launch, NDEP came apart piece by piece in the DC pressure cooker. McGahern, the energetic program manager, was moved out in the spring of 2010. Centralized summer training for DoD STEM professionals and teachers at Garrett College ended. LabTV filming and promotion stopped. The updating of the website ceased. Program evaluation was suspended. The annual conference of site coordinators was discontinued. Monthly conference calls tapered off, before being dropped altogether.

BEST hung on. Before leaving, McGahern had agreed with the army on renewed contractor support as our grant expired. The Picatinny Arsenal made a follow-on, five-year award to us with a broad statement of work, a year of DoD baseline funding, and a high ceiling of $24.5 million. McGahern's highly qualified successor, Kim Day, worked as closely as she could with us on a short leash. A career science and math teacher, she was not replaced after she returned to the DoD school system in late summer 2011.

The end of active management at the hub decentralized the K–12 program. The Office of the Secretary of Defense still owned it, but most funding went straight to individual labs. The White House zeroed out K–12 funding in its 2014 budget in a move to consolidate STEM education programs across the federal government. Even if Congress restored funds, the department would have to remake the case for its K–12 commitment. The wheel had turned full circle since the heady days when DoD was going to lead the federal government by example with MWM.

Meanwhile, STEM outreach in San Diego gained momentum. Hundreds of navy scientists and engineers got involved working with teachers, coaching teams, and mentoring students. Carmela Keeney, the ranking civilian engineer at the systems center, made participation in outreach a factor in the performance ratings of new hires. She and the base commander handed out awards to ninety-nine scientists and engineers for robotics activities alone. A bilingual Science Night series and introduction to engineering for girls sprang up. As the culture of community engagement took hold, volunteer hours topped 7,500—the equivalent of seven full-time teachers' yearlong engagement.

Other labs created their own variations of local success. The Naval Surface Warfare Center at Carderock, a few miles from our Bethesda townhouse, trained a group of middle school teachers in an underwater robotics program, SeaPerch, which the navy developed with MIT. Strong content and the availability of DoD support during the school year led the surrounding Montgomery County school system to adopt SeaPerch in its curriculum. Not stopping there, Carderock engineers designed a follow-on underwater glider activity for high schoolers.

For its part the Picatinny Arsenal viewed itself as more than an implementer of STEM programs developed elsewhere. While coaching dozens of FIRST robotics teams, Picatinny engineers also created their own low-cost, do-it-yourself robot with a unique simulation component. In addition, they took the lead in introducing 3-D printers to teachers in northern New Jersey. Ed Petersen, the experienced educator who directed the STEM Office at Picatinny, summed up his lab's approach: "An R&D center should never stand pat when it comes to getting teachers and kids engaged."

A new opportunity for BEST opened up as community-based outreach caught on. Labs needed third-party help to pay for materials, transportation, training, and teacher stipends. My crack financial team, led by advisor Diane Peluso, created a clearinghouse for six army labs and ten navy labs. Each kept part of its NDEP funding on account with BEST. Stephanie Martin Peluso, our bookkeeper, kept track of orders and filled them with precision. We processed $6 million in local program support, feeling the love as notes of appreciation flowed in. BEST was helping DoD establish itself as the powerful grassroots force that Hopps had predicted it could be.

We remained closest to the systems center in San Diego. The stable leadership there, removed from the hectic pace of DC, knew what success meant: creating local awareness, recruiting DoD volunteers, and widening the pathway for historically underrepresented groups into the lab. Jim Rohr reminded me that Hispanics accounted for almost half of K–12 enrollment in San Diego County and less that 5 percent of the systems center workforce.

Rohr had the personality and skills to move his agenda. His modesty wore well. Despite the doctorate, he presented himself as an amateur educator who loved engineering and wanted to help. He saw early on that undergraduate STEM majors were more effective communicators than middle-aged navy civilians. An undergraduate support team tapped that resource. He favored rich learning experiences over one-time events. The goal was to find candidates for internships, especially from underserved populations. UC San Diego named Rohr its alumnus of the year for public service in 2013. He put on a suit for the first time in years for the occasion.

The most poignant setbacks and successes of San Diego outreach had a personal edge. The systems center had to rescind a full-time offer to a Latina, the first in her family to go to college, who proved herself as an intern and worked her way through the undergraduate engineering program at Cal Poly. Even with the technical director of the lab on her side, her grade point average had fallen a fraction below the navy's 3.5 minimum. On the other hand, a disadvantaged high school junior did so well at the lab that she worked there part-time through community college, won a navy summer internship, and transferred to the UC San Diego electrical engineering program.

To my chagrin personal stories never found their way into the briefing slides that went up the chain of command. Headquarters wanted data, not anecdotes. The Pentagon's loss of touch with the field extended to areas with far higher stakes than mine. In his 2014 memoir, *Duty*, Secretary of Defense Robert Gates recounts his off-the-charts frustration with the inability to get life-protecting troop carriers to the front lines of Iraq and Afghanistan. Every hour of delay exposed soldiers to lethal explosive devices. The system couldn't register and respond to heartrending losses of life and limb. Gates experienced them whenever he met a wounded warrior or signed a letter of condolence to a grieving family (which he did every night). Angrily, he declared war on the bureaucracy that reported to him.

The personal dimension riveted me too. Rohr and his talented codirector, Chris Deckard, were trying to reach as many high-potential students as possible. Operating outside the K–12 system, they knew they couldn't lift all boats. Ten years of experience had put me squarely in their camp. With regret I doubted that a grand strategy of school reform would ever succeed. But going all out for a limited number of underserved students was a fallback to believe in. Kids grew up to become scientists and engineers one at a time. Every outcome mattered.

The San Diego educator whom I respected most, Paula Cordeiro, wasn't ready to give up on large-scale reform. As dean of SOLES, the School of Leadership and Education Sciences at the University of San Diego, she dedicated herself to strengthening the system. The dynamo with the soft brown eyes put SOLES on the map as a nationally ranked developer of K–12 leaders in less than a decade—a feather in the cap of a midsized Catholic institution.

Cordeiro offered me an office in Mother Rosalie Hill Hall, SOLES's state-of-the-art new building, when BEST's future was up in the air. Strictly speaking, I didn't need to keep current on teacher preparation, education policy, and technology in the classroom to execute the DoD grant. The department was interested in the output of the K–12 enterprise, not its inner workings. I, however, didn't want to remain stuck in place. SOLES gave me a chance to deepen my knowledge base and tap into ground truth outside Washington. I rarely used my office but joined the dean's advisory board and came to campus regularly.

What I saw reminded me of CSIS. Just as Abshire's think tank enriched government policy makers, SOLES expanded the horizons of superintendents and principals. Up-and-coming administrators flocked to the pioneering leadership development academy that Cordeiro had founded in 2000. There they found the research insights, know-how, and contacts that they couldn't get in their consuming day jobs. The power of a growing countywide network of school leaders strengthened every facet of SOLES—its degree programs, research, interdisciplinary centers, and technical assistance to school districts.

Cordeiro needed a second act. In education that meant an endowment to support a world-class program or researcher. After putting my head together with two thoughtful members of the advisory board, Todd Gutschow and Peter Sibley, I suggested a mobile technology initiative. The chairman of BEST's board, Irwin Jacobs, cared a great deal about that fast-growing area. He had called my attention to an innovative pilot program in North Carolina, Project K-Nect, which used smartphones with Internet safeguards and imaginative curriculum for Algebra I. The first cohort of eighty high school freshmen liked mobile math so much that they kept their specially programmed phones for geometry. Many of them kept going all the way up to advanced placement statistics. Jacobs and his wife, who supported the extension of the Qualcomm-funded project, wanted to continue pushing the envelope. Perhaps SOLES could help.

Cordeiro liked my thinking. Jacobs had an unmatched reputation for integrity. The school of engineering at UC San Diego carried his family name. A gift to the University of San Diego from Joan and Irwin Jacobs would take SOLES to the next level. I had no reservations about providing advice. I believed in Cordeiro and was not asking for BEST.

Jacobs accepted an invitation to explain smartphone math to a small group of superintendents and SOLES faculty. He followed up by taking a delegation of ten on his private jet to the Project K-Nect site in Onslow County, North Carolina. Eyes opened wide as the San Diegans saw what happens when you travel—even for a one-day visit—with a benefactor. The state and district superintendents welcomed the group at dinner. They applauded K-Nect and its director, Shawn Gross, for the gains that had been made in only a few years. We observed students using their smartphones in small groups in a classroom setting. Then we interviewed them along with teachers and administrators. The delegation returned bleary and enthusiastic.

Cordeiro invited me to assist her with an endowment proposal. She envisaged a cutting-edge research center under the SOLES umbrella. I drove with her to Jacobs's home for support when she presented the blueprint in person. She made her case with the right blend of conviction, deference, and warmth. SOLES received eighteen months of operating funds to show what it could do. The start-up phase, led by Scott Himelstein, a canny former acting secretary of education for California, scored early successes. Jacobs himself suggested the next step. In the spring of 2013 I looked on as cameras rolled and he pledged $3 million toward the SOLES Mobile Technology Learning Center. It felt great making a difference.

DC didn't offer rewards like this. A contractor's opportunity to add value hinged on the government sponsor. Our program manager held BEST at arm's length as the DoD K–12 program wound down. We submitted weekly reports and followed orders.

A change in leadership, however, brightened the outlook for BEST. A talented new political appointee, Reginald Brothers, won approval and secured funding to launch a three-year campaign to advance STEM diversity at the department. The campaign took us back to our founding mission. The support team included my pal Rodriguez, who knew the issue as well as anyone in the country. We added a resourceful executive coordinator, Karen Harper, to the full-time team. Her energy and people skills made for a perfect fit. My new colleague was a force of nature in the best sense. I struggled to keep up with her. She brought spark to BEST as our vice president.

As the DoD effort took shape, I caught up on the latest attempts to move the needle nationally. The Obama White House backed STEM mobilization to the hilt. Business leaders responded by forming a nonprofit, Change the Equation, to align the philanthropy of one hundred major companies. CEO Linda Rosen, my close colleague from the early days of BEST, skillfully campaigned for investment in a limited number of programs with hard evidence of effectiveness.

Entrepreneur Larry Bock, a San Diegan, brought hometown enthusiasm for STEM to DC with a USA Science and Engineering Festival. These events, showcasing hundreds of exhibits and dozens of eminent speakers, filled the Washington Convention Center with children, parents, and teachers every two years.

The National Governors' Association brokered a voluntary agreement among forty-five states to mesh math, science, and language arts under a strong set of common core standards. Predictably, this high-potential reform hit the partisan political divide as soon as the Obama administration embraced it.

These separate initiatives revealed the heart of the challenge at the national level. There was no commander in chief for education. The slow unraveling of Bush's No Child Left Behind initiative highlighted the limits of top-down reform. States had the last word in deciding what students learned and measuring their achievement. Fifteen thousand local school boards had the final say on hiring the superintendents who ran local school systems.

The piecemeal alternative came at the price of coherence. There were too many moving parts to manage. STEM advocates worked on their piece of the puzzle based on their own interests, resources, and views. Washington provided a less robust platform for overall leadership than many people realized.

While it helped professionally to spend half-time on the East Coast, the real pull was personal. My top priority was Diane, who had left San Diego at her lowest point ever. She didn't make her move back a family project, paying for and furnishing a compact two-bedroom condominium without dipping into our joint savings. This was the first statement of personal need she had ever made. Her choice, a high-rise in North Bethesda across the street from a metro stop and Rock Creek Park, was just right.

It took longer than expected for Diane to attend to herself. Laura's struggle with anorexia wasn't over. Our daughter dropped below ninety pounds near the end of her first semester at American University, scaring the daylights out of everyone. She never returned to the dorms, taking a year off and living at home the rest of the way.

Diane began to retool professionally as Laura inched toward recovery. She wanted to build a small business on her own. Her choice was professional coaching. Coaches were catalysts, not therapists, who practiced with a certificate credential. She enjoyed the training and liked her colleagues but found it difficult to attract more than a handful of clients.

The quiet determination that I hadn't seen for a long time came back. Diane invested in herself, learned new marketing skills, and networked like crazy. She decided to specialize in business coaching to take advantage of her own accomplishments in real estate. Before I knew it, my wife was a new members' ambassador at the DC Chamber of Commerce and president of a toastmaster's club. She spoke naturally and with great poise in a feature interview on local cable television. Diane would not have been able to regain such confidence in San Diego.

We bought a larger place in downtown Bethesda in the fall of 2010. I pushed for closure on a three-bedroom townhouse a block away from the metro. The location introduced us to urban-suburban life. A good library, gyms, restaurants, and the bike trail to Georgetown were blocks away. Friends parked in a visitor's slot, and we took off on foot. I especially looked forward to long weekend walks with Tyson Tuchscherer, an award-winning teacher who brought a wealth of classroom experience to navy outreach. We talked kids, DoD politics, and foreign travel. I called him my "Half-Marathon Man."

Lisa moved in with us before long. She and I got closer during her last two years of college. We spent ten memorable days together during her semester abroad in Nantes, France. She joined me for occasional weekends in Los Angeles. I was flattered that she arranged for me to speak to her business fraternity and capstone international business class. She graduated Redlands with many friends and warm memories. The photo of her dazzling smile at commencement was one my favorites.

Hard knocks followed. Lisa tried the DC job market, which looked stronger than California. She landed three administrative positions, none of which lasted more than six months. She was devastated. Her friends helped her through hard times. Her determination finally paid off at Sixth and I, a restored synagogue with a citywide following for great evening programming for young professionals. She moved up from volunteer to full-time cultural associate, managing several events a week with frequent celebrity speakers. I saw her set the stage for Nobel laureate Daniel Kahneman so beautifully that eight hundred guests clapped for her introduction to the introduction. She overcame such a rough start. I couldn't be prouder.

Laura faced life-threatening adversity that twice led her to the brink of hospitalization. The searing experience turned her inward. She studied health when she returned to school. The questions she asked were big and, unlike the ones I had asked in college, very personal. Why did this happen? How can I stop it from happening again? What can others learn from my story?

Little by little, as she realized that eating disorders were about much more than eating, Laura regained weight. She graduated with highest honors and a book manuscript. Balboa Press published *Sick* in November 2012. The brutally honest account made for painful reading. Laura didn't believe in feel-good endings. She doubted the value of outside help. She used creative writing, instead, to help herself.

228

Laura's journey brought her from the townhouse in DC to the townhouse in San Diego in the fall of 2013. She took a course in a healing exercise system catching on around the world. She was finishing a second book. She revisited the places that hurt in order to put the pain behind her. We walked through the surf in solitude for miles every day, feeling the tide come in and go out as the sun set over the ocean. We looked east to the mountains. "I like it here, Dad," she said. "I might come back to recapture everything I missed growing up."

20 SHIFTING GROUND

I thought about my public service journey during the long walks with Laura. The vivid expression of a great French historian, Pierre Renouvin, gave me perspective. I had devoured his classic account of European diplomatic history as a nineteen-year-old in Paris. He put little emphasis on the role of individuals. The drivers that really mattered were economics, demographics, and technology. Renouvin referred to them as "les forces profondes"—the deep forces.

No doubt a handful of people made a huge difference in my life. Things would have turned out differently if I hadn't taken Brombert's course at Yale, if Monnet hadn't needed help, or if I hadn't met Abshire and Volcker at csis. But personalities didn't make me love or leave Washington. Deeper forces shifted the ground under public service.

Three such forces shaped the policy arena that I entered in the mid-1970s. Compromise was woven into the structure of both major parties. The concentration of power in Congress increased the odds of cutting a deal. The limited flow of information protected backroom negotiations. Moderates like me had a place in this insiders' game, in which splitting the difference was not a sign of weakness. I managed to gain the confidence of major players on both sides of the partisan divide through performance, not politicking.

It's hard to fathom how much has changed. The political center where compromise used to be reached has fallen apart. The hierarchy that made closure possible has been leveled. The mainstream media channels that protected deal making have given way to digital age transparency. Separated by a few decades, the worlds that pulled me in and pushed me out feel ages apart.

The Democratic and Republican Parties overlapped when I got my start.

Their internal divisions drew them closer together, not farther part. The Democratic split separated rural southerners from urban progressives. The southern bloc, hawkish on defense and fiscally conservative, had fought but survived the civil rights revolution. Its old guard and young moderates stuck together in the face of a growing Republican challenge. Southern Democrats wielded immense power in Congress. Their survival spelled the difference between keeping or losing the Democratic majority. They remained a force into the 1990s, pulling the party away from the left.

I crossed paths with Senator Fritz Hollings, a senior member of the southern bloc, through CSIS. Tall and self-assured, he chaired the Senate Commerce Committee. We traveled together to Seoul for a U.S.-Korean parliamentary dialogue. He had national ambitions and welcomed an international platform. Korean textile exports were crushing his state's most important industry. Other members of Congress joined him in calling out Korean trade practices, but they also found time to excuse themselves to shop for hand-tailored suits at deep discounts. Hollings stayed at the table throughout, erect and articulate. He wouldn't budge on trade but made clear that commercial friction shouldn't stand in the way of close U.S.-Korean security ties. His good manners and nuanced views couldn't help but impress his Korean hosts (or me).

Across the aisle conservative Republicans couldn't ignore their party's Rockefeller moderates. They were pro-business internationalists like Brooke of Massachusetts, Javits of New York, and Weicker of Connecticut. A CSIS regular, Senator John Heinz of Pennsylvania, put the interests of the beleaguered steel industry above Republican free trade rhetoric. He also didn't buy the idea of shrinking the role of government across the board, especially when it came to workforce training. Independents like Heinz had their place within the big Republican tent.

The lack of a pure brand in either party put both the votes of southern Democrats and Republican moderates in play. Divided government—the norm during all but two years of the presidencies of Reagan, Bush, and Clinton, from 1981 to 2000—made it essential to do business across party lines. Personal friendships bypassed political boundaries. The bond I observed at CSIS between Sam Nunn and Pete Domenici, who attended the same small prayer group, was typical.

Dealmakers thrived in this fluid setting. None was more successful than Bob Strauss, the lawyer from Dallas who combined lucrative client work with high-level political assignments. The arc of his career from Democratic partisan to Republican appointee seems implausible today. Over the course of twenty years he brought the Democratic National Committee back from the wilderness, served as Jimmy Carter's trade negotiator, advised Ronald Reagan privately on getting along with Democrats, and closed out his public service as George H. W. Bush's ambassador to Russia.

Strauss kept in touch with me at csis to hear what his successor in the trade job, Bill Brock, was doing. He liked to live large, reminding me that money was the only surefire sign of success that Washington understood. But he had no interest in creating a public persona. A good quip behind closed doors took him a lot further than a good media interview. He never zeroed in on substance right away. Relationships controlled the tempo of business, not the other way around. Once he gave me a salty lesson on the use of the telephone. "John," he said, "God made the telephone to say hello into. You never ever announce who you are when you pick it up. That labels you as a flunky."

The hierarchy of Washington made life easier for the power brokers like Strauss by limiting the number of key players. The pecking order in Congress made the biggest difference. "Congress is the permanent presence in Washington," Abshire reminded me. "Administrations come and go." Presidents were expected to lead, but they only had four years at a time. Legislators could accumulate influence for decades.

Power in both the majority-ruled House and more deliberative Senate flowed to their longest-serving members. The seniority principle wasn't absolute. Leadership positions were filled by election, chairmanships were not automatic, and the House delegated considerable authority to subcommittees. Nevertheless, old hands still ruled. Freshmen waited their turn for committee assignments and for their share of budget earmarks to bring home the bacon.

For all its drawbacks the club that ruled Capitol Hill held up its side of the bargaining relationship with the executive branch. The system produced a staggering range of legislation from the mid-1970s through the mid-1990s: the creation of new education and energy cabinet departments; airline and telecommunications deregulation; the Reagan tax cuts; the shoring up of Social Security; a revamping of the tax code; the Tokyo and Uruguay Rounds of Multilateral Trade Agreements; the North American Free Trade Agreement; and welfare reform. Neither Republicans nor Democrats marched in lockstep on any of these mainly economic issues. There was room for give-and-take.

The inside game ran on inside information. Disclosure killed compromise by undermining the ability to make concessions. The secrets that deal makers kept were mainly from their allies, not the other side. As *Washington Post* editor Meg Greenfield observes in her memoir, *Washington*, collusion and press leaks were standard operating procedure. Paradoxically, the close hold on sensitive information deepened the circle of trust among those in the know.

Although Watergate had pierced the culture of secrecy, the news media went along with the insiders' game for years afterward. The concentration of power in the news business mirrored that of government. Perhaps a dozen major broadcast and print outlets commanded the most sought-after segments of the audience. Of these only the *Wall Street Journal* took a staunchly conservative editorial stance. As Katharine Graham makes clear in her revealing *Personal History*, a handful of players wielded great influence. Their main objectives were commercial, not political. They competed fiercely within the closed system that they dominated.

Reporters and columnists fought to break stories. Government players cultivated them to spin the news their way. Enterprising mainline journalists took full advantage of their privileged access. The Pulitzer Prize–winning DC bureau chief of the *New York Times*, Hedrick Smith, wrote a 750-page chronicle of the Carter and Reagan years, culling insights from dozens of insider interviews. *The Power Game* didn't confine itself to process and personalities. The prodigious Smith analyzed outcomes in every important sphere. Years later he explained that he and others didn't cozy up to government sources. "We were skeptical," he said. "The government had lied to us during Vietnam and Watergate. We weren't going to be megaphones."

I found my career legs at CSIS in this old-time Washington. My mentor Abshire knew how to play the inside game as well as anyone. He deliberately focused on overarching strategic issues to sidestep bloody turf battles and personal feuds. His skillful appeal to higher national purpose created a refuge in which I came into my own.

Abshire pulled off a remarkable feat. He catered to self-interest to build an institution that served the public interest. The luminaries got their offices and support. The government officials got their visibility. The donors got their access. Yet csis stayed true to its higher mission—providing the policy community with a credible, independent resource to analyze and debate U.S. global strategy.

The Council on Competitiveness, like csis, aimed at setting national direction for policy by making its case to the establishment. Both nonprofits operated inclusively. I called their capacity to bring together high-level people over issues of substance "convening power." Some came for the networking. Some were looking for a platform. Some simply wanted to be part of the conversation. All felt that they were getting enough to justify the time.

Bill Bradley, the pro basketball star turned senator, made a memorable case for the use of convening power. The setting was a small meeting room in the Capitol. The race to succeed Ronald Reagan was gearing up late in 1987. Bradley, who had just led a bipartisan effort to restructure the tax code, was jockeying for position. He and a Senate rival, Al Gore, both agreed to make comments to the csis Advisory Board. Looking every inch the former Rhodes Scholar, Bradley shambled to the podium after Gore's brief talk on climate change.

"Big decisions are made in these chambers," he said. "Everyone who makes them has a mental map of how the world works. We rarely talk about these maps and don't have time to think critically about them. More often than not, we're stuck in the past. Think tanks can make a unique contribution by helping decision-makers bring our mental maps up to date. You have the time and the tools. We don't."

Bradley nailed it for me like a three-pointer from corner. My motor ran on analysis, not advocacy. I wasn't a born political infighter. Grappling with mental maps gave me much more job satisfaction than pushing policy prescriptions. Debates around policy always turned on tactics, whereas debates about the fundamentals remained strategic. I wanted to own the process of brainstorming that produced fresh insights. There was a market for them because neither Republicans nor Democrats had fixed positions on the big issues surrounding U.S. interests in the global economy.

Bill Brock used the convening power of the CSIS Quadrangular Forum to touch off a rich discussion that had real-world consequences. In 1983 he asked the American working group about the relative importance of manufacturing and services for the nation's economic future. The financial service industry claimed that U.S. policy had been skewed toward manufacturing for too long. The service sector accounted for 70 percent of U.S. output and all of the recent growth in U.S. employment. America's strongest competitive advantage in the global marketplace lay in services. The manufacturers fired back that their sector accounted for almost all of U.S. R&D investment as well as the lion's share of cross-border trade. The global standing of the United States hinged on the capacity to make things. Manufacturing anchored the service economy.

This debate at CSIS and elsewhere did more than push the intellectual envelope. While U.S. trade policy remained attentive to manufacturing, the growth of U.S. service exports moved front and center. Political muscle alone didn't account for the shift. The mind-set in Washington had changed.

I developed a provocative slide show for CSIS audiences during Reagan's second term. The PowerPoint presentation—which I turned into a slim monograph in 1988, *U.S. Global Economic Strategy: Challenges, Choices, and Priorities*—contrasted two alternative U.S. international economic strategies.

The territorial strategy drew the bottom line of U.S. interests around our national borders. The United States could no longer afford its post-1945 commitment to a liberal economic order. The new realities of cross-border competition demanded an assertive response to level the playing field on trade and to rebuild the U.S. manufacturing position. The logic of the territorial strategy argued for shielding the U.S. market where needed, restricting access to U.S. technology, applying bilateral economic leverage, and weakening the dollar to boost exports and attract job-creating foreign direct investment.

The global strategy looked at the well-being of the global economy as the touchstone of U.S. interests. It stressed the need for system-wide U.S. leadership. The United States had a stronger voice in managing the world economy and gained more from its prosperity than any other nation.

The logic of the global strategy called for keeping the U.S. home market open, taking advantage of global technology flows, strengthening the multilateral trade framework, and maintaining a strong dollar to serve as the world's reserve currency.

Heads nodded when I presented the slides. Beleaguered manufacturers and organized labor identified with the territorial approach. Multinationals and large financial institutions embraced the global view. A working group at the World Economic Forum in Davos, Switzerland, appreciated the insight into U.S. choices. I didn't come down one way or the other. Stirring the pot provided all the return I was looking for.

The Council on Competitiveness defined the new reality of global innovation by drawing on the wisdom of a small crowd. The lightbulbs went on when 120 chief technical officers of U.S. multinationals all realized they were in the same boat. Each one was growing R&D overseas more rapidly than at home. The collective judgment of companies such as Boeing, IBM, Merck, Motorola, Procter & Gamble, and UPS carried weight. All of the council's previous work had reflected the brilliance of a single academic, Michael Porter, who handpicked his own small teams. Now we were able to apply group experience to put Porter's insights into a fresh context. The message was clear, compelling, and able to be documented in case studies. The United States had to strengthen its own innovation platform.

The council's effort to deliver the message in the spring of 1998 reflected the old ways of Washington. I didn't hire a director of communications or a PR firm. Paying scant attention to media coverage, we played the inside game of engaging key decision-makers at MIT. Host Chuck Vest, council chairman Bill Hambrecht, and I relied on our personal contacts to fill the program. We asked council members to give up an evening and most of a day to serve as the audience. The bipartisan turnout of DC notables and the strong council presence more than justified the effort.

The old-fashioned gathering of principals in Cambridge, Massachusetts, took place against a background of disruption in Washington. The master disruptor, House Speaker Newt Gingrich, would have enjoyed the summit at MIT. I had seen the policy side of the former Georgia college professor at CSIS. He had great curiosity, a lively mind, and a genuine interest in science and technology.

Gingrich the politician, however, rocked the DC establishment. His unconventional strategy broke the forty-year Democratic hold on the House of Representatives in 1994. Ingeniously, he put candidates across the country on record to support his handcrafted "Contract with America." The contract combined populist congressional reform with hard-right commitments to balance the federal budget, cut taxes, dismantle regulations, and toughen up welfare. Its provisions defined congressional freshmen politically, won their allegiance, and enabled the new Speaker to undercut the old boys' seniority system. Once he firmed up his base, Gingrich used his leverage to confront the Clinton White House. As I wrote at the time in the *Christian Science Monitor*, the Speaker was a dismantler of government, while the president was a reformer. Their battles over policy and over Clinton's personal conduct lasted for four years, until Gingrich's own indiscretions forced him to resign.

I watched the drama unfold with growing dismay. Republicans saw confrontation as a winning strategy. The civility that Dave Abshire had taught me to cherish was vanishing. Luckily, the Senate still had enough for the Council on Competitiveness to launch the Frist-Rockefeller staff briefings on technology issues.

I hit a tipping point in 1999. The press reported that the majority leader of the House was applying loyalty tests to K Street lobbyists. He held up legislation to pressure a large trade association to remove its president, a former Democratic congressman. I knew the target, a bright pro-business Democrat who specialized in national security. The gambit didn't work, but the very thought of loyalty tests and political cleansing felt perverse. It was time to leave DC if another opportunity opened up.

Multiple forces changed Washington from a town I loved to one that I was ready to leave. They took years to gather. Their ascendance marked a pivotal shift from the politics of compromise to the politics of confrontation.

First, realignment within the Republican and Democratic parties hardened the division between them. Republicans redrew the electoral map by winning over socially conservative white voters in the South. They picked up seats little by little, often making their most important gains in open elections when Democratic stalwarts like Hollings and Nunn retired. The success of their "Southern Strategy" marginalized the wing of the Democratic Party that had produced Presidents Johnson, Carter, and Clinton as well as Vice President Gore. A traditional counterweight to urban, liberal-leaning Democrats all but disappeared. The Republican Party, in turn, followed its expanding base and moved to the right. Before long its moderates became an endangered species. A polarized Congress lost its large centrist buffer.

The collapse of the center saw differences over policy escalate into a struggle for power. Following the Gingrich playbook, Republican congressional leaders drew the battle lines from day one of the Obama administration. The scope and intensity of their opposition, reflecting the rightward pull of the populist Tea Party, increased when they gained control of the House after Obama's first two years in office. Voters mistakenly thought that splitting their tickets would create checks and balances. Divided government fostered brinksmanship, deadlock, and unilateral White House action.

The stalemate resulted from a second tectonic change: the chasm that opened up over the size and reach of the federal government. The federal role wasn't a hot button when Kennedy asked Americans to do more for their country. The Great Society programs of his successor, however, set Democrats on a course of sweeping domestic activism in civil rights, education, health, and welfare. The Republican response took shape under Ronald Reagan, who pledged to cut government back by starving Washington of resources. When push came to shove, Reagan went along with revenue increases to ensure the solvency of Social Security. But the conversion of his rhetoric into an ironclad commitment never to raise taxes set the stage for the shoot-outs that followed. By taking any increase in revenues off the table, Republicans placed the entire burden of dealing with the nation's red ink on the spending side—a nonstarter for Democrats.

The Republican position rested on a fierce critique of the public sector. I challenged Gingrich politely before he became Speaker, when we happened to be seated next to each other at a CSIS lunch. Wasn't it counterproductive, I asked, to demonize the federal workforce? Weren't Republicans putting a target on the backs of the entire civil service? "Look, John," Gingrich answered shrewdly, "we need excellence in the limited areas like national defense where the government belongs. Running a smaller government will require the best talent available." In public he stuck to the party line that government only needed to be cut, not improved.

A third new development, the year-round political campaign, created demands that reordered public life. Fund-raising took priority over just about everything else. Candidates followed the same dogma, outsourcing strategy to pricey consultants, building war chests, and outspending their opponents on attack ads. The continuous campaign compressed the congressional workweek to a few hectic days. Incumbents returned home rather than treating DC as a second home. The grind increased reliance on staff, chipped away at subject matter expertise, and limited time with colleagues.

My congresswoman from San Diego, Susan Davis, a Democrat, regularly took the last Friday evening nonstop from DC. Anyone who wanted more than a fifteen-minute meeting with the four-term representative made an appointment in her San Diego office. Once she reflected wistfully: "The only real time I get to sit down informally with other members of the House Armed Services Committee is when we travel together on official business. That's when I'm reminded that Republicans can be smart and thoughtful." The brainstorming sessions with Nunn and Domenici at CSIS belonged in a different era.

Fourth, the billions of dollars that poured into Washington redefined the character of the city. The unquenchable thirst for influence gave insiders a chance to cash in as never before. Well-connected people coming out of government earned top dollar with soft skills of doubtful market value anywhere but in Washington. Lobbying grew into a $3 billion a year industry, not counting the strategic advisors and public relations firms that didn't have to register. The revolving door generated stunning personal wealth regardless of the performance of government itself. A one-time colleague bought a $4 million mansion less than a decade after leaving a senior post.

Senior Republicans and Democrats routinely joined forces in the influence industry. Respected former cabinet officers got in on the action. They worked the system on behalf of their clients—often taking Congress, the regulatory agencies, and the executive branch deep into the weeds. Their compensation sent a message that stirred envy in some, anger in others, and cynicism all around. Public service could pay off big-time.

The outsourcing of government services added icing to the cake. While the federal headcount held steady, spending on contractors grew by 87 percent in real terms from 2000 to 2012. Many in Congress didn't hesitate to claim that they were checking federal growth and taking advantage of lean private sector business practices. This budgetary sleight of hand didn't fool anyone paying attention to the real cost of government. By 2012 the $500 billion cost of outsourcing exceeded the federal payroll by almost $200 billion. The service providers, known to all as "Beltway bandits," offered their own set of exit opportunities. It was no accident that six of the twelve highest-income counties in the country surrounded the nation's capital.

Finally, the media revolution removed the protective shield of doing business out of the public eye. The old establishment had reduced risk by withholding sensitive information. Johnson cajoled Congress on civil rights in private. Nixon broke the taboo of opening relations with China in secret. George H. W. Bush made concessions on taxes without informing the Republican leadership. Government tried with mixed success to manage the news cycle around the deadlines of print journalism and network TV. But twenty-four-hour cable news, the explosion of online readership, and social networking created a new normal: instantaneous, worldwide transparency.

Advocates with a hard edge thrived in the new environment. The social media were tailor made for the politics of confrontation and the continuous campaign. Senators Ted Cruz on the right and Elizabeth Warren on the left jumped to national prominence in record time in the second decade of the twenty-first century. Likewise, Donald Trump came out of nowhere to upend the Republican race for the White House. His slash-and-burn attacks harnessed the power of the media to connect with millions, cracking open the GOP establishment in short order.

The same wireless world that propelled insurgents also checked presidential power. Opponents of compromise used their capacity to mobilize online early and often against proposals floated by the Obama administration. Their new weapon thwarted insider bargaining that used to be routine. Occasional accommodations, such as the two-year agreement engineered in 2015 to avoid a government shutdown, amounted to little more than a pause as Republican and Democratic combatants girded for the next round of the fight.

Confrontation made media positioning the most important game in town. The narrative of the shootout drew an audience, especially for cable news, whether government worked or not. As Mark Leibovich points out in his 2013 portrait of the power elite, *This Town*, the brightest media stars coped nicely with the story line of dysfunction. Off camera and off the record, they socialized with top policy makers and high-earning former officials. The journalists and their sources needed each more than ever when Washington wasn't getting much done. Their closeness struck a vivid contrast with the Watergate years.

I took myself out of the policy loop when I realized that the middle ground where I had made my career was shrinking fast. My departure was one marker among many of a changing of the guard. Congressional leadership in both parties shifted from conciliators to combatants. The past and future Republican majority leaders of the Senate Howard Baker and Mitch McConnell weren't cut from the same cloth. Neither were Democratic Speakers of the House Tom Foley and Nancy Pelosi. Staffers mirrored their bosses in style and outlook. A parallel shift occurred within the executive branch, where political operators gained an increasing voice over policy.

My move across the country led to an unexpected and satisfying kind of public service. I'd have dismissed grassroots action as too limited in my twenties and thirties. Not so in my sixties. I felt a deep sense of accomplishment putting together a small team to help DoD scientists and engineers reach out to schools in their communities. We assisted them with advice, bill paying, communications tools, and the drafting of reports. Many of the same skills that worked in Washington were just as useful linking the Pentagon and the field. I stayed in BEST's support lane without regret, passing up chances to get into the policy mix. No one in the upper reaches of DoD had the slightest idea what my virtual organization did with a $25 million grant.

From the sidelines I saw the clamor for access and leverage propel the think tank world that I had left behind. Its numbers increased from about seventy, when I got my start in DC, to well over three hundred today. The old standbys—AEI, Brookings, and CSIS—grew their budgets, widened their issue coverage, and bulked up on experts. The Heritage Foundation came into its own as a conservative powerhouse, luring a senator to take its presidency with a seven-figure salary. A libertarian outpost, the Cato Institute, consolidated its presence with millions from the hard-right Koch brothers. One latecomer, the New America Foundation, moved into the top tier in short order by tapping digital age wealth. A steady stream of policy research shops with more limited agendas opened their doors.

The line between policy research and advocacy faded as funds flowed in. Heritage led the way. Its leadership and financial backers had no interest in detached analysis. They wanted to overturn a mushy left-leaning Washington consensus. Without apology Heritage marshaled evidence to advance a point of view. This approach wasn't the outlier I had once thought it was. The aggressive marketing of conservative policy positions won a loyal following in Congress and supported an $80 million annual budget.

Many think tanks followed suit, gearing up their media game regardless of political leaning. The Council on Foreign Relations, to which I belonged, boasted its own formidable communications machine of conference calls, blogs, webcasts, and publications, including *Foreign Affairs*. The $60 million a year operation, backed by more than seventy in-house experts and adjunct fellows, covered just about every facet of U.S. global engagement. I marveled at the volume and quality of programming. Heads of state, leaders of international organizations, cabinet officers, military top brass, members of Congress, and CEOs spoke regularly. CFR president Richard Haass, with whom I went back forty years, ranked with Abshire as a gifted think tank head.

Yet the high standing of CFR didn't translate into a comparable policy impact. Its experts got plenty of exposure on headline issues, presenting a welcome range of personal views. But building policy consensus proved much harder. The council's bipartisan task forces of high-profile leaders outside government took on trade, immigration, cyberspace, the U.S.-Afghan-Pakistan triangle, and other contentious problems. The careful analysis and balanced recommendations that came out of these groups rarely made more than a ripple in a polarized environment.

Social scientist Andrew Rich illuminates the new reality in a deeply researched book on the politics of expertise. He finds that think tanks as a whole have mastered the art of political positioning. They've given short shift, however, to the neutral, scientifically designed studies that used to set the standard. Old-school rigor has declined because expert knowledge doesn't count as much as it once did. Commentary often suffices to build an audience and funding base. Rich concludes that gains in visibility have not been matched by increased influence. Instead, think tanks are producing a ready supply of well-versed partisans armed with issue briefs and talking points.

Today's Washington teems with policy warriors. The sense of community I once felt has been lost. Opposing sides see government as a stake to be fought over. Career officials live with the risk of getting caught in the crossfire. It's a harsh and self-serving environment. But the need for public service is as great as ever. The question is, what to do?

21 REALITY CHECK

My Kennedy-era commitment to public service rode the prevailing tide of faith in government. I got too wrapped up inside the Beltway, however, to feel the tide turn. Public opinion polls tracked a fifty-point decline of confidence in Uncle Sam over a fifty-year span. Today almost three out of four Americans see big government as a threat to the nation's future. The numbers spiked 17 percent after 2008, following the worst financial crisis since the Great Depression. The Bush bank bailout and the Obama stimulus package may have broken the free fall of the economy, but they also heightened fears that Washington was going too far.

My thoughts drift back to LBJ unveiling his vision of the Great Society and NASA putting a man on the moon. The narrative around the government has changed since then from soaring ambition to serial failure. Politicians haven't taken the hit alone. The slide of the public sector has battered a silent majority of civil servants too. Volcker tried to intervene twice, chairing national commissions on civil service reform in 1989 and 2003. His recommendations to reduce federal program overlap, strengthen management, and update personnel practices fell on deaf ears. The incoming Clinton administration chose to go its own way on reform instead of leaning on independent outsiders. Congressional committees resisted any threat to their oversight. Cabinet officers defended their turf. The political will wasn't there to challenge business as usual.

A cottage industry of research and commentary has sprung up, picking federal performance apart. It's the academic counterpart of the public souring on government. I can search the literature in a few clicks—a far cry from poring over the card catalog in the old days. I imagine myself as a Woodrow Wilson School student plowing through the reading list I've assembled.

At the top is Francis Fukuyama's treatise on the American political model, *Political Order and Political Decay*. The renowned Stanford professor, a one-time optimist, has turned 180 degrees. He sees entrenched special interests shackling both branches of government. The defining feature of the American state is ineffectiveness, not strength. Public distrust makes things worse by tightening the constraints on government. Fukuyama offers no way out except shock treatment from an external source.

Congressional experts Thomas E. Mann and Norman Ornstein paint as bleak a picture on a smaller canvas in *It's Even Worse Than It Looks*. Their blow-by-blow account of federal shutdown and near financial default in 2012 depicts partisan warfare at its worst. They hold the far right accountable for blocking the give-and-take that the constitutional system needs in order to function. Their proposal for pie-in-the-sky electoral reform has been tried and came up short in the past.

In *Why Government Fails So Often* law professor Peter Schuck looks under the hood at the cost effectiveness of federal programs. Going back more than a century, he finds only a handful of initiatives (like Social Security, the GI Bill, and the Interstate Highway Act) whose benefits exceed their price tags. He concludes grimly that reform is only possible at the margins. The forces of dysfunction are too deeply embedded to change much.

Political scientist Paul Light, a protégé of Volcker, signals his views in the title of a Brookings research paper, "A Cascade of Failures." The miscues encompass both operations and oversight. Their rate has doubled during the Bush and Obama presidencies compared with their predecessors. Light, however, believes that the public sector is fixable. Streamlining could produce large gains in efficiency and at least $1 trillion in deficit reduction over ten years. All it would take is a meeting of the minds between Democrats and Republicans. That's the rub.

In his recent book, *Bring Back the Bureaucrats*, conservative John DiIulio attributes federal decline to the farming out of public functions. Federal spending on contractors, nonprofits, and state and local governments has exploded to some $2 trillion a year since the 1970s, while the headcount of the civil service has held steady at about two million. Too few civil servants are chasing after too many federal proxies. DiIulio's diagnostic hits the mark, but the tongue-in-cheek title of his proposal to tame big government will never fly.

I wonder how the numbing negativity would have affected me if I were starting out. Would I have been as determined to join the foreign policy establishment if I knew then what I know now? I think so. Nothing could erase my year of study at Sciences Po. The exalted French view of government shaped my expectations of federal service back home. I left Paris in 1964 dead set on becoming a player in transatlantic relations. I couldn't do that without becoming part of the U.S. policy community.

But I've had my opportunities. What's at stake is the future of the federal workforce. It's still the cornerstone of public service. The nonprofit space in which I found my niche is only an offshoot of government. A weak foundation threatens the much larger edifice that rests on federal decisions and dollars.

The nagging question is whether government can attract sufficient numbers of the highest performers. U.S. interests are more varied, conflicts run deeper, and cross-pressures are more intense than they used to be. The Cold War choice between guns and butter looks easy compared to today's policy trade-offs. I rattle off a few and barely scratch the surface: narrow the income gap without stifling growth; wind down U.S. debt without compromising the social safety net; reconcile privacy and national security in cyberspace; and respond to climate change while meeting domestic demand for energy.

Tests like these demand the A team of technical experts, program managers, and policy analysts. A continuous inflow of high-caliber people may not save the day, but without them things will keep going downhill. Every organization I've ever been around has flourished or floundered based on the quality of its workforce. I see telltale signs of trouble at every level: respected lawmakers who have left Congress in frustration; presidential appointees who must run a gauntlet of personal disclosure and political scrutiny; and bureaucrats whose morale has hit rock bottom. Will the most able job seekers from places like my old grad school commit to such a system?

I draw up a list of pluses of federal service. It's substantial. No career offers an opportunity to make an impact at a comparable scale. The government's authority to legislate, regulate, negotiate, and act is unmatched. "The only place I'll get an overall grasp of the U.S. health care system is at the national level," a young professional with many job options tells me. Another ranks working for the federal government a step above advocacy. "It's better to be the one who decides than the one who asks," she says.

Job security and compensation clearly count—but not as much. The most able civil servants I've met, like the best teachers, feel a calling. Some of the careerists at the top set an extraordinary example. "I worked very late last night," my navy pal Jim Rohr tells me. "As I left near midnight, I knew I'd see the light burning in my executive director's office. She's responsible for a multibillion-dollar facility and doesn't earn much more than I do. She is the most dedicated person in the lab."

Technical experts can make fulfilling contributions in research, management, and government operations. The federal employee of the year in 2015 pioneered the use of the body's immune system to fight cancer. The career achievement awardee led studies that decreased the use of antibiotics in commercial poultry. The national security and international affairs winner coordinated the U.S. response to the Ebola crisis in West Africa. These federal workers excelled in their specialized lanes.

But the other side of my ledger runs long. Pay remains a drawback for the highly skilled. Advanced degree holders earn about 25 percent less than their private sector counterparts. Coming off a three-year pay freeze, federal workers received a 1 percent salary increase. A long-term commitment to government boils down to a choice between mission and money.

A bigger negative: reliance on contractors has eroded the knowledge base and management skills of civil servants. "When I was at NASA," a friend recalls, "we couldn't hold a meeting on the agency's information system without our contractors. It was beyond embarrassing to stand by silently while they worked the problem." The inability to manage contractors undid the Bush administration's response to Hurricane Katrina and hobbled the Obama administration's unveiling of the Affordable Care Act website. In the defense sector, which employs about 40 percent of the federal workforce, I've seen that deep investment in future military leaders has no civilian counterpart. Contractors are the on-call resources who have taken much of the interesting work as well as direct accountability out of the hands of the civil service.

Federal employees endure a burden of process unlike any other. It starts with the filing of a job application online. Wait times to land an interview, receive an offer, and get a security clearance have an unreal quality for anyone who has been through the experience. When new hires finally get to the inside, they often find a workplace weighed down by rules, layered management, data calls, and internal coordination. Small indignities pile up. "It takes me about ten computer screens, filled with near microscopic headings, just to submit that I worked this week," a veteran DoD colleague sighs.

The rise of privately funded public service has changed the race for talent most of all. Options to give back from outside government scarcely existed when I was at Princeton. They've multiplied many times over since the mid-1970s, when the nation's big tax-exempt charities began to coalesce into the nonprofit sector. Organizations registered as 501(c)(3)s have grown faster than any other part of the economy since 2000. Embedded in the trillion-dollar sector are more than one million service providers, hundreds of public interest groups, and seventy mega-foundations with $1 billion or more in assets. Slews of entrepreneurs have joined them by launching for-profit ventures to create social value.

This transfer of private wealth into the public space has opened a raft of new career entry points. They encompass public interest advocacy, grassroots mobilization, think tanks, nongovernmental organizations, philanthropy, and social entrepreneurship. There's plenty of room in this space for activists who want no part of government as well as those interested in taking the political route. More than a few of the open doors lead to greater mobility, more hands-on experience, a higher public profile, less red tape, or better pay than a job in a federal agency.

Whereas I saw my charge in a public policy nonprofit as building consensus, the new breed of 501(c)(3) organizations sees theirs as making change. "We're in the business of fostering advocates, not supplicants," a key player tells me. Today's times call for engagement with a tight focus and a hard edge. Welcome to public service 2.0.

This is uncharted territory for me, but others know the new terrain well.

One is business consultant William Eggers, who advised the Bush administration on improving federal performance. He asserts with confidence that government and privately funded public service complement each other. Government, he writes, can't escape the cross-pressures of politics. The First Lady fights child obesity, while the Department of Agriculture subsidizes sugar. The Department of Transportation pushes mass transit, while low gasoline taxes encourage car use. Inconsistencies and constraints are facts of life in government.

Nonprofits and socially minded companies, on the other hand, can take purposeful action. In *The Solution Revolution* Eggers and coauthor Paul Macmillan present dozens of examples highlighting disruptive technologies, innovative finance, and scalable business models. They point to breakthroughs in health, waste management, education, and urban ecology. Wave makers led by the Bill and Melinda Gates Foundation have pointed the way by bringing resources, private sector discipline, and the culture of risk taking into the public arena. True to form, the foundation has begun to make equity investments in addition to its grants to nonprofits.

The Solution Revolution proposes that cash-strapped, rule-bound government reposition itself in this fast-changing landscape. Federal agencies should move away from directly providing services wherever there are more cost-effective alternatives. Instead, they should leverage their most valuable assets—dollars and access to data—in collaborative public-private partnerships. That strategy would unlock the know-how, ingenuity, and agility of a wider circle of players. "Public-private partnerships can put government back at the center of innovation," Eggers tells me. "This isn't old fashioned outsourcing. It's cracking the code."

Eggers pushes me out of my comfort zone. Even though he's writing primarily for a business audience, he makes a powerful case for rethinking public service. His upbeat tone gives me a lift, whereas my lit search in the field of public administration brings me down. I can imagine a career that jumps back and forth between policy work in Washington and implementation in the field. That would be truly complementary. Perhaps my old-school view putting government at the core is a relic of the sixties.

Still, I can't buy into the vision of hybrid public service unconditionally. The blurring of public and private boundaries glides by the question of ac-

250   REALITY CHECK

countability. CSIS taught me that sheltered money confers great power with few checks on its use. The risks can't be wished away. Mega-foundations and social entrepreneurs can contribute to the public good, but they aren't its stewards. Only government can fill that bill. And what if there isn't enough talent to go around? Privately funded initiatives stand a chance of syphoning off the next generation of Kennans and Volckers.

The pace of change inside and outside government is another sticking point. Government is playing catch-up on just about every front. Budget deficits have thrown the public sector into retrenchment mode most of the time. High-powered entrepreneurs and fast-moving companies are in growth mode. They're at the New Frontier. Government isn't. Is public service in such different environments really interchangeable?

I take the train up to Princeton for a reality check at the Woodrow Wilson School. Its alumni have pursued a much wider set of public service options than I ever thought possible. Their wayward choices angered the supermarket heirs whose endowment paid my way. The Robertson family filed suit against the university for disregarding its intent to prepare students for diplomatic careers. A six-and-a-half-year legal battle, ending in a costly out-of-court settlement, drew the line between narrow and broad definitions of *public service*. The school went all out to push the federal track but couldn't restore a bygone era. This year's recruiting brochure features twelve midcareer graduates, among whom one holds a federal job.

Starting at Princeton, I meet with twenty gifted Millennials committed to public service. Some have won prestigious Truman scholarships that combine a stint in government with federally supported graduate study. Others are competing for presidential management fellowships or working as part-time interns at federal agencies. Their accomplishments and backgrounds are dazzling: command of Chinese and Arabic; U.S. Marine Corps service; leadership on campuses across the country; and immigrant success stories. All have found a merit-based inside track into Washington.

None of these men and women share my Eurocentric view of the world. None have been schooled as intensively as I was in geopolitics. They see an international community in which the United States is a key player, not the leader of the Free World. They feel much more globally connected than

I did. They don't draw a sharp line between domestic and international issues. Every issue has a global dimension in the Internet age.

Differences in worldview fade as we compare notes on public service over pizza, burgers, or Thai food. I observe familiar qualities at the personal level: a strong sense of duty; a streak of altruism; a readiness to forgo big bucks; and a desire to make a mark.

The Millennials with whom I speak welcome a chance to help me out. They're used to lending a hand. Service is threaded into high school, college admissions, and undergraduate life. "It's expected," a Truman fellow tells me, "but the channels to get involved are clubs and nonprofits. The federal government has nothing to do with the ethic of volunteering that we feel."

The government doesn't ask as much of Americans as it used to, a Woodrow Wilson student adds. "The end of the draft took shared national sacrifice off the table," he says. "Washington stopped setting the expectation that young people had a responsibility to the country." He supports the grassroots effort led by retired military leaders to reestablish national service.

A long-term commitment to a single employer is also long gone. A typical career means a variety of jobs across different sectors. The important thing is what you want to do rather than where you want to work.

One of the most compelling reasons to move around is to move up. "Even presidential fellows run into glass ceilings in government after a few years," a recent DoD intern says. "The career path of leaving and coming back as a political appointee looks better." A Woodrow Wilson student sees in-and-out in his future for a different reason. "The federal government can't match the private sector in developing management skills. I'm going to start in the public sector and then move out to learn how to run an organization."

A future foreign service officer across the table begs to differ. He needed a scholarship as an undergraduate. The one he got leads to work in the diplomatic corps. He's ready to make a career commitment because, after two good summers in overseas embassies, he knows what he's getting into.

Having an inside track is as valuable as it was in my day. A student working at a DC nonprofit describes how she succeeded in winning a hard-to-get internship at the Consumer Protection Finance Bureau. "A strong sponsor vouched for me after my informational interview," she explains. "That's the opening I needed. I could get a career position if I do well. It helped to target a small start-up bureau. My friend who applied cold to a large agency had a much rougher experience."

An early career professional recounts how the loss of an inside connection turned a good job into a loser. "My new boss shunted me aside as soon as the supervisor who brought me in left," she says. "It made no difference that I had more experience deploying technology in the field than anyone else in the office. He got away with ageism and sexism because I was just a contractor."

The verdict on the federal hiring process is unanimous. It's utterly broken. The biggest gripe I hear is over lost time. Savvy applicants do whatever they can to avoid the one-stop shop government website, USA Jobs, which they dub the "Black Hole." The security clearance process can be just as trying. A Council on Foreign Relations fellow who can offer his expertise to a government agency for free is about to bale out when his clearance comes six months late. "The difference between federal and private sector recruitment is day and night," a Princetonian reminds me. "One is time-consuming and impersonal, while the other is fast-moving and hand tailored."

In contrast, views on the standing of federal service vary widely. A Truman scholar believes that the war on government has made working in the federal enterprise much less appealing. "I face ridicule from folks outside of DC—sometimes friends and family from back home—for working in a public sector that is said to be inherently inefficient, oppressive, and corrupt. The attackers have done an effective job of chipping away at the prestige public service once had."

A centrist fears that politics will override analysis inside government. "When I look across federal agencies," he says, "my first goal is to understand whether politics or policy dominates decision-making. I've found space for pragmatism in pockets of the executive branch, such as defense and national security. But there is a real risk that the partisan divide will affect less politicized areas too."

A nonprofit intern from George Mason University is upbeat. The civil service allows her to stand for something bigger than individual ambition. "It's a privilege to work on behalf of the public good," she tells me, "even if it means accepting a degree of anonymity. I don't plan to compromise my values, one of which is tolerance. My generation has a better chance to bring the country together than our parents' generation because we're more accepting."

Too much has changed for me to put myself in the shoes of the generation that's coming of age. A hostile superpower drew me to public service. The challenges they face aren't that limited, nor are they purely external. I saw myself safeguarding a force for good in the world. They see a wider gap than I did between America's promise and performance. They want to close it, while I was hardly aware of it.

I had larger-than-life public servants to look up to in high school and college. My classmates and I were following in the footsteps of public service giants like Dean Acheson, George Kennan, George Marshall, and Paul Nitze. Millennials don't see figures of this stature in the public arena. They've grown up in a world in which Silicon Valley innovators tower over the political class in Washington. They equate high achievement with starting something new rather than moving up a government or corporate ladder. We have different visions of success.

When I think back on my start as a federal employee, I never recall having to explain myself. The disfavor heaped on Washington has added a burden of self-justification on Millennials that I was spared. Partisanship increases the strain. A Yale and Princeton grad tells me about growing up in a rock solid household of Fox News watchers. She has kept up the family tradition of military service but has shifted to the left politically. There's no getting around the undercurrent of disapproval. The children of first-generation immigrants feel less pressure. A federal job will validate their family's journey to America.

Above all, the public service universe has expanded nonstop since my day. The growth in demand has occurred entirely outside the federal workforce. Schools of public affairs send nine out of ten graduates elsewhere. The pyramid of public service that I knew—with Washington at the top—has given way to interconnected spheres. An aspiring city planner sums up the new configuration: "My internship in a cabinet department showed that city government is nimbler and more entrepreneurial than the federal bureaucracy. That's where my future lies."

These changes are bound to make it harder to attract and keep talent in the federal enterprise. There's no shortage of top-notch people. The challenge is institutional. The pool from which the civil service draws has more entry-level choices, shorter time horizons, and more lucrative off-ramps from government than my generation did. If the bureaucracy can't compete, it will soften in the same way that the U.S. teacher workforce began to weaken in the 1970s. That's when large numbers of high-achieving women, who might have chosen to teach, sought other fields in which to expand their career horizons. A lot is riding on whether Washington can step up to its recruitment challenge.

22   TALENT SEARCH

I head back to DC to find out how attuned the powers that be are to the competitive landscape. Three presidents in a row have tried to strengthen the civil service as a whole. Clinton promised to reinvent government through agency-by-agency performance reviews. Bush focused on improving the delivery of federal services in targeted areas. Obama appointed a chief technology officer.

But government morale and performance keep going down. The job satisfaction of federal workers has hit a succession of all-time lows. Seven out of ten civil servants give the government a failing grade for its lax approach to low performers. Six out of ten rate their agencies below satisfactory in providing leadership or rewarding creativity. The grim trends stir no outcry. The faltering of the public sector fits Shirley Ann Jackson's definition of a quiet crisis—urgent but largely unnoticed.

To its credit the Obama administration acknowledges the federal workforce problem publicly. The White House has no across-the-board solution. A second-term response has focused on the vulnerability of information systems across government. The key is bringing in innovative outsiders like those who rescued the U.S. healthcare website in the fall of 2013. A Presidential Innovation Fellows Program parachutes in a few dozen high-flyers, mainly from Silicon Valley, on one-year rotations. To retain them, the White House has established a small unit, the U.S. Digital Service, with big plans to deploy some five hundred world-class technologists in small teams within every major agency.

The president himself has taken part in the talent search. His personal call to public service clinched the decisions of some of the administration's biggest West Coast catches. Yet the White House concentration on a single sector—even one as important as information technology—looks too narrow. The administration may think it has found a silver bullet. Experience tells me there aren't any. Computers in the classroom, higher standards, and smaller class sizes were all supposed to transform k–12 education. None proved to be a miracle solution. An elite technology corps alone won't solve the problem of government performance.

I look for answers by meeting with the president of the Partnership for Public Service, a well regarded nonprofit, for perspective on the reform agenda. The Partnership was set up in 2001, the year we moved to San Diego. It's at the heart of a loose coalition of good governance organizations. A young staff of about one hundred exudes the same energy I used to feel at CSIS. Max Stier, a Yalie, greets me in a sweatshirt. He used to work for a thoughtful moderate Republican congressman, Jim Leach, who habitually wore a baggy sweater. I like the iconoclastic statement. You don't have to defend the middle ground in the usual DC uniform.

"The civil service needs a complete overhaul," Stier tells me. "It's based on a sixty-year-old code. But implementing the blueprint we've provided takes more political capital than the White House and Congress have been willing to expend. The American system rewards crisis management and policy development far more than getting government operations right."

This insight recalls my time at State, in the 1970s, where the sharpest foreign service officers all pushed for the political career cone. Lesser lights ran the machinery of the department. Yet it's the machinery that's breaking down across government. The piling on of complex management challenges—outsourcing, regulatory mandates, court rulings, and the data revolution—has pushed the civil service far beyond its limits. The splintering of congressional oversight rules out a unified response. The Department of Homeland Security alone answers to some 120 House and Senate committees.

If revamping the entire enterprise is a long shot, government will have to compete for talent a single hire at a time. The best way to do that, Stier explains, is through competitively awarded student internships. "That tool rewards capacity," he says, "whereas posted job descriptions reward experience. Internships enable the employer to judge quality and fit better than any test, interview, or recommendation. They also get a higher grade of applicant."

I find, however, that veterans and the federal employees' union have derailed the fast-track internship that the Clinton White House put into place in 2000. The Obama administration dropped the program in 2010, following charges that it had skirted hiring procedures. The successor Pathways program is designed not only to be more user-friendly but also to allow high achievers to convert automatically to permanent positions.

Good intentions run into a brick wall of bureaucratic caution. Having declared victory with its policy announcement of Pathways, the White House lacked a strategy for its implementation. Federal agencies don't use the flexible tools at their disposal. Their lawyers want to avoid the perception that they're playing favorites at all costs. The least-risky option is to continue posting every opening on a federal jobs website that fields a million applications a year. The number of interns dropped from sixty thousand in 2009 to less than fifteen thousand in 2014. Those that convert into full-time hires account for 6 percent of entry-level slots.

The botched introduction of the Pathways program has galvanized good governance nonprofits. Stier's organization has gotten into the trenches with the Volcker Alliance and the Robertson Foundation, going after the barriers—misinformation, conflicting guidelines, and risk aversion—that stand in the way of making government more accessible to highly qualified young people. It's rough going that sometimes leads to reading regulations aloud to stubborn personnel officers. The sustained support of senior White House staff would help immensely. But a recruitment initiative without a newsworthy focus doesn't get that kind of attention.

Meanwhile, veterans take full advantage of their edge in the hiring process. They get an added boost from the personal engagement of the First Family. Armed services veterans filled 30 percent of the positions available in the federal government in 2014. "The collective guilt in Washington over what we have asked of them in Iraq and Afghanistan can't be measured," an insider explains. "It doesn't matter whether they knock more qualified candidates out of the running."

The hiring gap between recent graduates and veterans shows that federal personnel policy is a moving target. There is no standard definition of what counts. Unions champion the seniority principle. Veterans and schools of public affairs fight for their own. Diversity is a must. Uncertainties over complex regulations run high. And federal agencies invariably try to game the system for their own purposes.

A civil service built on this foundation isn't poised for generational change. Millennials make up less than 10 percent of the headcount, compared to almost one-quarter of all U.S. workers. I hear about a case in point when a senior official explains why more positions have not opened up at DoD labs. He says that large numbers of retirement-eligible scientists and engineers decided to hang on after the financial shock of 2008. The turnover that DoD expected hasn't materialized, nor has it occurred in many other agencies.

Taking a step back, I realize that the federal government can't infuse fresh talent by trying to fix everything or recruiting individuals piecemeal. There's productive space in between to meet the talent imperative. The example to look at is the country's other large public enterprise, K–12 education. That system, like government, has been tagged for decades for not delivering. Its three million teachers and administrators have felt just as much heat as federal workers. Likewise, comprehensive school reform has come up short.

But meager system-wide improvement hasn't stopped the achievement of excellence at hundreds of schools across the country. These schools and the programs that support them serve as magnets for the kind of young talent that federal service needs too.

Teach for America (TFA), a two-year tour of service on the front lines of educating disadvantaged children, has recruited almost thirty thousand high-performing undergraduates from the nation's most selective universities. The nonprofit AVID deploys a corps of another thirty thousand career teachers to close the college-going achievement gap. Innovative charter schools like High Tech High in San Diego and the KIPP network continue to draw more gifted and talented educators into the K–12 system.

Government has pockets of excellence too. The Defense Advanced Projects Research Agency, or DARPA, has made risky, breakthrough investments in R&D since 1958. The Peace Corps, with its five-year service limit, has provided a launchpad for thousands of high-quality volunteers to transfer to other federal agencies since the 1960s. The Millennium Charter Corporation has been widely praised for its disciplined venture capital approach to funding economic development projects in low-income countries.

Another possible winner was set up within the General Services Administration, or GSA, the main support arm of the federal government. In 2014 GSA created a home inside the bureaucracy for some of the tech talent that the Obama White House convinced to come to Washington. They took the name 18F after their headquarters' address at Eighteenth and F Streets, Northwest. A team of designers, developers, and product specialists competes for federal business as an in-house resource. Early demand for consulting and delivery of services has boomed, growing the headcount at 18F from fifteen to almost one hundred within a year.

Still, government doesn't have a sufficient number of success stories to change the perceptions of the public or the federal workforce itself. Excellence in the K–12 enterprise, on the other hand, is widely recognized as attainable. There simply isn't enough of it.

I see a rich opportunity if the public sector is able to take a page out of the educational reform playbook. What's needed is a critical mass of federal pockets of high performance. These beacons may not be a cure-all, but they will instill confidence, quiet naysayers, and above all attract talent.

It may be harder to make headway within the federal enterprise than in the K–12 system. Local control of schools allows for more room to experiment in education than what is possible in government. Reformers have used philanthropic funding to press for innovation, an option that does not apply to the public sector. K–12 pockets of excellence are easy to identify because educational achievement is measured regularly at the state and national levels. The far-flung missions of government agencies don't allow for the same kind of across-the-board measurement.

My experience suggests that the most important barriers standing in the way of improved performance are structural and cultural. Lowering them will lead to a workplace whose features resemble the private sector and nonprofit norm.

More empowerment. Human capital would be treated as the most valuable asset in an exemplary government workplace. That translates into lightening the burden of process, cutting back dependence on contractors, and engaging core staff more deeply in the issues they're responsible for.

Fewer layers. Middle management has had more staying power in the public sector than anywhere else. Harried supervisors with little authority and overflowing inboxes slow the pace of decision-making. A high-performing federal workplace would use the same lean management model that companies do.

Less insularity. Organizations that have a payroll to meet must look outward, but the pressures within government agencies turn them inward. Insularity undercuts both the appeal of federal service and its capacity to handle complex, interconnected problems. A high-performing workplace would allow sufficient freedom to operate responsibly without the monitoring I've observed at DoD.

More top-level access. Effective CEOs keep a close eye on internal management. Most senior political appointees, however, lack the time, interest, or authority to change much of the machinery that reports to them. Pilot efforts to reshape the federal workplace won't get off the ground without a policy audience that uses them strategically.

Higher expectations. Companies feel pressure to perform from the CEO suite to the lowest-level employee. The intense demands that pound the upper reaches of government, however, get lost in translation on the way down. An exemplary federal workplace, with tough hiring standards and term limits, would prevent civil servants from losing their edge.

GSA's 18F start-up tells me that I'm not asking for the impossible. Standards there are extremely high. The hiring process is fast. Positions are limited to two-year terms, with the option of a two-year extension. The organization is flat. The business model is driven by client work rather than congressional appropriations. And the president of the United States is keeping tabs on the agency's progress directly.

Is 18F a template for government-wide restructuring or a one-of-a-kind exception? I ask John Kamensky, a careerist turned IBM senior fellow, who knows federal performance inside out. He reminds me that corporate CEOs can set goals and align the organization around them. Government restructuring doesn't work that way. The hands of the president are tied unless Congress buys in. He remembers what Vice President Gore told a small team that he convened in the early days of the Clinton administration: "We're going to reinvent government without changing the org chart. Moving the boxes around is a nonstarter."

There are other telling constraints. Federal managers can't offer big performance bonuses, nor do they carry a big stick. The strong must bide their time as they move up, while the weak have the protection of due process against reassignment or dismissal. The principles of hierarchy and seniority are locked into the general classification of civil service jobs. Kamensky stresses that many obstacles blocked reform before partisan divisions grew so wide. "Polarization saps political energy and limits attention to the here and now," he says. "But the roots of the performance problem run deeper."

Nevertheless, there are bright spots. The Partnership for Public Service has identified them every year since 2003 by culling federal survey data on job satisfaction. It's a classic effort to turn lemons into lemonade. Even though federal employees as a whole are unhappier than ever, some still like their jobs and say why. The agencies that rank highest are deemed the best places to work in the federal government.

The Partnership's case studies of success all highlight leadership at the top of the organization. Its core components are listening and engaging. I don't discern a shred of coercion. The secretary of transportation sets the tone for collaboration by making peace with flight controllers. The director of the Patent Office involves first-level supervisors in management decisions. The NASA administrator solicits input from scientists and engineers on innovation. The Mint holds focus groups and town hall meetings. Nothing improves morale (and presumably performance) more than the simple act of taking the career workforce seriously.

But collaborative leadership only goes so far. The innovators whom I've met in the K–12 arena feel passionate about excellence. They're inspirational and demanding. I think of Mary Catherine Swanson's struggles to get AVID off the ground in the early 1980s. She persevered in the face of tremendous skepticism that low-income kids with no college background could excel in advance placement courses. She overcame the doubters with results.

Leaders with Swanson's qualities will be required in government to press for the changes needed to reach best in class. The faint of heart need not apply for resetting the balance between civil servants and contractors, removing deadwood, breaking down insularity, and raising the bar. The degree of difficulty argues for limiting the initial scale of a federal workplace initiative.

My imagination turns on again. I'm a close advisor to the next president-elect of the United States. It's time to shift gears from campaigning to governing. My portfolio includes the federal workforce. I compress my thoughts into a tight, one-page memo.

To: the President-elect
From: John Yochelson
Subject: Your Executive Branch Management Strategy

The two million civil servants who support you are going to have a significant impact on your presidency. Their morale is low. Many are performing below their potential. Although your capacity to act independently is limited, you can drive change within the current civil service framework. Here are three recommendations that will mark you as a take-charge CEO of the country's largest workforce as well as the nation's commander in chief:

1. Enlist the government's top career executives to help you succeed. Your predecessors have largely overlooked the seven thousand senior executives who have made it to the top of the career pyramid. Instead, they have focused on the four thousand political appointees who come into government with each new administration. But it will take about a year to get your appointees on board. You will need additional help during the first six months, when you will set your agenda and act on your biggest ideas. You should engage the corps of senior career executives early on. Ask them to step up to make the transition of your incoming administration a success. Seek their input and support in strengthening the executive branch. Tell them you will provide top cover when it comes to innovative performance and delivery. Designate a chief operating officer of government operations—someone like the vice president or your deputy chief of staff—to spearhead your efforts.

2. Compete for the nation's best talent at all levels. Designate your director of the Office of Personnel Management to be recruiter-in-chief for government service. His or her portfolio will not be limited to the political side of the house. Your personal backing will be needed not only to drive home the message that human capital counts but also to push the bureaucracy to take action. Your recruiter-in-chief should be directed to ensure that federal agencies have the latitude, authority, and will to compete as aggressively as the private sector for the best and brightest at all levels. Recruitment strategy must be aligned with the reality that many high achievers do not expect to spend an entire career in government. Strengthening the quality of the federal workforce will not take a new law, but it will require a new mind-set.

3. Create model high-performance workplaces within every cabinet agency. You can take the lead in creating best-in-class government units that break the mold. Pockets of excellence such as DARPA, the Peace Corps, and the Millennium Charter Corporation set the standard. So does a start-up within the General Services Administration that is competing with contractors to bring the digital know-how and creative spirit of Silicon Valley to federal agencies. Your administration will make a lasting contribution by developing many more such high-performance workplaces. Their goal is not to extend the reach of government but to demonstrate its proficiency. All of the key agency heads that you bring into government should be directed to establish units that truly reward initiative and innovation. Let them pick the areas in which they will break new ground. They should be challenged to submit proposals for action to your chief operating officer that involve no net increase in resources. I will follow up with a detailed memorandum if you wish to explore this option further.

Reality snaps back. I'm at the Ruben Fleet Science Center in San Diego 2,500 miles away from the power game. My friend Jim Rohr, who has worked with dolphins for twenty-five years, is sharing hands-on activities with elementary school teachers. He invites a half dozen of them to bang spoons tied to strings against a table. Half of them bang with their strings suspended in the air, while the other half hold their strings firmly against their ears. The tinny sound of listening through the air is nothing like the rich, deep sound of listening through the string. In simple terms Rohr explains why sound waves that travel through different mediums make different noises. The teachers nod. This will be perfect for their third graders. DoD is funding the event through my nonprofit BEST. What could be more satisfying?

I'll be in DC next week. BEST will brief higher-ups at DoD on a campaign to make the department's laboratories an employer of choice for women and minorities. I'll also meet with interns from the Partnership for Public Service. They're starting the same search I did a half century ago. I'll try to interest them in fleshing out an initiative on high-performance workplaces in government. Perhaps the Partnership will run with the idea. I'd love that too.

My cross-country travel marks almost a decade of compromise. It's not a perfect solution. I accept the wear and tear to avoid painful choices that would leave holes I couldn't fill. I don't plan to stop anytime soon. Splitting the difference has always come naturally. The harder the going gets in Washington, the more determined I am to stand by the middle ground.

SOURCES

Balter, Ben. "The Difference between 18F and USDS." Blog post, April 22, 2015. http://ben.balter.com/2015/04/22/the-difference-between-18f-and-usds.

The Best Places to Work in the Federal Government. Report. Partnership for Public Service. Washington DC, April 1, 2015.

Bowie, Robert, and John Yochelson. "Federalism: The American Experience." *U.S. Federation, Swiss Confederation, German Federation, European Communities*. Lausanne, Switzerland: Fondation Jean Monnet pour l'Europe, 1972.

Breul, Jonathan D., and John M. Kamensky. "Lessons from Clinton's Reinventing Government and Bush's Management Agenda Initiatives." *Public Administration Review* (November–December 2008).

"A Bridge for All: Higher Education Design Principles to Broaden Participation in Science, Technology, Engineering, and Mathematics." Report. Building Engineering & Science Talent, February 2004.

Center for Responsive Politics. Lobbying database. www.opensecrets.org/lobby.

Chenock, Daniel J., John M. Kamensky, Michael J. Keegan, and Gadi Ben-Yehuda. *Six Trends Driving Change in Government*. Washington DC: IBM Center for the Business of Government, 2013.

Choate, Pat. *Agents of Influence*. New York: Knopf, 1990.

DiIulio, John J., Jr. *Bring Back the Bureaucrats: Why More Federal Workers Will Lead to Better (And Smaller!) Government*. West Conshohocken PA: Templeton Press, 2014.

Domenici, Pete, Sam Nunn, and Debra L. Miller. *Strengthening of America: First Report*. Washington DC: CSIS, October 1992.

Eggers, William D., and Paul Macmillan. *The Solution Revolution: How Business, Government, and Social Enterprises Are Teaming Up to Solve Society's Toughest Problems*. Cambridge MA: Harvard Business Review Press, 2013.

Endless Frontier, Limited Resources: U.S. R&D Policy for Competitiveness. Washington DC: Council on Competitiveness, 1996.

"Federal Contracts and the Contracted Workforce." Letter from the Director to Congressman Chris Van Hollen. Washington DC: Congressional Budget Office, March 11, 2015.

Feuchtwanger, Lion. *The Oppermanns.* New York: Viking Press, 1934.

Fox, James W., and Lex Rieffel. *Strengthen the Millennium Challenge Corporation: Better Results Are Possible.* Washington DC: Brookings Institution, 2008.

Fukuyama, Francis, *Political Order and Political Decay.* New York: Farrar, Straus & Giroux, 2014.

Gates, Robert. *Duty: Memoirs of a Secretary at War.* New York: Vintage, 2014.

Gertner, Jon. "Inside Obama's Stealth Startup." *Fast Company,* June 15, 2015. www.fastcompany.com/3046756/obama-and-his-geeks.

Going Global: The New Shape of American Innovation. Washington DC: Council on Competitiveness, 1999.

Graham, Katharine. *Personal History.* New York: Knopf, 1997.

Greenfield, Meg. *Washington.* New York: Public Affairs, 2001.

Jackson, Shirley Ann. "The Quiet Crisis: Falling Short in Producing American Scientific and Technical Talent." San Diego: Building Engineering & Science Talent, 2003.

Katz, Eric. "One-Third of New Hires in the Federal Government Last Year Were Veterans." *Government Executive,* March 23, 2015.

Kennedy, John F. Inaugural Address. January 20, 1961. American Presidency Project. www.presidency.ucsb.edu/ws/?pid=8032.

Land of Plenty: Diversity as America's Competitive Edge in Science, Engineering, & Technology. Report of the Congressional Commission on the Advancement of Women and Minorities in Science, Engineering, and Technology Development. Washington DC, September 2000.

"Leadership for America: Rebuilding the Public Service." Report of the National Commission on the Public Service. Paul A. Volcker, chairman. Washington DC, 1989.

Leibovich, Mark. *This Town: Two Parties and a Funeral—Plus, Plenty of Valet Parking!—in America's Gilded Capital.* New York: Blue Rider Press, 2013.

Light, Paul C. "A Cascade of Failures." Research Paper. Washington DC: Brookings Institution, 2014.

Mann, Thomas E., and Norman J. Ornstein. *It's Even Worse Than It Looks: How the American Constitutional System Collided with the New Politics of Extremism*. New York: Basic Books, 2012.

McKeever, Brice S., and Sarah L. Pettijohn. "The Nonprofit Sector in Brief: Public Charities, Giving and Volunteering, 2014." Washington DC: Urban Institute, October 2014. www.urban.org/sites/default/files/alfresco/publication-pdfs/413277-The-Nonprofit-Sector-in-Brief--.PDF.

NASPAA. "Annual Accreditation Data Report, 2012–13." Washington DC: Network of Schools of Public Policy, Affairs, and Administration, September 2014.

Partnership for Public Service. Samuel J. Heyman Service to America Medals. "2015 SAMMIES Recipients." http://servicetoamericamedals.org.

Porter, Michael E. *Competitiveness Index 1996: A Ten-Year Strategic Assessment*. Washington DC: Council on Competitiveness, 1996.

Porter, Michael E., and the Monitor Group. *San Diego: Clusters of Innovation Initiative*. Washington DC: Council on Competitiveness, 2001.

Porter, Michael E., and Scott Stern. *The New Challenge to America's Prosperity: Findings from the Innovation Index*. Washington DC: Council on Competitiveness, 1999.

Renouvin, Pierre, and Jean-Baptiste Duroselle. *Introduction à l'histoire des relations internationales*. Paris: A. Colin, 1964.

Rich, Andrew. *Think Tanks, Public Policy, and the Politics of Expertise*. Cambridge: Cambridge University Press, 2004.

Rising above the Gathering Storm. Report of the National Academies of Science. Washington DC: National Academies Press 2007.

Schuck, Peter H. *Why Government Fails So Often*. Princeton NJ: Princeton University Press, 2014.

Schwallenbach, Nick. "Is the Federal Civilian Workforce Really Growing? Some Important Context." Washington DC: Center for Effective Government, February 11, 2014.

"Scope of the Nonprofit Sector." *Independent Sector* blog. www.independentsector.org/scope_of_the_sector.

Smith, Hedrick. *The Power Game: How Washington Works*. New York: Random House, 1988.

Sorenson, Ted. *Counselor: A Life at the Edge of History*. New York: HarperCollins, 2008.

Stirling, Catherine, and John Yochelson, eds. *Under Pressure: U.S. Industry and the Challenges of Structural Adjustment*. Boulder CO: Westview Press, 1985.

Stoga, Alan, Marina Whiteman, and John Yochelson. *Breaking the Economic Impasse: An Urgent Quadrangular Agenda*. Washington DC: CSIS, 1987.

"Urgent Business for America: Revitalizing the Federal Government for the 21st Century." Report of the National Commission on the Public Service. Paul A. Volcker, chairman. Washington DC, January 2003.

U.S. Census 1950. Population of the 100 Largest Urban Places. Table 18. Washington DC: U.S. Bureau of the Census, Internet release date, June 15, 1998. www .census.gov/population/www/documentation/twps0027/tab18.txt.

"What It Takes: Pre-K–12 Design Principles to Broaden Participation in Science Technology, Engineering, and Mathematics." Report. Building Engineering & Science Talent, April 2004. www.bestworkforce.org/PDFdocs/BESTPre-K -12Rep_part1_Apr2004.pdf.

Winning the Skills Race. Washington DC: Council on Competitiveness, 1998.

Yochelson, John. "The American Military Presence in Europe: Current Debate in the United States." *Orbis* (Fall 1971).

———. "Dismantlers vs. Reformers." *Christian Science Monitor*, January 3, 1995.

———. "MBFR: The Search for an American Approach." *Orbis* (Spring 1973).

———. *The Quest for Strategic Focus: The U.S. and the World Economy in the 1990s*. Washington DC: CSIS, 1999.

———. *U.S. Global Economic Strategy: Challenges, Choices, and Priorities*. Significant Issues series. Washington DC: CSIS, 1988.

Yochelson, Laura. *Sick: In the Name of Being Well, I Made Myself Sick*. Bloomington IN: Balboa Press, 2012.

Yochelson, Sam, and Stanton Samenow. *The Criminal Personality: A Profile for Change*. Lanham MD: Jason Aronson, 1976.

INDEX

Dr. Scholl Chair in International Business and Economics, 143–44
Duty (Gates), 223
Dynes, Bob, 197
Dyson, John, 46

Eagles, Republican, 172
economies: European, 80–82, 100, 153, 159–60, 161, 167; global, 149–50, 153, 166–67; Japanese, 158–59; U.S., 108, 133–34, 152–53, 236–37, 245
education: No Child Left Behind and, 205, 226–27; pre-k–12, 202, 205, 208, 217, 258, 260–61; STEM and, 6, 194–95, 208–12, 216. *See also* Building Engineering & Science Talent (BEST)
Eggers, William: *The Solution Revolution*, 250
18F, 261, 262
ENA. *See* l'Ècole Nationale d'Administration (ENA)
Endless Frontier, Limited Resources (Council on Competitiveness), 189
Engler, John, 173
Épinal, France, 71
European Community, 82, 153, 176
European Roundtable of Industrialists, 167
European Union, 82, 161
Eurósclerosis, 153
Everhart, Tom, 187, 189
Ewing Marion Kauffman Foundation, 211
exchange rates, 152–53, 174

Falk, Richard, 49
Farren, Michael, 183
federalism, 80–82
Feketekuty, Geza, 151
Feldman, Sandra, 196
Fessenden, Nick, 23
Finley, Murray, 188

Fisher, George, 186
Fisher, Max, 172
Foley, Tom, 242
Forbes, John, 46, 48, 73
Ford, Gerald, 107
Foreign Affairs, 243
foreign-born workers, 209
foreign service officers (FSOS), 109, 112–13
foreign service reserve officers, 108, 109
Fort Benning, 58–61
Fort Gordon, 61–62
Fort Knox, 54–57, 61–62
Fox, Galen, 48
Fox, Marye Anne, 212
France: Bordeaux, 163; and European security, 82–83; Paris, 33–40, 88; study abroad in, 31–40; Tours, 31–33
François-Poncet, Jean, 154
Frist, Bill, 193
FSOS. *See* foreign service officers (FSOS)
Fukuyama, Francis: *Political Order and Political Decay*, 246
fund-raising: Council on Competitiveness and, 186; political, 240; President's Export Council and, 171–73

Gallego, Augie, 211, 212
Gallois, Pierre, 76
Gasteyger, Curt, 84
Gates, Robert: *Duty*, 223
GATT. *See* General Agreement on Tariffs and Trade (GATT)
Gelb, Leslie, 92, 113–16, 197
General Agreement on Tariffs and Trade (GATT), 175
General Services Administration (GSA), 261, 262, 265
geographic clustering, 195–96, 199
Georgetown University, 28, 45, 219
Georgia Tech, 206
Gergen, David, 179

Mancinelli, Paolo, 166, 167–68

Mann, Thomas E.: *It's Even Worse Than It Looks*, 246

Mansfield, Mike, 84, 136–37

manufacturing sector of U.S. economy, 152–53, 236–37

Marchick, David, 181

Materials World Modules (MWM), 216–18

MATHCOUNTS, 219–20

Mathews, Jessica Tuchman, 115

MBFR. *See* mutual and balanced force reduction (MBFR)

"MBFR" (J. Yochelson), 101

McClees, Tim, 216–17

McConnell, Mitch, 242

McGahern, Bob, 220, 221

media, 147, 204; Germany and, 70; politics and, 9, 231, 234, 241–42; Quadrangular Forum and, 152; think tanks and, 129, 243

Mendershausen, Horst, 92

Mendès-France, Pierre, 33

Merck, 195, 237

Mersky, Esther, 13

Mersky, Laura, 192

Mersky, Nathan, 13

Millennials, 10, 251–54, 260

Millennium Charter Corporation, 260–61, 265

Miller, Debra, 179–80

minorities in science and engineering, 6, 203–4, 206–7

MIT, 97, 190, 191, 201, 220, 222

Monnet, Jean, 3, 4, 84; European integration and, 80; John Yochelson paper with, 80–82, 94, 98

Moore, Gordon, 189

Morella, Connie, 207

Morgan, Edmund, 26

Morita, Akio, 146–47

Mosbacher, Bob, 157, 171, 172

Murray, Alan, 152

mutual and balanced force reduction (MBFR): about, 94–96, 101–2; and arms control, 100

MWM. *See* Materials World Modules (MWM)

Myers, Ken, 128, 130

NAFTA. *See* North American Free Trade Agreement (NAFTA)

NASA, 195, 215

National Association of Manufacturers, 195

National Defense Education Act, 216

National Defense Education Program (NDEP), 217, 219, 220–21, 222

National Governors' Association, 226

National Innovation Summit, 191–92

National Institutes of Health, 19

National Journal, 152

National Science Foundation (NSF), 6, 197–98, 204, 209–10

NATO, 75–76, 94–96, 111–12, 128, 130–31

NDEP. *See* National Defense Education Program (NDEP)

Neumann, Robert, 134

New America Foundation, 243

New York Times, 9–10, 37, 153

Nichols News, 16

Nichols School, 14–16; college acceptance and, 14, 19; religious training and, 18

9/11 attacks, 202

Nixon, Richard, 62, 92, 97, 107, 241; administration of, 75, 84, 92, 94; and Brookings Institution, 92

No Child Left Behind, 205, 226

nonprofit sector, 7, 8–9, 246–47, 249–50

North American Free Trade Agreement (NAFTA), 79, 84, 167, 234

NSF. *See* National Science Foundation (NSF)

Nunn, Sam, 178–80, 232
Nye, Joseph, 99–100

Obama, Barack, 29, 239, 245–46; administration of, 226, 241, 248, 257–58, 259, 261
oil, 108, 149–50
Olivetti, 165–68
Operation Reforger, 64–65
Orbis, 84, 101
organized labor, 68, 188, 194, 259
Ornstein, Norman: *It's Even Worse Than It Looks*, 246
Ostpolitik, 77, 78
outsourcing of government services, 241
Owen, Henry, 84, 91

Partnership for Public Service, 258, 263, 266
Peace Corps, 260
Pelosi, Nancy, 192, 242
Penner, Rudy, 180
"Pentagon Papers," 113
Pepperdine University, 161
Perle, Richard, 193
Perry, William, 192
Person, Carl, 206
Personal History (Graham), 234
Petersen, Anne, 212
Petersen, Ed, 222
Pfaltzgraff, Robert, 84
Picatinny Arsenal, 221, 222
Plaza Accord, 153
political center, collapse of, 231, 239
Political Order and Political Decay (Fukuyama), 246
Porter, Michael, 5, 188, 195–96, 199, 237; *Competitiveness Index 1996*, 189; and geographic clustering, 195–96, 199
The Power Game (Smith), 234
Prechter, Heinz, 165, 171–72, 173
Presidential Innovation Fellows Program, 257

President's Council of Advisors on Science and Technology, 185
President's Export Council, 4–5, 171–73
Princeton University, 44–45, 46–49, 53–54, 93–94, 251
privately funded public service, 249–51
Public and International Affairs, 51
public opinion, 245
public-private partnerships, 250–51
public service, vii, 10, 53; careers in, 47, 54, 76, 93, 217, 241, 247, 251; education in, 34, 43–44, 48; infrastructure of, 92; John Yochelson's calling to, 2–3, 7, 19, 34, 121, 139, 231, 242–44, 245; Millennials and, 251–54; privately funded, 249–51; shared interest in, 46; student internship in, 223, 252–54, 258–59. *See also* civil service

Quadrangular Forum, 149–54, 181, 236
Qualcomm, 197, 198–99
"The Quiet Crisis" (Jackson), 207

RAND Corporation, 92–93
R&D. See research and development (R&D)
Reagan, Ronald, 135, 151, 239; administration of, 133, 171, 185
Reckford, Tom, 133
recruitment, federal, 253, 255, 257–61, 265
Rees, William, 218
Rémond, René, 36
Renouvin, Pierre, 36, 231
Republican Party, 173–74; confrontation of, with Democratic Party, 242; internal divisions of, 231–34; Southern Strategy of, 238–39
research and development (R&D): by BEST, 209; by Council on Competitiveness, 186, 188–92, 194, 195, 237; by Department of Defense, 215, 260; federally funded, 8, 180; investment in, 236

State Department (*continued*)
108–9; European Bureau of, 111–12;
John Yochelson and, 4, 49, 76, 105, 154,
171; Politico-Military Bureau of, 111,
113–16
Steere, Bill, 190
Stein, Herbert, 92
St. Elizabeths Hospital, 19, 117
STEM education, 6, 204, 208–12
Sterling Library, 25
Stern, Scott, 195
Stier, Max, 258–59
St. Maurice, Madame de, 37–38
Stokes, Bruce, 152
Strauss, Bob, 233
Strengthening of America Commission,
178–81, 182
Sullivan, Brenda, 206, 212, 218–19
Summers, Lawrence, 204
Swanson, Mary Catherine, 205–6, 263
Sweetbriar College, 28, 31–35
Szilagy, Peter, 23

Taft, Bob, 46, 53
"The Talent Imperative" (BEST), 209
tanks, 54, 61–62
Tarnoff, Peter, 110–11, 113, 116, 197
Taylor, Bill, 133
Teach for America, 260
Tea Party, 239
technology, government upgrading of,
257–58
think tanks, 9, 129, 242–43. *See also specific think tanks*
Third International Math and Science
Study, 194–95
This Town (Leibovich), 242
Thomson, Jim, 94
Today Show, 181
Tours, France, 31–33, 64
Toyoda, Eiji, 135, 138

Toyoda, Shoichiro, 138
Toyota Motor Company, 9, 135–38, 159
trade: deficits and, 175, 179; globalization and, 108, 166–67, 172, 181, 236–37;
imports and, 152–53; Japan and, 158–59;
Quad Forum and, 150–54; South Korea
and, 232
transparency, 231, 241–42
troop stationing, 75, 84–85, 94–96, 102
The Troubled Partnership (Kissinger), 145
Trump, Donald, 241
Trupin, Bob, 22
Tuchscherer, Tyson, 228
Tung, C. H., 147
Tuthill, Jack, 80, 84

Ullman, Dick, 49, 94, 102
Under Pressure, 152
unions, labor, 68, 188, 194, 259
USA Jobs website, 253
U.S. Army civil affairs school, 61–62
U.S. Army Europe, 63–73
USA Science and Engineering Festival, 226
U.S. Digital Service, 257
U.S. Global Economic Strategy, 236
U.S. trade representative, 150, 151–52

Vance, Cyrus, 113, 114
Vander Ark, Tom, 14
Vanderpool Films, 219
Van Opstal, Debbie, 186–87, 190–91, 196;
Going Global, 191
Vernant, Jacques, 82
Vershbow, Alexander, 114
Vest, Charles, 187, 190–92, 237
Vest, George, 111
veterans, 259–60
Vietnam War, 43, 53, 56, 61–62, 107
Vogel, Ezra: *Japan as Number One*, 159
Volcker, Paul: about, 3–4; and commissions on civil service, 245; contribution
of, to *Competitiveness Index 1996*, 189;

CSIS and, 5, 174–77, 231; inflation and, 174; Quadrangular Forum and, 154; values of, 4, 176–77, 183
Volcker Alliance, 259

Wallenberg, Jacob, 147–48
Wallenberg, Marcus, 147–48
Wallenberg, Peter, 147
Wallenberg Group, 147–48
Wall Street Journal, 5, 152, 234
Ward, Wanda, 204–5
Warren, Elizabeth, 241
Warsaw Pact, 94–95
Washington (Greenfield), 234
Washington, Bill, 206
Washington DC: changes in, 176–77; congressional reform and, 237–38, 242; continuous campaigning and, 240; global economy and, 236–37; government size and reach and, 239–40; insiders game and, 233–35; lobby industry and, 240–41; outsourcing and, 241; pace of, 251; political parties and, 231–33, 238–39; think tanks and, 242–44; transparency and, 241–42
Washington Hebrew Congregation, 118, 119
Washington Post, 97
Watergate controversy, 97
Weinberger, Caspar, 150
West, Bing, 46
West Germany, 77–78, 83. *See also* Germany
Westinghouse, 133
"What It Takes" (BEST), 208
Whitehead, John, 154
Whitman, Marina, 151
Why Government Fails So Often (Schuck), 246
Wilburn, Bob, 49
Wilburn, Jim, 162

Wilson, Charley, 56–57, 61
Wilson, James Q., 118
Wince-Smith, Deborah, 186, 189, 194–95
Winning the Skills Race (Council on Competitiveness), 193–94
Wolfensohn, James, 174–75, 176
women in science and engineering, 6, 201, 203–4, 207, 209
Woodrow Wilson School of Public and International Affairs at Princeton, 44–45, 46–49, 53–54, 93–94, 251
Woodward, Bob, 23
Worms cemetery, 70
Wright, Julie Meier, 197
Wright, Marion, 42

Xerox, 182, 190

Yale University, 2–3, 21–28, 41–42, 44; admission to, 13–16, 19; family history with, 11; and study abroad, 27, 31–40; Timothy Dwight College of, 27–28; Yochelson lecture in forensic psychiatry at, 28, 119–20
Yeutter, Clayton, 151
Yochelson, Bonnie, 17, 29, 57–58, 87–88, 95, 117, 118, 125, 140–41, 169, 202, 213
Yochelson, Diane Kamino, 120–25, 140, 154–156, 157, 169, 182, 197, 212–13, 227. *See also* Kamino, Diane
Yochelson, Fannie, 12
Yochelson, John: "The American Military Presence in Europe," 84; *Army in Europe*, 65; birth of children of, 154–56; calling of, to public service, 2–3, 7; childhood of, 1–2, 11, 13–19; courtships and weddings of, 71–72, 89–91, 120–25; divorce of, 89–91; European security focus of, 4, 7, 54, 75–76, 79, 82–84, 98–104, 112; family of, 11–14, 19; grade school education of, 13–16; health of, 207–8, 213; internship of, 43, 77;